"...connecting some tough or unsavory aspects of the real world with the meditative, inner reality Ragir encountered through Buddhism are the book's most consistent strengths. The prose is clear and unadorned throughout, which deepens the sense that the author is sharing a warts-and-all spiritual odyssey. Likewise, the mindless, blissful tone of so many accounts of Buddhism is pleasingly absent here. Ragir delivers plenty of critiques of the Zen path—which makes her embrace of it all the more intriguing to read about. A plainspoken, engaging, and very realistic account of a Buddhist journey" —*Kirkus Reviews*

"Judith Ragir—a Zen teacher, a mom, a Jew, a sexual assault survivor—splits open her heart and fearlessly pours out the hate, internalized anti-Semitism, and unquestioned rule-following that blocks her love. This book is at once a love letter to Zen practice and a critique of late-twentieth-century American Zen. Judith inspires us to investigate our own karmic knots, and in the middle of this suffering, she invites us to walk quietly down the backyard steps to the neighborhood pond and take a cooling dip in the moonlight." —**Natalie Goldberg, author of *Writing Down the Bones, Long Quiet Highway, Three Simple Lines*, and many other books**

"In *Untangling Karma*, Judith Ragir
Zen teacher has done: shows us ea
ness and healing. And she does sc
ness, and transparency." —**Tim I**
Holy About It and *Zen in the Age of* ⌐ ......⌐

D1279967

"This is not the book you'd expect from a Zen teacher and senior Zen priest. Full of pain, passionate intensity, and brutally honest, Judith Ragir's writing shows us what Zen looks like under the hood, in the context of an American woman's lived experience of trauma, abuse, and intergenerational pain.... An uplifting, and searing, read." —Norman Fischer, Zen teacher and author of *Sailing Home*, *The World Could Be Otherwise*, *When You Greet Me I Bow*, and many other books

"*Untangling Karma* deals head-on with the pain of living, with hurting and being hurt—and with the many dimensions of healing. Here are hard-earned lessons in which Judith Ragir recognizes and recovers from several strands of trauma woven intimately into her life, personally and multi-generationally, based on gender, race, and religious prejudice." —Jan Chozen Bays, author of *Mindful Eating*, *The Vow-Powered Life*, *Mindfulness on the Go*, and many other books

"*Untangling Karma* is a stunning book that weaves together Zen, Judaism, family, trauma, healing, and much more. Judith Ragir opens her heart and writes with remarkable honesty. I felt she was speaking to me as an intimate friend. You, too, will be encouraged by this courageous woman." —Susan Moon, author and editor of many books, including *The Hidden Lamp*, *This Is Getting Old*, *Being Bodies*, *Not Turning Away*, and *What Is Zen?*

UNTANGLING KARMA

INTIMATE ZEN STORIES ON HEALING TRAUMA

JUDITH RAGIR

Monkfish Book Publishing Company
Rhinebeck, New York

Paperback ISBN 978-1-948626-69-9
eBook ISBN 978-1-948626-70-5

Library of Congresss Cataloging-in-Publication Data

Names: Ragir, Judith, author.
Title: Untangling karma : intimate Zen stories on healing trauma / Judith
   Ragir.
Description: Rhinebeck : Monkfish Book Publishing Company, 2022. | Includes
   bibliographical references.
Identifiers: LCCN 2022000223 (print) | LCCN 2022000224 (ebook) | ISBN
   9781948626699 (paperback) | ISBN 9781948626705 (ebook)
Subjects: LCSH: Healing--Religious aspects--Buddhism. | Zen
   Buddhism--Psychology. | Zen Buddhism--United States. | Karma. | Ragir,
   Judith.
Classification: LCC BQ4570.H43 R34 2022 (print) | LCC BQ4570.H43 (ebook)
   | DDC 294.3/927--dc23/eng/20220222
LC record available at https://lccn.loc.gov/2022000223
LC ebook record available at https://lccn.loc.gov/2022000224

Front cover quilt by Judith Ragir
Book design by Colin Rolfe

Monkfish Book Publishing Company
22 East Market Street, Suite 304
Rhinebeck, NY 12572
(845) 876-4861
monkfishpublishing.com

This is the sixty-sixth autumn I have seen.
The moon still lights my face.
Don't ask me about the meaning of Zen teachings—
Just listen to what the pines and cedars say on a
windless night.

—Ryonen (1646–1711), "Death Poem"

CONTENTS

Introduction
A LANDSCAPE OF HEALING

Hatred never ceases by hatred,
But by love alone is healed.
This is the ancient and eternal law.
—Dhammapada

I have spent more than fifty years enamored with Buddhism. It started when I was a hippie teenager in the late 1960s, listening to Alan Watts on the radio and later being inspired by Zen in the kitchen thanks to *The Tassajara Bread Book,* published in 1970. This cookbook was created by the cook (or *tenzo* in Zen terminology) who was then serving at Tassajara Zen Mountain Monastery in California. On the back cover of a subsequent book, *Tassajara Cooking* (1973), I found a startling line drawing of a bald person in full Buddhist priest regalia with a radiating halo on her head. And where was this extraordinary being pictured? Cooking in a kitchen! The image represented what I wanted: kindness, presence, and peace of mind in daily life. This image is what Katagiri Roshi, my root Zen teacher, would call the "original inspiration" for my spiritual practice. That vision of a life well-lived was incredibly important for me as a wounded and alienated teenager. Could Zen be the path out of the pain of my childhood?

I fell in love with anything Japanese and proceeded to fall in love with a Japanese man, Dainin Katagiri, who moved into my Minneapolis neighborhood in 1973 and started teaching Zen. He was my teacher and mentor for seventeen years until he died in 1990. Through my continuing devotion over the years, I was trained in Katagiri Roshi's manner, which was a combination of classic Zen and his simplification of it for Americans. Now, having engaged in the full training of Zen; having served in all the temple officers' positions, including as head teacher; and having participated in many decades of the ritual of *sesshin* (meditation retreats), I have come back to the image of the priest in the kitchen. It is still what I want. I want what I have learned from formal Zen practice to be fully integrated into my daily activities—to move through life, with its ten thousand sorrows and joys, with my feet grounded in each step, my heart open, and my mind as clear and fully present as possible.

When I began to write this book, little did I know that combing through my life stories and their concomitant traumas would produce a hard-met but welcome transformation in me. I had a head full of questions about the efficacy of Zen training for American women. What is transferrable from one culture to another? I laugh now when I see that as a young woman I was drawn to Japanese culture, which actually resembled the culture of my Jewish family of origin: achievement oriented, compulsively overworking, and hierarchical. I realized that I had made an unconscious choice to gravitate toward qualities that felt like my family or home—both of which I had actually rebelled against. My youthful decision-making was a cleverly disguised return to habit and safety. This shock of insight stopped me in my tracks.

The questions raised by my many years of Zen training grew in urgency as I looked at the influences of Eastern modes of thought and our Western accommodations to them, as well as the prevalence of psychology in our spiritual lives. The understanding of a "self" in a modern Western mind seems quite different from its interpretation in the East. How does this divergence change our Buddhist training in America? Questions like this one became so profound for me that I needed a sabbatical from teaching to allow fresh wisdom to come forward, from my own experience. What had I learned from being a woman, a mother, a feminist, and a Zen teacher? And how should I go forward in my life?

I was searching for a way to feel more connection and to have more inner availability for love in my life. This new direction and healing that I was asking for seemed like it would have to come from a different source than I had previously known. I saw that I needed different tools in my spiritual toolkit.

This wish for change was especially strong, as some of my students had started to call me "Roshi," which is an honorary title reserved for a mature Zen Teacher. Did I deserve that title? I wanted my insides and my outsides to be congruent. I thought a lot about Einstein's quote: "No problem can be solved from the same level of consciousness that created it." I felt trapped by my "role"—the rules and rituals that surround a Zen priest—and wanted for myself a change that was very personal, self-connected, and lovingly intimate with other people. I finally had to recognize that if the leap I wanted could have happened within the Zen system, it would have already occurred.

And so began my "pause," when I stopped my usual activities to engage in the personal investigation I needed. I am deeply grateful for the privilege I have that allowed me to pause, recognizing that many people cannot afford to slow down. I really didn't know how to manifest the spiritual quantum jump I knew I needed to make, but I trusted that it would unfold if I carved out the space and time to listen for my inner guidance and see where it led me.

Audre Lorde, the African American womanist poet, offered inspiration: *"The master's tools will never dismantle the master's house,"* she wrote, and her words certainly applied to my sense of the feminine in Zen Buddhism. How could Zen's orientation change when the ancient structures made by Asian men are so strong and formidable? This same attitude adjustment also applied to me and my way of practice interiorly. How could a woman who grew up in and conformed to the men's hierarchy and rituals, who even taught those same rituals, open to a new way of being? I wanted to step into a format that retained the baby of Buddhist wisdom but could let go of some of the bath-water that no longer applies to our time and culture. It took four hundred years for Buddhism to transform into its current form in Japan; we have been developing an American Buddhism for only a paltry hundred years.

This book chronicles my delving into the most painful and challenging dimensions of my life and how I have struggled to investigate them fully and lay them to rest. I used to think that exploring my personal karma would open a Pandora's box of infinite pain. I was afraid to open that box. It is better, I thought unconsciously, to use religion, somehow, to cover up that pain or try to escape or transcend it.

Here, my addictive personality shows itself. There was a part of me that wanted, at all costs, to run away from pain. Is it possible to use something as profound as Zen practice in an unwholesome way? I have found the answer to be *yes*. But as I matured in the practice, something different began to occur. Instead of trying to escape my problems, I started to face them directly. I found that, to the contrary of the myth, Pandora's box is actually finite. Exploring that box of darkness and shadows is what, in many religions, is called self-purification. But *how* we do this is very important. We cannot avoid cleaning up the wreckage of our individual past and childhood, but it is also illuminating to explore our ancestral heritage. The past generations influence us, culture influences us. These are the external conditions that produce our life.

The writing of this book required my reliving some very daunting periods of my life, and as the process unfolded, I found that I was being transformed. My entering in the darkness allowed for a new light in my mind. I am hoping that the reader, in participating in my journey with me, may encounter moments of clarity that shine the light back on her own life. While I have been a Buddhist priest for many years, I offer the experiences in these pages as a woman and ordinary person struggling to understand her life and trust that they will communicate with readers on a spiritual path. I set out to explore the repercussions of unhealed trauma both in myself and in the larger culture. I offer this description of that exploration to readers who may resonate with my struggles and perhaps share in my effort to shake off trauma's consequences and find a path to acceptance and peace. This book is about consciously, as much as possible, bringing these conditions to light, for if we do this, we can help ourselves let them go—and finally accept them enough, heal them enough, to forget them.

Now that I am in my late sixties, I look back on a full life that was formed in the latter part of the twentieth century. I have lived through many stages of the developments of feminism and I was in the first round of American women to step into the roles of spiritual leadership and teaching in America. I have also, perhaps controversially, imbued my understanding of Buddhist practice with an amalgamation of twentieth-century psychology. All of these ways of seeing have deeply informed this writing. To tell my personal stories and history might seem to break some kind of mold of how a Zen Teacher should express herself. I think perhaps it's a woman's way of teaching. Can someone else learn from my deepest struggles? Do I dare to drop my façade of the calm and centered Zen Teacher who has transcended her problems and show you the real underpinnings of my awareness and growth? In these stories, I expose the underbelly of my life, wanting to know why my heart is sometimes still hardened and closed. Even our reactions to the worst stories in our lives can become an incentive and a seed for tenderizing our hearts. And certainly, in the twenty-first century of global communication, practice cannot be narrowed down to a focus on our interior life or personal history, but we must have some understanding and relationship to our world.

In its essence, this book is about healing trauma—individual trauma and the trauma that is held in the collective memory. It includes my personal struggles with illness, identity, social injustice, caregiving, parenting, and domestic life—all of which has been absent from the male-inspired monastic Buddhist tradition for a long time. As I approached the wounds within myself, I saw that a lot of our inner violence comes from the consequences of violence, war, and oppression in our culture and history. This harks back to the Buddhist teaching of karma: that there are previous conditions and causes for everything that appears in life. These external conditions and the collective consciousness affect us deeply, creating the circumstances for our attitudes and upbringing.

Because of writing this book, I can now see the helix of healing I am going through. This spiraling journey takes me to a place where I can love my whole, integrated self—the good and the bad, together. I have learned that we cannot feel whole unless we make an effort to gather up our splintered-off selves and knit them back together, without judgment, into one functioning, alive, interconnected being. This weaving of our personal tapestry requires much kindness, gentleness, and forgiveness. From this place of personal integration, we have the foundation of equanimity that can birth our understanding of interdependence and the Buddhist concept of no-centralized self.

I have included some Buddhist vernacular and presented Zen koans (or teaching stories) in a few of the chapters. My hope is that I have explained the language as we go, and that my unpacking of these Zen stories will make them accessible to any reader.

Chapter One explores the effects of World War II on my family and myself and delves into my father's rage, in the context of Jewish identity after the war, with its internalized anti-Semitism. It looks at the consequences of global war. I have learned that place and geography can become a fertile ground for learning. Place becomes the teacher, which allows for the teaching to be viscerally experienced. In the Zen community, in the late 1990s and early 2000s, retreats began to be organized around historic sites. First, I went to Auschwitz/Birkenau with Zen teacher Bernie Glassman and the Zen Peacemakers Order. A few years later, to continue my probe into World War II, I went to Hiroshima/Nagasaki on the Jizos for Peace Pilgrimage on the sixtieth anniversary of the nuclear bombings, with a trip organized by Great Vow Zen Monastery in Oregon. I was able to watch my mind and heart in the dire atmosphere of these historic sites, all of them places of total devastation, and see what arose in me. I examined the labels of victim and perpetrator by putting myself in those very different sites of violence. I, as a Jew, was a victim at one of the sites; I, as an American, the perpetrator at the other.

Chapter Two takes the reader along to my Dock Retreat. I had heard and read about hermits who climbed to the mountaintop to sit. I yearned to have that solitary experience and had always wanted to meditate outdoors in nature. In my dock retreat, I combined these ideas, but my circumstances were quite radically different from the yogi's in his mountain cave: my husband and I were parenting two elementary school children and had a good-sized house to take care of. Nevertheless, I devised a schedule for myself that was retreat-like, meditating for five hours a day but at a place located smack dab in the middle of the suburbs. I sat on my meditation cushion on a dock alongside a suburban pond, in my backyard, and right in the middle of family life. These retreats allowed me to go deep into meditation practice but required me to turn on a dime and immerse myself in integrating practice into the ordinary life of children and spouse.

Chapter Three, "Untangling My Karmic Knots," explores the theme of healing from trauma and life's ever-present suffering. The First Noble Truth in Buddha's teaching is that suffering and disappointment are always a part of life. Because of this condition, we can learn to hold our individual stories of pain in the arms of a universal perspective. In this chapter, I tell the story of my bottoming out with illness, drugs, and self-destructive behavior and how the combined modalities of a twelve-step recovery program, Zen, and psychotherapy supported me through some of the hardest periods of my life. This chapter describes my recovery from addiction and, very surprisingly to me, healing from what used to be my ever-present severe asthma. It is a celebration of the healing gifts I have already been given, and the underlying life-affirming attitudes that are embedded in spirituality: humility, forgiveness, acceptance, and compassion for suffering.

"Wash your bowl," a Zen koan from the ninth century, as set forth in Chapter Four, is probably the most quintessential instruction for mindfulness in Zen. It directs us to be present to what is actually happening in this moment. I explore different stories of wholesome mindfulness in this chapter and also some of my failures at exactly that, which led me to discussing parenting as a mindfulness practice. Parenting continues to be one of the most challenging if not *the* most challenging aspects of my life, which is still carrying on, even as a parent to adult children.

Chapter Five, "Do Not Misuse Sexuality," examines sexuality and healing. Although this chapter was written before the explosion of the #Me Too movement, it raises many similar issues, from my personal perspective. I investigate the repercussions of my own sexual molestation as a child, which largely determined my early development as a sexual being, and my being raped as a young woman on a street in Chicago. Threaded into its exploration of sexuality, this chapter weaves the use of Zen koans written by women from the eighth, twelfth, and fourteenth centuries. I used these stories from our ancestral mothers as support for my psychological work and to get some understanding of women's sexuality in the context of the Zen world.

Many parts of life, many phases of healing our difficulties, require Inner Fortitude, the subject of Chapter Six. Zen practice teaches us a great deal about patience, fortitude, and perseverance. That is one of the assets of the Japanese-style structure and strictness. Though I do complain about what some people call the "militarism" of the Zen rituals and retreats, one thing I have gained from this style is a strong sense of my own inner fortitude and a lot of practice in getting through life's difficulties breath by breath. I share stories about my ski accident, giving birth to my first child, and going through the darkness of deep grief with the underpinning of grace and grit learned from years of Zen practice.

"Malissa and the Legacy of Enslavement," Chapter Seven, plunges us into the very sensitive issue of racial justice. This chapter begins and ends with my relationship with Malissa Hyman, the African American woman who worked for my family from my high school years until her death in 1982. She was one of the most important mentors in my life and, in some respects, gave me my strongest experience of love from my childhood. The memories of our relationship activated my current investigation of racism in my own mind and in the culture. This exploration was also steeped in "place." I traveled to Greenville, Mississippi; Ghana, Africa; and Montgomery, Alabama; to learn about the history of slavery and its brutal oppression and aftermath. Drawing from my personal story of being raised by Black domestic help, I braid my own experience into this narrative. This writing taught me that racial injustice in America cannot heal until white Americans face the violence and terrorism of slavery and its current impact, and until we begin to comprehend the consequences of this violence, personally, for our nation, and for the conditions that keep racism alive.

I have been on the frontline of the many transitions that are happening as Buddhism comes to America. My practice and teaching have incorporated Western psychology, a mix of several of the different geographical sects of Buddhism and their practices, and the feminism that I inherently bring as a late twentieth-century woman Zen teacher. Many of my generation of Buddhist practitioners are forging new paths as we begin to understand a more integrated Way to practice within the mind of our own culture. But, ultimately, my message in this book is an intimate one, a call to each of us to turn toward our life experience with curiosity and courage, to excavate, investigate, and burn up the residue of our suffering. And with what pain remains, may we find the acceptance and kindness to embrace our wholeness and our humanity. With this soothing of our personal misfortunes, I pray that we can face and alleviate some of the pain of our world.

I meditated for fifty years with my eyes shut; now I want to live with eyes wide open.

Chapter One

WORLD WAR II AND NO-SELF

You need to recognize the suffering within you—and to see the ways it carries within itself the suffering of your father, your mother, your ancestors, and your people.

—Thich Nhat Hanh

A man emerged from the stream of passersby on a Hiroshima sidewalk and began to shout at us. Red-faced, arms wildly gesticulating, he raged for an hour (I clocked him on my wristwatch). Not understanding Japanese, I could only watch him and hear the sound of his fury. I learned afterwards that he was raging with anti-American, anti-Buddhist, and anti-religious sentiment. This is what I had feared most: that the presence of Americans at the memorial services for the sixtieth anniversary of the nuclear bombings of Hiroshima and Nagasaki would arouse hatred in people and not the hoped-for reconciliation. I was on a pilgrimage, traveling with a Zen-based group called "Jizos for Peace Pilgrimage." Our group was resting and waiting for the next activity of peace demonstrations, when, on the periphery of our group, this outraged Japanese man approached the Japanese teachers who were a part of our contingency and started his tirade. The Japanese Zen teacher sat on the bench with his hands in his lap, quietly nodding his head and listening. For an entire hour, he received this harangue! After this explosion of resentment, the man calmed down. He actually ended up smiling and shaking hands with our host teachers. I was shocked by the whole encounter. When I went up to the teacher afterwards to learn what he had said to this irate man, he replied, "I did nothing. I just listened and listened until he calmed down." He had gently and lovingly witnessed this man's rage and was able to hold his very agitated energy. This was a teaching moment for me, suggesting that there might be a healing for the righteous anger that is born out of trauma.

* * *

I am a second-generation American Jew, born in 1951, directly after World War II. I lived with a high level of anger and rage within my family when I was a child. My father was a little like the angry Japanese man I encountered: filled with the violence of World War II and finding no place to heal. And I have lived with that rage inside myself as a consequence. I have studied and practiced Buddhism for many years—nearly my whole life—so why am I still very anxious?

As a child, I was sorrowful and full of pain. I would play with my dolls in my bedroom and rearrange the furniture to be like my grandmother's very small apartment. Then, I would pretend that my husband had died and my baby doll was extremely, mortally sick and I would cry all afternoon. How did that sorrow come to an eight-year-old? One could say that it came from the dysfunction of my family, but could it also come from my Jewish heritage?

This big question—"Why am I still very anxious and

paranoid almost all the time?"—has haunted me. It seems to me that I have digested most of my personal karma, that which happened to me in my own history, so what is it that still needs to be healed in order for me to have peace? This disturbing question led me on a journey to explore the causes of my deep-seated anxiety. Usually we think that Buddhism is teaching us to let go of the storyline of our personal history, but my intuition asked me to go directly into my storyline. The teaching of *karma*, which is that every effect has a preceding cause, led me to look more deeply at World War II, which shaped my parents, who carried forward a grievous legacy that was extended down to me. I wanted my investigation to be experiential and not academic. I wanted an embodied teaching, so I went on two meditation retreats that had a place of civic devastation as their teacher.

I have been reading lately about the molecular biology of intergenerational trauma. Scientists are investigating how genetic information is changed by the effects of post-traumatic stress disorder (PTSD). They are finding that PTSD may actually change our DNA and our chromosomes. Because of extreme stress and PTSD, the telomeres—the DNA caps on the end of the chromosomes—are actually shortened. The next generation of a traumatized people often share common psychological features, including numbness, sadness, inhibition, anxiety, hyper-vigilance, and a not-unreasonable sense that the outside world is implacably hostile. They ruminate on death and dead relatives. Some people call this "embodied history" or "historical trauma" or "collective trauma."

In Buddhism, we call it karma, which is accumulated lifetime after lifetime. Our karma resides in our bodies like knots of emotional, physical, and psychic energy. We untangle these knots by intimately exploring the conditions that made them and then by spending time in deep meditation, allowing them to be metabolized and hopefully discharged. If we can break the habits and patterns of inherited karma, seven generations before us and seven generations after us will feel the release of this karma. The frozen places within ourselves, which are the effect of collective trauma, can begin to melt. This belief has given me some hope.

With this new understanding, I began to explore my personal and ethnic history. I immersed myself in two very provocative sites of World War II, one in which I, as a Jew, was the victim; and the other in which I, as an American, was the perpetrator. In 1998, I went to Auschwitz-Birkenau with the Zen Peacemaker's Order, and in 2005, I went with the Jizo for Peace Pilgrimage to Hiroshima and Nagasaki for the sixtieth anniversary of America's nuclear bombing of those cities. Both of these retreats taught me that there is no "other." If we allow the opposites of the labels "victim" and "perpetrator" to isolate us and cause us to fight the "other" within ourselves and the world, we just get stuck in hate forever.

There is a dynamism that swirls in the opposites of victim and perpetrator. Longfellow wrote: "If we could read the secret history of our enemies, we should find in each person's life sorrow and suffering enough to disarm all hostility." A victim can turn into a perpetrator, and a perpetrator has a victim within. People can swing from one side of the polarity to the other. A concentration camp survivor can go to Jerusalem and become the terrorist. My mom's older cousin was such a person, fighting with the Irgun (an underground paramilitary Zionist group) for a Jewish state. Survivors can swing towards such a deep-seated depression that they can no longer live life. The secrets of the horrors they witnessed fester so much inside them that they cannot open to love or connectedness.

Sometimes they lose their ability to live beyond the suffering they have endured.

Is it true that violence begets violence, as the Buddhists preach? These crimes against humanity need to be revealed and examined for any possibility of healing to occur, or we will continue to act from the seeds of the effects of violence within us. These breaches of humanness are a very deep level of karma when we consider the plight of historically oppressed people—in my case, the Jews, but this is also true for African Americans, Native Americans, the Hmong, the Cambodians, and so many other oppressed and traumatized peoples. The world, including America, is "hurt" by these unacknowledged and unprocessed fissures in our societies.

Auschwitz-Birkenau

When you visit a concentration camp, your first reaction tends to be a mental shock that stops your thinking. We cannot fathom the horror of this violence. This is particularly true at Birkenau, which was the largest death factory ever built by human hands. Perhaps that is why it has become such a symbol of genocidal terror and such a poignant place to do retreats. Your brain stops and your heart flies right open—and all of the stored personal pain in your own heart bursts forth too.

Bernie Glassman, the late Zen teacher and activist who introduced bearing witness retreats at sites of great historical violence (which he called "plunges"), offered an interpretation of the three refuges in Buddhism which steered me through my uncontrollable reactions to such places.

The first instruction is that the teaching in such places is to come from "don't know mind." This is quite an easy concept to understand when you enter a place like the Auschwitz Museum.

Who can even imagine such horror? All of your long-held concepts and beliefs explode in your brain in your first five agonizing minutes at the museum as you walk through rooms full of suitcases, shelves of human hair, forgotten dolls, mounds of pots and pans, wristwatches, eyeglasses, and gold dental fillings. You see photographs of lines of people being designated to work or to die. You see train cars being used as prisons filled with people, just their hollowed eyes exposed and their fingers sticking out of the iron bars of the small windows at the top of the train's sliding doors. You might glance at a photo of a mother being pulled away from her child. All of your "ideas" go out the window. There is no intellectual understanding to help you face these abhorrent images. None of us knows how to "fix" anything we see at Auschwitz. We immediately understand that all our concepts are too small.

The second instruction is to bear witness. We simply allow our heart, mind, and body to live with the Great Sadness and Great Grief of these locations. Each place has a voice and can teach us if we are willing to "hear the cries of the world," which is the translation of the Buddhist name for the embodiment of compassion, *Avalokiteshvara*. We bear witness with a torn and bleeding heart.

The third instruction is to love or do a loving action—to do *that one small thing* that might help. From the bottom of the pain of bearing witness, you can sometimes intuit a kind act or kind word that might fit the situation. For instance, sometimes I am flooded with the suffering of the world and the small thing I can do is make soup for friends and *sangha* members who are ill or in distress. I actually do this—make soup and bring it to three people one afternoon a week—calling my project *Byakuren's* (my Buddhist name, which means White Lotus) *Soup Kitchen*. What I have learned from this small action is that it is not the soup that is important, but the small amount of presence and love in the interaction during the transfer of the soup that offers a connection or a blessing.

Most of us know the name Auschwitz. Although there is a small camp named Auschwitz I, which houses the main historic museum of the holocaust, and is the place where the horrific medical experiments on prisoners took place, the general name "Auschwitz" actually designated a network of Nazi camps: three main camps and forty-five satellite camps. I spent most of the weeklong bearing-witness retreat in Poland at Auschwitz-Birkenau, which is also known simply as Birkenau and often called Auschwitz II, as it is one of Auschwitz's three main camps. Birkenau is an enormous camp. It takes about forty-five minutes to walk from one end to the other. The architectural footprints of the original camp still exist and show what a killing factory it became. In 1942, as Hitler moved toward the "Final Solution" to the "Jewish Question"—that is, the annihilation of the Jewish People—Birkenau was repurposed from a political prisoner camp to a combination labor and extermination camp. By 1943, it had four continuously working crematories. One gas chamber could kill two thousand people in twenty minutes.

Every day at Birkenau, we meditated as a group on the train platform where Jews, gypsies, homosexuals—and all of the "others"—disembarked the train and were selected to either go to the work camp or be killed. Children were dragged away from their parents. Husband and wives were separated. Sometimes there were so many people waiting to be killed that there was no housing for them and they had to camp out in the forest next to the gas chambers, where the dust of human remains from the chimney stacks of the crematories fell down around them like snow. We meditated in a great circle on that train platform and read the names of those who had been killed in the gas chambers and burned in the crematoriums of this very place.

It was very cold outside. I wore all my high-tech gear: polyester and "smart" wool underwear, hats, mittens, and special rain gear. Even so, with all of us bundled up in such layers, we shivered in the freezing cold and the rain. During one downpour, we all sat in one of the still-standing barracks, lit by candlelight—approximately one hundred and fifty retreatants doing *zazen*, the Zen term for seated meditation. Two sides of the barrack were lined with large platforms with partitions, each one three rows high, with bunks to accommodate several people sleeping. When the camps were running, these sleeping enclosures were stuffed with so many people that they even slept on top of each other. Such conditions were devastatingly unhealthy, with the only advantage being that people could use each other's body heat to fight the cold. The occupants of the barracks far exceeded the number of people that were expected when the housing was built. Each barrack housed over seven hundred prisoners. The overcrowding was ignored; it was only one more horrifying condition that contributed to killing the spirits, if not the bodies, of all these imprisoned people.

In the barrack, we sat in the candlelit darkness, listening to the rainfall outside. The names of the dead were read, and after each name, we took a breath. Many people were crying; there were the quiet sounds of meditators sniffling and of arms moving in synthetic parka sleeves against jacketed torsos as people blew their noses and dried their eyes. We faced the terror of what had happened there together, more directly than I could have ever imagined. We were supported in this by the tender poignancy of nature—the sound of the raindrops and the beauty of the candlelight.

One night there was an all-night vigil in the children's

WORLD WAR II AND NO-SELF

barracks. We were all bundled up in our state-of-the-art gear, and I still felt uncomfortably cold. But I knew that the children who once were housed here wore thin cotton prisoner garb and maybe, if they were lucky, huddled under a blanket. I had read in one of the books assigned as homework before the retreat, that the limbs of the children sometimes froze. In one gruesome incident, two babies had actually chewed off their frozen little fingers. Even as I write, I can feel how much I don't want to face those images again. I don't want to imagine my own Jewish children in those barracks or bring them anywhere near this scene.

In our group, there were a good number of Jews and many Germans, each with their own view of the suffering in their cultures. What stood out for me was that each culture had tremendous suffering, and yet they were on the so-called opposite sides of this enormous field of pain. The Germans were dealing with the guilt and surrounding secrecy in their families of having had a relative as a Nazi or employed as a guard at a concentration camp. They faced the anguish of what their people had done. And of course, the Jews faced the horror of having had their relatives annihilated.

But intercultural awareness occurred between the two groups. One very poignant example of this was the meeting between the daughter of a commandant of a certain camp and the son of a survivor from that same camp. At first, when they realized their second-generation connection, they avoided each other as if they were polarized magnets. But little by little, their polarization began to wear down. During our evening discussions, people from all sides shared their personal stories. We began to see a commonality of feelings rather than our differences. All of us began to see that no side was exempt from this deep, layered suffering. There was no escape from the enormous psychic damage of this brutality. Finally, near the end of the retreat, when the daughter of the commandant and the son of the survivor sat down and talked, they found that their experiences as children of Holocaust survivors and perpetrators were ironically similar. Their childhoods had been shrouded in numbness and extreme secrecy, with a mandate not to talk about the pervading sorrow and enervation that they perceived in their relatives and in themselves. All of this deep-seated pain and secrecy produced an unwholesome atmosphere in which to grow up, regardless of which side of the conflict. Against all cultural odds, this man and woman began to empathize with each other's suffering. And theirs was not the only conversation of this kind. As I watched and heard about these conversations among people, I felt the dichotomy between victim and perpetrator slowly dissolved. I saw how our prejudices produce the pain of our *samsara*—the wandering-in-circles world of suffering.

Each day on retreat, Kaddish, the Jewish memorial service for the dead, was performed at the crematories. These services provided extremely emotional catharses, especially during the chanting of the prayer for the dead, which many Jews know by heart. I am a totally assimilated American Jew who became a Buddhist teacher and doesn't follow the faith into which she was born. At certain moments, like during the Kaddish services at the crematories, I wondered how I could forgive myself for turning away from Jewish life. I felt that I had betrayed my own people and all of the Jews who had died in the concentration camps. I was overwhelmed by Jewish guilt. There is a proclamation, both stated and unsaid, among Jews that one should never turn one's back on being Jewish. Because of Jewish oppression comes a very deep enmeshment with family, relatives, and culture. If we don't stick together, what do we have? My parents' entire social circuit was Jewish except for some business acquaintances. If my father had a choice of business partner, they would always be Jewish. My heart broke open with grief beyond grief as I felt the full meaning of having broken with my family and rejected my inherited religion. How had this happened? How dared I? Was there anything that, as a formed adult and as a Buddhist teacher, I could do about the unbearable sorrow I felt about what I had done?

As a fallen-away Jew, I had the chutzpah to ask the rabbi if I could hold the Torah during one of the Kaddish services at the crematorium sites. It was an itty-bitty Torah I could hold in my hand; I covered my heart with it. I was holding the Torah—I who had always hated being Jewish, hated my crazy relatives, and hidden my Jewishness for years. But even though I never spoke about my past or my family during my young life, I failed to hide being Jewish. My hand gestures, my mannerisms, the intonations of my speech—they all gave me away though I never *told* anyone that I was Jewish. Now, I held this miniature Torah to my heart, crying and crying, just asking for forgiveness. I had betrayed all these people who had been sacrificed for their faith. What could I do about my unending regret of being a Jew who was now a Buddhist? The pain of this was very much beyond my understanding. It scorched me and shredded my heart. How could I deal with the very complicated karma of my rebellious past and my ancestors' pain? There is an old Yiddish saying: "The history of the Jews is written in tears." The only thing for me to do was cry, let go, and feel.

Standing in the middle of the Birkenau concentration camp, I realized the causes and conditions that had made my father, my so-called enemy, and he became a human being in my eyes. I saw beyond my limited and preconceived intellectual understanding of who my father was, and the conditions that had shaped his psyche. My heart opened to the causes of my father's rage. It struck me like lightning in a moment of insight and release as I was moving in a long stream of retreat participants toward the front gates for a lunch of bread and soup. All of a sudden, with no warning or intention, I found myself dropping to my knees, my head bent over and my hands on my heart. People were streaming past me on both sides as if I were a rock in a stream, the water rushing past. In this moment out of time, huddled forward over my knees, I forgave my father and asked him to forgive me. Crying and howling with grief for my ancestors, for my parents, and for me, I saw the many repercussions of the violence and dehumanization that had happened in Birkenau and in my people's lives and their connection with my own life.

I could see how my parents' values had been formed by the lifetime projections on them of anti-Semitism and the atrocities of World War II. I saw them struggle with a loss of human connection and their own pride. My parents spent their entire life, from the moment they woke up each morning until their heads touched the pillow at night, working, proving their worth, and gathering status. For better or worse, in terms of human values, I admire my parents for their diligence. What I observed was that the acquisition and accumulation of wealth and power seemed to them like their only safety net. When my father was dying, he told me, "All I can give you is money and the security that money provides. This is all I have and what I give to you." Hearing him say that out loud, my heart broke a little bit more than it already had. That which I had imagined to be true, he had stated audibly. Either he didn't know how or wasn't willing to take the time to love, forgive, or accept his children as they were. Indeed, my father set me up for a life with no financial worries, for which I'm grateful, but my brothers and I have a mental legacy coming from the psychological violence in the family and my parent's priorities. My parents definitely succeeded in finding a place in the society of wealthy Chicago Jews and thrived in business, proving that they were not animals to be slaughtered—they could rise up, and they did.

My father was indeed a great demonstrator of rage-fueled aggression, and at Birkenau I came to understand the conditions that had caused that. He was a keg of dynamite ready to explode at any turn. In fact, he often did explode. I had seen over and over through the years what happened to people, especially men, who were subject to my father's berating abuse. My father insisted on his absolute status of top dog. He was proving to himself over and over that he was worthy, a success and not a denigrated beast, even though, sometimes, through my eyes, he didn't succeed at this last goal because he seemed like a brute to me. If you challenged his authority in any way, he would aim his psychic revolver at your forehead and, without hesitation, shoot. My brothers barely survived my dad's vitriolic screaming at the dinner table. Caustic acid shot out of my dad's mouth as we ate. He aimed psychic bullets, actually more like machine-gun fire, into my brothers with his "good-for-you" criticism. Meanwhile, I, as the only daughter—the youngest and the perfectly behaved, silent, princess—would shovel the food served on a silver platter by a maid into my mouth in an effort to numb myself. Then, once I felt stuffed, I would slide out of my seat onto the floor and hide under the table, out of shooting range. I witnessed my brothers being killed psychologically by my father's furor, night after night over the course of our childhood.

At Birkenau, as I stood with the Torah next to my heart, my young Jewish life passed before my eyes. I still have a vivid image of being dressed by my mother for my Bat Mitzvah, which in the Jewish tradition, formally welcomes a young woman into the congregation. In the 1960s, concurrent with early feminism, the Jewish community in my conservative congregation began to acknowledge the girls by holding Bat Mitzvahs. But a young girl could only have a Bat Mitzvah on Friday night, not on Saturday morning like the boys did, and not with a reading from the Torah, the book of the law given to the Jewish People by Moses. My mother dressed me in a yellow dress with a pair of matching, dyed silk, low-heeled, yellow pumps and a Jackie Kennedy-style yellow pillbox hat—it was 1964. I was an awkward, embarrassed, thirteen-year-old girl with braces and tiny breasts. Standing in front of the congregation, dressed to the nines, in a newly remodeled, very expensive, fancy temple, I read my section of the *haftarah*, which is a reading from the Book of Prophets in the Hebrew Bible, not the main reading from the Torah.

Then a terrible thing happened. Laughing, the rabbi rolled his eyes and joked that my recitation had been sung way too fast. I was mortified. I watched closely the two front rows of twelve- and thirteen-year-old kids, looking for their reaction. They weren't real friends of mine—in fact, did I have any friends? Of course, they weren't paying any attention to me anyway, but I have an almost cartoonish vision of the whole audience roaring with laughter. My stomach was already in a knot just from the exposure of standing up there at the pulpit, but the rabbi's comment reeled me out of my body.

Oh dear, the rabbi's one flippant indiscretion crushed my young heart and closed my connection to the spirituality of Judaism. I would not continue my religious education to confirmation, which happens around the age of fifteen—not after that humiliation, no way. I would just continue nurturing my hatred for Jewishness. I realized that the Bat Mitzvah, a so-called religious event, had not been for me or my spiritual development but was actually for other people, like the rabbi, my mother, and the congregation, and I was angry. How dare the rabbi insult me after my year of studious preparation! I hadn't wanted to do that stupid celebration anyway. I hadn't wanted to be the center of attention. Even at age thirteen, I perceived how inauthentic the scene was. The essential meaning of a Bat Mitzvah, welcoming a thirteen-year-old into adulthood and the Jewish community, was completely lost. This was it—the end of Jewishness for me.

The closest to a religious Jew that I knew was my grandfather Harry, whose last name was originally Libinsky, but when he landed at Ellis Island, he'd changed it to Libin—more American, he thought. He would sing and pray in the backseat of the car, almost mumbling. My family would joke that Grandpa was "deedle-diddling" whenever he did it. During the High Holidays, he would serve as an associate cantor at his synagogue. When I would ask him about religion or what he was doing, he would smile and say, "I don't believe in it; I just like to sing." His words still reverberate in my mind. How disappointing to me that he would not claim his spirituality. I wanted to ask him, "Is there no deeper meaning for you, Grandpa?"

But I had a healing moment and connection to Grandpa at Birkenau. I was standing at a gathering with a tallis, a Jewish prayer shawl, draped over my head. I may have been using the tallis to hide my face, so I could continuously cry. Someone asked for a song. I knew one Jewish song in Yiddish that my grandfather had taught me, "Oyfin Pripetchik," a nineteenth-century song that's famous as a memory of pre-Holocaust times. I remember him teaching me the song in the back seat of the car, having me repeat it after him. That had made him happy. He had laughed with me at my attempts to memorize the song.

Now, at Birkenau, I stepped forward into the field of a Jewish annihilation camp, and, with the tallis covering my head, shoulders, and body, I sang this song of my ancestors with my whole heart.

My alienation from my Jewish heritage had many causes. What does it mean to assimilate? Sometimes, it seems to me that assimilation is a way to cover up the pain of internalized anti-Semitism. We were white-skinned, so Jewish assimilating in America was possible. However, assimilating did not address our deep-rooted inner shock and the submerged lacerations of the Holocaust. Our trauma was buried. Assimilation became for me a disconnection and dislocation. What I lost was the richness, the interconnection with community, the deep sense of belonging. I became detached from my history and culture and that dissociation left me feeling cold and alienated.

One afternoon at Birkenau concentration camp I saw what has become for me one of the symbols of the retreat. It was a searing illustration of the statement: There is no "other." Across from me, a Japanese Zen monk who was teaching in Germany and spoke fluent German was dressed in many layers. First, worn over his parka were his *koromo* and *okesa* (the robes of a Japanese Buddhist priest), and then, over those robes was an oversized tallis, covering him from shoulder to ankle in blue and white. The Japanese, German, Zen, and Jewish cultures, with their differences, were living in peace and harmony in this one man. I couldn't take my eyes off him.

Hiroshima/Nagasaki

Corresponding to the image of the Zen monk wearing a tallis, which was burned into my brain, is my own image of myself, years later, standing in the middle of Hiroshima, Japan. I had gone there on a Buddhist pilgrimage with the Jizos for Peace Project, organized by Great Vow Monastery. Standing and sweating in extremely hot weather in Hiroshima on August 9, 2005, the day of the sixtieth anniversary of the United States' nuclear bombing, I saw through to the bottom of any sense I had of a "conditioned, solid, one-identity self" in utter amazement. There were so many identities within me interchanging. There I was, dressed in traditional Japanese clothes as a Zen monk, with my head shaved. I was an American, Jewish, female, feminist, dressed in traditional Japanese clothes, and bald. Being bald was deeply emotionally emblematic for me. On the one hand, I felt like I was masquerading as a man, and layered on top of that, I felt like a Jewish woman entering a gas chamber, a breast-cancer survivor, or a Zen priest letting go of her attachments. The complexity and superimposition of these images triggered my sense of the unraveling of my identity. Who was I? These multidimensional references left me totally baffled. I was standing in the spot where my country had committed the worst atrocities of war: nuclear, mass, and civic destruction. I was standing there for peace. However, in many people's eyes, I was still the enemy.

Part of our pilgrimage involved talking to atom bomb survivors, called *Hibacksha*. One older woman kept repeating, "But you're an American, but you're an American," in disbelief that we were there in peace. Or that we were actually Zen Buddhist priests. I was filled with questions. Was I just an outrageous symbol of appropriation?

Nagasaki and Hiroshima have been completely rebuilt and one would never know simply from looking at these cities that, now more than seventy years ago, they were totally destroyed. In Hiroshima, only one square block of ruins remains as part of the Hiroshima Peace Memorial Museum. But even though the appearance of the cities belies the devastation, when you talk to people and scratch the surface of their stories, all the pain of the last generation is completely present.

On the outskirts of Nagasaki, the Jizos For Peace participants visited an eighty-five-year-old nun. Her temple was far enough into the country that it was just outside the perimeter of the destruction from the bomb. She answered our questions in a quiet and tender manner, but her stories were quite terrifying. She told us that in the days that followed immediately after the bombing, when she went down in the mornings to open the front gate of her temple, there would be mounds of bodies. People would bring their dead and pile them up at the front gate, hoping that they would be cremated and buried according to Buddhist tradition. The temple also took care of the wounded and people who were dying. She said that the nuns did first aid on the injured and burn patients and held people's hands while they died. The situation was so dire that blood from the second story seeped through the floor and dripped down from the ceiling onto the first floor. She said that people were all crying out for water to quench their thirst from the bomb's enormous ball of fire. Seared into my soul: my country had dropped this bomb.

On this trip, I also learned about Japanese war crimes. No side was spared the horror of seeing its own country do terrible things. The most famous of the Japanese massacres is the Rape of Nanking, which took place from 1937 to 1938, during which the Japanese military massacred as many as three hundred thousand Chinese civilians and prisoners of war. This slaughter in Nanking is just one of many examples; the burying of Chinese POWs alive is another. To my regret, I also found out that Japanese Zen Buddhism was used in the training of the kamikaze pilots. The Japanese military used the discipline of *sesshin*, our retreat style, and the theology of being unafraid of death to train young Japanese boys not to be afraid of killing themselves in suicide plane missions for their country. This is ironically similar to the training for the religious-based suicide bombers today. And so it goes: No country or no religion is spared the ugliness of war. My idealization of Japanese Zen was irrevocably cracked when I learned these things.

Whether amidst or because of my internal chaotic reactions to what I was experiencing, from out of nowhere, an insight into "who I am" or, more accurately, "who I am not" dawned on me. I had long expected that my startling perception of the main Buddhist teaching of no-centralized self, *non-self*, would happen on the *zafu*, or meditation cushion, in the classic way in a meditation hall. But, ironically, the diffusion of my sense of a solid identity—an "I" with ownership of her choices—occurred in the middle of the overwhelming situation of a peace demonstration in this place of nuclear devastation. Thich Nhat Hanh, the famous Vietnamese Zen teacher, has taught over and over, "*I am made up of non-I elements.*" According to this teaching, we are not isolated units of being but instead are completely interdependent and formed by the causes that preceded our life or the conditions that produce the current moment. I began to clearly see all the *non-I* elements that produced the construction of myself.

I came to realize that I, Judith, was a reaction to all the issues of the previous generation. My life had been a reaction to my parents, to World War II, to the cultural influence of "hippies," and to other events. It seems that all of the most important decisions of my life—who I would marry, what my religion and career would be—had been made from an aversive reaction to my parents' and Jewish history. Choosing Zen meant choosing the religion of the enemy—the Japanese. My blue-eyed, blonde, *goyish* husband, who has German ancestors, fits into this same scheme of oppositional defiance. I was aware of how rebellious my sad, angry, hurt, teenage self had been, but I had not understood the extent of her conditioning and reactivity. Now I realized that I was made up of all these non-I elements.

Even though I had studied the teaching of Buddhism for many years, still I had unconsciously presumed that there was a central place in myself that had made many of the major decisions of my life. This was my delusion of being in control. The core of me, my deeply held beliefs, loves, and choices, I now experienced as a response to outer conditions. This was far beyond psychology. My choices were not produced, as I had previously thought, by a brilliant "I." Instead, I saw that "I" was merely a reaction! This revelation stunned me. My "I" felt deeply betrayed.

This deep untangling of identity and my understanding of choicelessness left me with the profound feeling of being lost. I wandered around Hiroshima and Nagasaki not knowing who I was and feeling a lot of grief, anguish for this history I was witnessing, and despair over losing my sense of self. Meandering through this Japanese city, I felt desolate, as if my life had been a sham. It was all a reaction, a kind of nihilistic, empty backlash. I felt like a ghost.

I had never questioned the core decisions in my life up until this point. I had always believed that these decisions came from a deep place in myself. Now I was heartbroken. I could see that many of my decisions had been sourced from the group-think of my generation. I joined a whole generation of hippies in defiance of the dominant culture and in opposition to what had happened in the '50s, which, in turn, was a reaction to what had happened in the '40s, etc. I had also joined a whole parcel of Jews who assimilated so well into American culture that we weren't Jewish anymore. Everything in my life had happened to me through the Buddhist term "interdependent co-origination," and not "me." In that moment, I saw this interdependence, and I was deeply changed forever.

I have a whole new relationship to my sense of choice now. I became, experientially, a systems thinker. I am a cog in a big machine. I have to keep my wheel turning with the best discernment and decision-making I can muster, but it is ultimately and always in relationship to all the other cogs. It is a letting go of a sense of individual power. Even if I don't know exactly what to do in any given moment, the momentum of the whole machine—the "Whole Works" or the "Total Dynamic Function"— as the great teacher Dogen Zengi from fourteenth-century Japan called it, this dynamism will keep me moving and functioning. I am learning to let go, and by default, learning to trust something larger than myself.

There were healing moments, too, amidst these overwhelming environments. Each morning at the family temple in Nagasaki, which housed us, we would all gather to do *zazen*, the Zen term for meditation. We joined the temple priest and his friend who did zazen there every day. Afterward, the friend would go into the Buddha hall and play his *shakuhachi*, or breath flute, for a half hour. Each day I would sit on the porch *tatami*, a woven flooring mat used in traditional Japanese rooms, and listen to the flute's melodious sound joined with my breath, the wind in the trees, the bells of the temple, and the blue, open sky singing of emptiness. The man would play for a half hour and then change from his sitting clothes into his suit and go to work, walking out of the temple with a briefcase swinging in his hand, and then the music would linger in my mind all day. It was a soothing sound, expressing the essence and goodness of life, which contradicted and also, in a sense, helped to ameliorate like a balm the desecrated humanity that I was facing during the day. The sound of the shakuhachi, the sound of the breath, combined with the feel of my deeply held heartbreak, began to, in some small, immeasurable way, mend me.

All over Japan, we were involved with water—the element of water and its healing properties. We poured water over the heads of statues of Jizo Bodhisattva, the Buddhist guardian of birth and death. On many street corners there would be a little Jizo altar maintained by the neighborhood. You could light a candle or pour water over the statues. We sent candlelit memorial boats down the river in Hiroshima with thousands of other boats in a city-wide ceremony of memorial. These little boats were made of cardboard or light wood, each with a brightly colored sail, lit by candlelight and moving slowly through the streams of the river and among thousands of boats. Each boat carried the radiance of the spirit of someone who had died. The beauty of these thousands of colorfully candlelit boats touched and soothed my heart.

What I experienced for the most part, was that the people of Hiroshima and Nagasaki were not filled with hate but with a deep reverent need to tell the world that what happened to them can never happen again. They asked us to remember this destruction and to bring forth the humanity of a different kind of conflict resolution. They were emphatically calling out to the world, urging us to figure out how to go toward living together in peace.

The Nagasaki Atomic Bomb Museum & Peace Park is designed around water. Many walls have water streaming down their sides—whole walls of water—answering the cries of thirst from the people dying from the burning ball of fire. Turn the corner inside the museum and you'll find a bench by a still pool. Here and there, right in the middle of displayed mementos of the devastation of this city and the projections of images of the dead on the walls are centers of respite and moving water's quiescent melody—just as there is a center of quiet right in the middle of our being. Right in the center of everything is the offering of a place to rest and heal, surrounded by the flow of water. Is there a possibility of healing from the traumas we inflicted upon Japan? Is forgiveness possible?

Gifts of Forgiveness

In 1985, when my teacher Katagiri-Roshi was still alive, Ikko Narasaki Roshi came to Hokyoji, a Zen monastery in Southern Minnesota, for a weeklong retreat. I particularly remember the ceremony he did for us: the *Ryaku Fusatsu*, or full-moon, receiving-the-precepts ceremony. At that time, Hokyoji had no electricity. The zendo was lit by kerosene lamps and was full to the brim with students. It was so crowded that our zabutons, or sitting mats, touched each other and were lined up even in the middle of the room, which is usually kept as an open space. During the ceremony, Narasaki Roshi pulled his *okesa*, Buddha's robe, over his head, looking just like images I had seen of the great Bodhidharma, who is known for bringing Buddhism from India to China. He began to sing the eerily melodic tune of the ceremony in the lantern light, and I thought to myself that this experience was completely other-worldly. I could have been sitting in a community on a mountain peak in the Himalayas. I didn't understand him as he was singing in Sino-Japanese, nevertheless I was punctured in my heart with the arrow of the dharma. It was a very poignant experience.

On the last lecture of the week, Narasaki Roshi, the distinguished Zen master from Japan, started to cry! He said that he had not wanted to come to America, the land of the enemy.

He said he had a lot of hatred in his heart for America and Americans after the catastrophe in Japan of World War II. He was just barely convinced to do it as a favor to Katagiri Roshi, but he had a lot of internal resistance. Now, he said, having sat zazen in the beauty of Hokyoji, in the *zendo,* or meditation hall, with all of us for a week, he had watched his hatred dissolve. Ikko Narasaki Roshi watched his mind as it changed. He began to see our humanness and hear our heartfelt stories. He saw our practice as the same as his practice. As he told of his transformation, the whole zendo began to cry. I think he left the United States a changed man, which he had not expected. We had all thought that the students would be changed, but in this atmosphere of truth, in a week of sitting together, we were all mutually transformed.

At the Birkenau retreat, there were also many transformations. By the time we had come to our last day at the concentration camp, I was cried out. My personal suffering around my Jewishness and the issues of my individual life seemed to have subsided, and I finally was clear enough to do what I came to do: pray for the dead.

I had read and been told that people on the previous Auschwitz-Birkenau retreat felt that many invisible spiritual beings were present on the land. Though I hadn't expected to connect with that type of extraordinary reality, I felt by the last afternoon that I was being touched by invisible beings. There was a mass of luminous healing energy there at the camps that counterbalanced the horrible evil. On the last day I chose not to follow the schedule. What I wanted to do was put on my *okesa* over my parka and do the slowest possible Zen walking meditation. On inhale, you lift your foot; on exhale, you place your foot; and, superimposed on these breaths, I did *tonglen,* a Tibetan

Buddhist practice. I began with the classic tonglen—breathing in the suffering and exhaling out healing, loving energy visualized as moonlight. I did this all morning and became very concentrated. At the crematories, I could not simply walk through and do tonglen in the areas of the killing field, which show up now as outlines on the ground where the foundations stood, because the energy in those places was totally overwhelming. I found that I could digest some of my feelings if I put only one or two toes over the line of demarcation. That was enough. I just tried to breathe in the pain of that square inch of land. I stayed in the killing field for quite a long time.

In this concentrated state, unexpectedly, the direction of my tonglen practice started to change. As I breathed in, rather than feeling the corrosive energy of pain and sorrow, I felt the energy of the place healing me, and as I breathed out, I felt like I was letting go. By the afternoon, my tonglen practice changed even further. As the directions were reversing, the opposition of in and out was dissolving. I couldn't control what was coming in or going out. Then I laughed and just let every part of the breath be filled with healing and gentleness. There was no inside and no outside. There was no victim and no perpetrator. There was no someone trying to heal others and no someone being healed. Just love flowing in and out and all around.

By the end of the day, I heard angels singing. This sound was a spangled opening through the mist in the gloaming. Was it internal or external? It seemed it was coming from everywhere. Through the shimmering silver light, a thin, beautiful, tremulous thread of voices pierced through the sky and the clouds, the shadows of the leaves, and my mind. In a pure, high, and clear voice, the angels were singing the three pure precepts—"Do good, don't do harm, and save all beings"—over and over in the twilight. *Do good, don't do harm, and save all beings.* The trees, walls, tiles, and pebbles at Birkinau were all singing the Three Pure Precepts. My heart and mind relaxed in a spacious moment of interconnection, freedom, and healing.

Chapter Two

DOCK RETREAT

What is the heart of this old monk like?
A gentle wind
Beneath the vast sky.
—Ryōkan (translated by John Stevens)

"The crazy woman of Mirror Lake," my husband laughed. What could the children on their bicycles possibly have thought of me as they passed me on the little-used dirt path? Or the suburban women dressed in their khaki shorts and pastel shirts, walking their dogs, side by side, intently talking? They would look up and notice me. Strange, they said, that woman—is she meditating? They became quiet as they pass behind me. When there was enough distance between us, they began talking again. They got used to me, finally, after months of seeing me. *Yes, of course, she's meditating.* And then there was the man with his two big dogs. Twice a day, he walked them off the leash— once in the early morning in the dark before he went to work, and once again, after he came home. There I was, still sitting in the dark. At first his dogs barked at me, but then day after day, they got used to me. They would just come up and sniff me and rub their noses on my back and then return to their business of running around the path of the lake.

Here is how they all saw me: as a fifty-year-old woman sitting alone on a single section of wooden dock pushed up against the edge of Mirror Lake, which is barely a lake, really—it's almost a pond, but big enough to be home to a lot of water creatures. This woman sat on a black pillow and mat with a canvas bag next to her. On some bright, sunny days she had a sun umbrella with her, and on some rainy days she sat with a large rain umbrella and two tarps, one for her and one for her bag. She sat, not moving, day after day in this quiet, slightly wild, suburban park. Such a strange sight, like an appearance of exotic fauna, like a moose sighting, or a red fox—oh my, a still woman!

* * *

One day on the dock, my eyes opened and I saw before me an ancient being that had swum up to the shore. It was very large, with craggily pointed spikes on its huge, wide shell. Cocking his head to the left, he looked at me. Our eyes met for a long time, and we both stayed completely still. Enough, he finally decided, and ducked down to disappear into the deep. Oh my, I realized, that was a snapping turtle! I closed my eyes again and also descended into the deep quiet.

It was all so unexpected. There I sat in the middle of a suburb, in the middle of family life—in the middle of minivans, grocery stores, dishes, and children's screams, laughter, and demands. In the middle of the chaos of family life, I did a solo retreat, outside on the dock by the lake in our backyard. Could you call it a "hermit practice?" I laughed. A hermit practice surrounded by family—not exactly what the ancient male teachers wrote about in their quiet huts at the top of the mountain.

I suppose the main reason I turned to solo practice is that I had left my sangha right before it blew up. The three assistant teachers, all women—I was one of them, already demoted from my title of coteacher—began to feel the toxicity of the environment. When I acknowledged to myself that these were grave ethical violations, when I felt pushed out of my position, I had to leave and to give up the group denial. The community wanted to ignore the misconduct, excuse it, or hide it, and I could no longer do that. I left the sangha in as dignified a manner as I could, taking two weeks to say goodbye individually to all my students. Then I was shunned. What I wanted to say, the members of the sangha didn't want to hear. I was taken aback, shocked by this failure of community, Buddhist teachings, and relationships in modern spiritual life.

Two years after I left, the sangha did explode. On May 10, 2004, an email was sent out to the community by the teacher in question, acknowledging the truthfulness of these sexual allegations. I was devastated and heartbroken and I didn't know where to go. I couldn't just go and quickly join another sangha. I needed to be alone and to digest what had happened and so, I sat by myself, outside on the dock.

Also at that time of my life, I was burning with Zen ardor and the desire to really know the truth about life. I had an incredible willingness to follow spiritual discipline; the sangha I had left was quite rigorous, so I was trained in using my willpower. I had a sentence repeating in my mind: "If I just sit quietly for some long, deep time, the quiet will dissolve all my doubts. If my mind is quiet enough, I will just *know*." I took this sad opportunity of disengagement from formal Zen communal practice, and just sat. I decided I would sit like the ancient hermits but do it smack dab in the middle of my suburban life.

I made a schedule in the Zen style, crafting a highly choreo-graphed container. I fit the container around the schedule of being a mother and found that there was quite a lot of time to sit. In that respect, it was quite similar to formal retreats and *sesshins* I had done with the sangha. You don't have to think, you simply follow the schedule. Here's how I arranged my day:

- 4:00-6:00 a.m: Sitting and walking meditation outside on the dock with a formal service
- 6:00-9:00 a.m: Prepare the children for school. Dress them, feed them, and drive them to school.
- 9:00 a.m.-12:00 p.m: Just sit and walk at the dock and the park path.
- 12:00 p.m. onward: The rest of the day was "regu-lar": chores, appointments, chauffeuring, phone calls, emails, exercising, food preparation, and family life.

What was equally important to me, besides finding the stillness that the Ancient Ones talk about, was integrating this deep knowing of silence and emptiness with the ordinary aspects of my life. This was then and continues to be my main explora-tion: How can I integrate my karmic life and my dharma life? This at-home type of retreat was ideal for seeing the disparity between my "retreat self" and how I act in my so-called regular life. Could I demonstrate my understanding of the source point of stillness and the mystery that is always within and surrounds me, even while seeing the habituated patterns of my personal life that come from greed, anger, and ignorance? Would that clarity of mind that comes from meditation help me to see and then choose to change my psychological patterns? From a very clear and focused mind, this type of retreat allowed me to observe myself as I failed at being a "good parent" and to watch my reaction to my failure. If I could not change my habits and reactions completely, could I at least soften them as I saw them in the huge perspective of the big sky, the quiet pond, the still mind?

Georgia O'Keeffe was once asked, "What is the most important thing about making art?" Her answer was so different from what I expected. She said, "You have to learn how to say 'no' to many, many, things so you can just paint." I took her advice to heart. During this time, in order to do a solo retreat, I had to say no to anything other than my sitting schedule and my family. I said no to Zen teaching, my students, dates with friends. If I were not strict about saying no, this retreat would evaporate before my eyes. I understood it as a renunciation. Saying no to the manifest world in all its appearances—the scheduling, the appointments, the chores—allows us to discover the underlying energy that runs through all life, through all moments and all time. It was, at least in the morning, a time of nondoing. I was doing nothing. That certainly went against my very strong achievement drive and my desire for enlightenment. But this retreat helped teach me that doing nothing can reveal a lot. I had to hold my "no" extremely dear. That "no" taught me how to say "yes" to what was exactly happening in the moment. Yes to the rain, the raccoon family, or the dark early morning sky. Yes to my children, crying or laughing. Yes to my mundane, ordinary life.

Before bearing children, I had practiced Zen for twenty years in the more usual circumstances of Buddhist centers and monasteries. Just after childbirth, I realized, "Oh, childrearing *is* monastic practice." You completely surrender all your time and thoughts to something beyond your egotistical desires, that is, to the needs of your children. The parenting schedule is also demanding and its intensity is as exacting as a monastic schedule. Nothing can be skipped. You do whatever is right in front of your nose to do. I remember realizing, just after breast-feeding stopped, "Oh my gosh, I have to make three meals a day! And after every single meal, I need to scrub the high chair and the surrounding floor." These were endless mundane actions I had never really even thought about in the joy of anticipating children or being pregnant or nursing them. Surprise! We surrender ourselves when we have to get up in the middle of the night, maybe several times, or change the diapers again and yet again. I needed to cultivate the patience I never had as I responded to my sick child. He brought many opportunities to be present whether I liked the circumstances or not.

I kept in my heart the stories of an East Indian woman, a Buddhist teacher who would meditate during the night while her family was sleeping. During the day, she did all the chores required in her role as wife and mother. She would repeat to herself, "It can be done, it can be done." A wife and mother can be enlightened. Another story I kept in my heart is that of the mother of one Tibetan teacher who was said to "practice in the gaps." When asked how she practiced, she said, "When there is a gap, I return my mind to my breath, to interdependence, to silence." Within her busy life, she became free.

I did five dock retreats of two-to-three months duration over the next three years. But in Minnesota, where I live, the fall and the spring are the perfect times, with moderate weather and no bugs. Eventually, I built a screen hut, so I could practice outdoors in the summer.

I kept my bag always ready for dock sitting. My large canvas bag held a fuzzy blanket, a hat with a rim, a water bottle, a journal and pen, binoculars for fun, a chant booklet, and two rain ponchos (one for me and one for my shoes and bag). I learned that around 30 to 40 degrees Fahrenheit was my threshold for the cold. Even in late fall or early spring, I would bundle up as if for winter with snow pants, many layers of coats, and a huge blanket as my final wrap.

I usually wore rubber boots to walk through the dew-filled grass, the high weeds, the cattails, and along a dirt path. My husband built a very haphazard stairway with wooden slats to get down the steep slope to the lake. Mirror Lake is so much like Walden Pond that there is a touching of two worlds.

The dock retreats seemed to have their own natural rhythm. The first few weeks would be an exhilarating relief from the chaos of life. My quiet meditations brought an intoxication of fresh air, sky and sun, cattails, red-winged blackbirds, dragonflies, butterflies, fish, raccoons, deer, dog walkers, and the sounds of children's soccer teams playing in a field down the way. But as I sat deeply and the retreat wore on, the mud of my unprocessed psychology was stirred up from the bottom of my mind. Through clear eyes, I started to see all the places in which I was stuck in my life and the parts of myself that I held in disdain. I sometimes went over and over in my head the moments when I yelled at my children. Or I would have non-stop cravings to go to my neighborhood coffee shop for muffins or chocolate cake. Or I'd think repeatedly of hurts that had happened to me in the past, even decades ago. Sometimes I called this part of the retreat "shoveling the shit out of my psyche"—it is not a high, and it is often painful. But perhaps, after all that shoveling, I would experience a period of deep quiet. So quiet that I wouldn't even recognize it happening. Often the endings of the retreats were not what I had planned—usually they were shorter than scheduled and dissolved into busyness without my realizing it as I responded to life's chores calling me. Sometimes an emergency would arise, like my husband or one of the kids becoming ill, and the retreat would automatically be over. I was always disappointed with those endings. I wanted them to be more like the ones that happen in a formal Zen retreat, when nothing interrupts the determination to go to the finish line. Finally, however, I softened as I realized that sitting alone without external support is simply different, and I let the ending of my solo retreats be a quiet dissolving of the container with no fanfare.

In those retreats, I was also challenged by my fears of darkness. The 4:00 a.m. sitting was usually in pitch blackness. I remembered the phrase, "Take back the night," which became the marching cry of protests against rape and other forms of sexual, relationship, and domestic violence as early as 1975, and later on, the lyrics for a Justin Timberlake song. "Take back the night" became a legitimized practice for me. I had to face my fears of sitting alone in a dark public park. Having once survived a rape, I found my victim fears wrapping themselves all around me. For the first several weeks, I sat in the dark imagining a man coming up behind me and grabbing me. I was afraid even though this was a suburban park and our older women neighbors assured us that there had been no crime in our neighborhood for fifty years. Still, I sat with my cell phone turned on, in case the boogey man suddenly came up to harm me. But day after day, I realized I was safe. Each day, like clockwork, at 5:45 a.m., the same two chatting men, walking their dogs, passed behind me on the dirt path that runs along the edge of the lake. I made sure to introduce myself. They were accepting and curious as they listened quite intently to my explanation of what I was doing. Soon, I left my cell phone at home. And soon, only the dogs with sniffing noses, wagging tails, and wet tongues cared that I was there, sitting still, in the dark of early morning.

After I relaxed about experiencing physical harm, I fought spiritual demons. Insidiously, these entities would find their way into my mind. During one of the retreats, I had a very convoluted fantasy. One of my students had been involved with African voodoo immigrant shamans and he was often afraid they had power over him. Because of our relationship, I fantasized that the shamans could enter my mind as well. The student became a psychic depot for reflecting the shamanic energy. Even as a teenager, I had been especially sensitive and had felt panicked that I might be the one person in the room who would become possessed. I never watch scary movies like The Exorcist, which my husband and children love.

My fear of the occult and spiritual demons may be what caused me to choose Zen all those years ago, because Zen is a most grounded spiritual practice. Now, in the dark, at the edge of my own backyard, my fears had gone wild. I felt I could be possessed by evil demons. For many days, maybe even a week, I did the practice I had learned from Machick Lapdron, an eleventh-century Tibetan tantric female teacher, who wrote about what she called "feeding the demons."

First, as much as possible, I would let go of my thoughts and return to the breath. Thinking is what produces the fear and the fantasy. If I could not release the feeling of malevolent spirits being present around me, I would begin to feed them all the kindness and loving energy I could. With each exhale, I sent them good, wholesome, kind, loving, generous energy, filling them up with rapture until they lay down and slept, completely satiated with spiritual nectar. Sometimes I would have to do this repeatedly over days. There is a tale in the Tibetan Buddhist lore of Milarepa, a famous Tibetan yogi and poet, sitting in his cave with demons. At first, he physically fought them, but that didn't seem to work. Then, he taught his demons the dharma. He loved-up his demons. Little by little, the demons left the cave. Finally, the last strongest, most persistent demon was left and Milarepa made that demon also dissolve by surrendering his body to the demon and putting his head directly into the demon's mouth. In an act of total bravery and abandonment, he faced his fear without hesitation. As I had learned in other more formal Buddhist retreats, the stability of *zazen* would protect me. I sat and sat and felt protected by emptiness. After a few weeks of fear, I could just sit, with nothing in my mind, in the complete dark.

This nothing-in-my-mind state was very different for me. Now, as I look back, I see that it was actually the deepest gift I received from these retreats. Silence and nothing. I just did not have the thought of self-referencing or wishing for more. I was completely at home and familiar with sitting, doing nothing, empty mind, and silence. What a deep relaxation! It was very unpretentious. Just sitting. The environment and my body-mind were completely the same. In many ways, I haven't experienced that again. This was utterly simple. I just sat outdoors in the backyard with no pageantry of formal Buddhism at all. I was empty, without thoughts.

Darkness and its accompanying silence became my friends. When the early mornings in the dark weren't cloudy, I noticed the stars. One morning I had a strange yet obvious insight. The stars were in the same place as the day before. Oh, I thought, those are the constellations! How silly of me, of course. I felt like an original ape-man realizing there were patterns among the stars. I bought a star map and learned all the constellations I could see; then I bought a telescope. In northern Minnesota, there are "boundary waters wilderness areas," and while on vacation there, I would get out my telescope at any hour of the night. In the pitch black, maybe at 3:00 a.m., by myself, I would stand in awe of our planets, galaxies, nebulas, and star clusters. My best sighting was the rings of Saturn. I was not afraid to be alone in the dark. I stood in astonishment before the universe. This, I thought, is the vastness of interdependence and emptiness. Universal perspective, Katagiri Roshi used to say.

Now I sometimes just turn to the dark silence for relief. For example, as a Zen teacher, I have a small room in which to see students one on one. After talking in relationship for hours in this closed room, if there is a moment between events, I'll just turn off the light and sit in the dark to refresh myself.

On the dock, there were many one-on-one meetings with animals. It was extremely exciting to have an intimate connection with them. My heart pumped, my adrenaline levels rose: *What's going to happen?* A raccoon family—a mom and five kits—often came to visit in the dark of the early morning sittings. They came out of the cattails. First, I'd hear a rustling sound and then their little heads would peek out from behind cattails or jut out above the grasses. Their little beady eyes asked, "What is that? A human? Why is she here?" Then they would trudge through the shallow water to avoid me. Once, one of them even crawled under the dock I was sitting on. My heart thumped: Was he going to bite me?

There was a weasel that would roll in the dry mud in front of me—long, slender, and sinewy. He may not have noticed the still person behind him. Didn't he smell me? After his rolling dance, the weasel would disappear into the weeds. I imagined his tunnels leading out from where I sat.

Sitting with my eyes closed one warm spring day with my cap on so its brim could shield my eyes from the sun, I felt something on the top of my head. My mind was very quiet, devoid of words. Quiet, quiet, quiet. But slowly, one sentence began to form: "Could... that... be... a... bird?" I felt two little feet push off and heard the swishing sound of fluttering wings. "Oh my god, that's a bird!" I thought. Pause. "I must be St. Francis of Assisi." Pause. "Calm down, you silly fool, calm down, let go, come back."

Once I opened my eyes as the sun was coming up. I was wrapped in a blanket to ward off the morning chill and when I looked down at my body, I noticed that my blanket was covered with very small, less than a half inch long, white things that looked like larva. What were these things, I wondered. How did I get covered with them during the hour that my eyes were closed? Were they insects, mosquito larvae? Or seeds? I never found out.

* * *

Between each sitting, I did a slow walking meditation down the narrow, foot-worn path alongside the lake to the circular turnaround that marked the end of our street. Especially in the spring, I could see the infinitesimal movement of nature's growth. One day there would be a bud, then maybe the beginning of a leaf, then a spray of baby leaves—all visible as I walked by in slow motion. In the fall, I could watch the leaves twisting this way and that as they fell.

From this quiet place, I would reemerge into my ordinary life. That reentry was as simple as walking up the hill and entering through the back door. There would be piles of dishes or laundry to be done, and screaming children fighting over their toys. Coming from a feeling of "nothing" on the dock, this whirlwind of activity felt completely strange. My hypersensitivity and vulnerability did not help me respond appropriately. Wearing an invisible cloak of disengagement, I could hardly cope. I kept crashing into the clumsiness of my habitual emotional patterning. I was in a refined state of energy from sitting and the coarseness of the ordinary patterns of family life disconcerted me. I was actually more impatient, losing my temper at the smallest things. It was hard to know what to do when my children fought each other or would defy my authority. I saw that I didn't know how to set a boundary without being angry. Even the dog barking could shatter my nerves.

I began to have a mindfulness practice called "putting on the children's snow gear." I noticed that I screamed at the kids every time we tried to leave the house and I had to put on their snowsuits, their boots, mittens, gloves, hats, and scarves first. One day we were in the small hallway by the garage, where we had cubby holes for all their outerwear. When I watched myself from a clearer mind that was produced by sitting more zazen, I noticed that I was quite obviously off kilter. I could feel my adrenaline start to rush and my hands begin turning into forceful claws, pushing and shoving the children into their snowsuits. And putting on their boots was another awful adventure altogether. It was frustrating to see one child get overly-heated while waiting for us all dressed up in their snow gear, while the other child was losing it trying to get their boots on. And Mom was losing it too! My mouth would be yelling at and speaking so harshly to my adorable, really innocent children—my precious ones. There was all this demand-energy, just because I wanted to get out of the house on a certain fixed timetable, and nothing and nobody was going to stop me accomplishing my task.

Finally, I just didn't want to do that anymore, especially after coming straight home from silence. So I decided to double the time, from fifteen minutes to thirty minutes, as my set-aside time for this newly devised meditation of preparing to leave the house with my children. I realized that this time was about me and my response and not about getting out of the house, so I made a vow that this half hour of mindfulness was the most important spiritual practice of my day. I smile now, as that seems like such an unusual priority. Snowsuits over silence and prayer? Could I get the kids dressed without losing my temper? Day after day I practiced. I was proud, in the end, that I improved. This seemed like a more truthful ranking of my mindfulness practices and felt deeply healing to me. Putting my children's snowsuits on them in relationship and love felt more important and harder than the formal practice of getting up early, sitting in silence in front of the fire in the fireplace, which is where I did my zazen when it was winter.

* * *

I remember walking down the halls of my children's elementary school, feeling like an exotic giraffe towering over the chaos of children half my height; it was a sea of children, running, laughing, and yelling all around me. I went to a PTA meeting and felt like an alien as I looked around at all the anxious moms really trying to do good things for the school. They had a lot of to-do lists and strategies. I felt thin-skinned and vulnerable. Who was I in this field of humanity? But this was actually a great grounding practice to weave back and forth from silence to activity, like a kite remembering that someone is holding the other end of the string, anchoring it to the earth. Could I find relationship and kindness in this madness? How could the calm of the dock help me in my life? I didn't go away to a monastery for this retreat, but its world of stillness and my own world of activity were both very visible to me and

I held them in close comparison. In some Zen literature and teachings, these two worlds are seen as one seamless whole. But at that point in my spiritual maturity, stillness and activity seemed to be miles apart from each other, even though I just walked up and down a small hill from one to the other.

Because my mind was quiet, I could observe my harmful patterns very clearly and see a whole list of human failings. How quick I was to judge and be angry with my children, my husband, the women at school. I had very little patience with the mundane chores of life. I saw with some regret the pace of my life, the pace of the Zen Center I had worked for, the pace of my ambitions and human desire to construct things. I could see that this pace often blocked my true connection with my children and the people in my life. The contrast between the lake and its creatures, the darkness and the quiet, and my automatic functioning in the afternoon of chores was quite stark. It exposed a new level of ego-driven tensions. I saw that I was always evaluating everything and everyone. In this comparing mind, I found myself a critical and sometimes unkind observer.

Practice is not just entering silence. It's also working with how we conduct our active lives. In these retreats, I saw both sides of life under a spotlight. This was the advantage of doing an at-home retreat. I saw no-mind and also the very difficult aspects of my egocentric patterns in relationships. I saw a long list of faults coming from my humanness. I didn't want my mindfulness to simply fall into the hole of self-denigration, but rather, to allow these deep observations of human frailties to inspire me to keep enlarging my perspective and my understanding of self and other. From this larger view of the world, I might gently be able to let down my defenses and therefore change my behaviors.

These observations of myself in activity were in such con-
tradiction with the world of the pond. I wanted to allow nature
to heal and teach me. The tree I observed day after day across
Mirror Lake was a beautiful expression of the flow of life and
impermanence. Over the course of the seasons, I watched it
grow leaves, flower, shed its leaves, and go dormant. In the
winds of autumn, on some days, there was almost a continuous
diagonal stream of falling orange leaves. It was so beautiful, the
tree letting its leaves fall and being generous and giving, even
in its "death" in the fall. The world seemed to work in peace at
the lake. As Dogen, the thirteenth-century Zen teacher said,
"The fish swim like the fish. The birds fly like the birds." My
dock retreats encouraged me to continue practicing forever—
practicing to find the ease of being truly myself, at one with my
environment. Just Judith being Judith. And practice is simple
and complicated at the same time.

It is still surprising to me that this period in my life came
to an end. I thought that I could always do dock retreats, but
the karmic conditions for such an endeavor have to be ripe.
Many things have to come together in retreat. I have to be especially disciplined to do it solo. It was a special time and I still
always hope for it to be repeated, but so far, it never has. But
its influence on my understanding stays with me. I am profoundly grateful to my past self for having the determination
to do those retreats, and for the life of the pond. During that
time, I became the environment of the pond with no separation between us. That experience was a great gift. This interdependence is always present, but seldom do we truly feel it.

One day around mid-morning I looked up to see a great deal
of turbulence on the surface of the water in the middle of the
lake. What was that? The Loch Ness monster? Having forgotten

my binoculars, I ran up to the house and as I crossed the lawn I realized that what I had seen were the turtles. I grabbed my binoculars and then disturbed my husband's morning work and dragged him down to the steps to the lake. On the steps he had built, through the binoculars, we watched two snapping turtles mating. They were rolling over and over each other. My husband and I had the once-in-a-lifetime experience of being turtle voyeurs.

The dark quiet I discovered during those years of solo retreat is still present in my life. Sometimes I can hear it in the middle of the loud world. The call of a red-winged blackbird will immediately take me back to the dock, even now. At night in my bedroom, before I go to sleep, I light the candles on the windowsill and sit in the beauty of the candlelight in my over-stuffed chair. I can still hear the call of silence. That silence has become my refuge. It can, if I let go, bring me peace.

The brambles of life are thick and full. I try to bring forth what I heard in those deep days and nights listening to the quiet and the dark. That kind of silence can help heal the bruises and cuts we get from untangling ourselves in a briar patch. I remind myself steadfastly to slow down and entrust myself to the dynamic energy of life itself. I practice seeing life without achievements and letting go of the results of my actions. There is so much freedom open to us if we can drop the fabrications of our minds. My energy is much more available, and I feel happy. There's no need to even cut the brambles.

In a moment, I can remind myself what is true. Do I need the tension of my mental constructions or not? Can I, in this moment, be immediate?

Chapter Three

UNTANGLING KARMIC KNOTS: A TALE OF HEALING

The wound is the place where the light enters you.
—Rumi

Recently a member of the Katagiri Roshi Sangha from forty years ago recognized my face and said, "Oh, you were the girl who cried all the time." Although I was slightly taken aback, I knew what she meant. In my early years as a Buddhist I was really an emotional mess—grief-filled and sick all the time. If my present-day sangha had only known me then! My meetings with Katagiri Roshi consisted mostly of me crying and he being bewildered by this very emotional, disturbed, young woman. I often wonder how that distraught girl could have become a Zen teacher.

Since my earliest days, I had suffered from acute asthma, and my emotionally difficult childhood had left me struggling with neuroses. When I discovered Zen practice, it became one of the tools that helped me develop awareness of my problems and find a measure of solace. In some sense, taking refuge in Buddhism saved my life, but while Zen has been my central path, I realize that I could not have healed by Zen alone. Zen practice did not offer sufficient instructions on how to deal with my painful psychological distress. I also could not have healed *without* Zen, because I needed the depth of my connection to the universal perspective and energetic truth, which I experienced through long hours of meditation practice.

During my dark times I thought that if I just worked hard enough, I could get the world to yield to my wishes. But I began to comprehend that healing comes in the opposite form: surrender. By surrender I don't mean passivity but the need to understand that I can't change the world by force to conform to my ideals, my perfectionism, or my own image of good health. I need to understand and conform to the way the universe actually works, which I sometimes can discern through Zen practice.

Maladies of Childhood — The Beginning

My mother often joked that I was allergic to the hospital receiving blanket. There was something wrong with my lungs and my health from the very beginning. If I'd been born before antibiotics and cortisone were discovered, I would have been the child who died. I'm sorry for both of us, my mom and me, as I remember how my asthma took its toll on my harried mother. As many people know, taking care of a chronically sick child is emotionally wrenching and physically demanding, requiring doctor's appointments, home treatments, special diets, and additional chores, ad infinitum. It is a mother's nightmare— watching her child suffer. My mom once told me that she had wanted a fourth child, but when I, her third child, became so time-consuming, she just decided three children were enough. Burdened by taking care of me and my brothers and managing the sometime outrageous behavior of my father, she knew she could not handle any more.

Besides my physical illness, there were many other threads in my life that led me to feel, by the time I was seventeen years old, that I was a broken person. As a young adult, I was afraid that if I opened the well of grief within me, I would not survive the tsunami of anguish that would burst forth. I didn't have any tools to help me through the trauma of what I was holding inside. It seemed that all my neuroses were inextricably braided together. Many aspects of myself—my asthma, overweight, anxiety, depression, and post-abuse symptoms—had all con-tracted together in dense and tenacious knots, both physical and emotional, embedded in my body. They felt inescapable. As a young person and also a person who didn't have much, if any, adult support, where was I to go? Who should I turn to?

I never thought in my wildest dreams that my asthma could be healed or I could find relief from the emotional distress I felt all the time. In those days, because I didn't have the fortitude or support to face my problems, I turned to substances that I thought would bypass my feelings. I overate, drank, and took drugs to try to alleviate the pain. To my despair, those strategies did not work and even made my life worse.

Hitting Bottom

Sometimes you have to go to hell in order to feel the desire to change and be willing to do all the work that growth requires. In this place of bound-up immobility, the only avenue left is to become *completely* disenchanted with the way you have been living and with your habits. In this deep, dark place, the seeds for change can be sown and then, hopefully, cultivated.

After I graduated from high school, some encouraging

things happened for me, but my inner life continued to deteriorate. I met Charley, who later became my husband. I had a group of friends, unlike in high school. I learned to dance and felt my personal power as an artist start to take shape. But my asthma and eczema continued to get worse. My despondency and inner turmoil was always with me. I felt like a vessel of shame about to burst. In reaction to this internal pressure, I began using more alcohol and drugs, and my worsening substance abuse became more obvious. This downward trend was encouraged by a crowd of friends who joined me in an intoxicated solution to our problems.

In 1970, I moved with Charley to Minneapolis, following a path that dance teachers recommended for me, and rented an apartment for $75 dollars a month. In the three years we lived there, we became engaged and then broke the engagement. I moved out of our apartment and lived alone in a rundown four-plex which became condemned within a year. I caught many mice in my kitchen: everyday, the sound of mouse traps snapping became a symphony in the lonely silence. I had a shower painted purple and a kitchen with a hippie pop-art mural in psychedelic colors on the wall. My next-door neighbor was a dealer—very convenient. He provided all the weed and any other type of drug I wanted, anytime—just ring the doorbell across the hall. Oftentimes I got high alone, and my isolation would just fuel my depression. Once, when I was alone tripping, I thought that taking a bath would help me calm down. I took my bath in a freezing cold Minnesota bathroom, with doctor-prescribed mineral oil poured in the warm water to moisturize my very irritated eczema. But in this bathtub of mineral water, I felt like a rotund, dying, beached whale covered in thick oil slick on acid. I didn't know whether to cry or laugh. Mostly I cried.

Several of my friends ended up in psych wards. Was I next? I put more and more distance between me and my parents, thinking that they were the source of much of my inner pain. I was in full grief because of breaking up with Charley. To hide the demoralizing decline and splintering of my spirit that was really going on, I overworked myself in my dance career.

In 1974, a year after separating from Charley and six months after meeting Katagiri Roshi in Minneapolis, I moved to New York City to study dance. I was still very much alone and isolated in my St. Marks Place apartment, so I spent my time familiarizing myself with the downtown dance scene. To my enormous surprise, in April, 1975, I was invited into the first dance company of the choreographer and dancer Trisha Brown, who was exploring a very innovative style of movement and composition. She was experimenting with whether or not other people could dance her quirky, unprecedented, organically-based movements, which have since become a standard technique in twenty-first-century modern dance. This was a pinnacle experience in my life, but underneath my facade and despite my real achievement of being in a dance company in New York City, I think it was also my emotional bottom. A high and low were happening for me simultaneously, and I probably would not have survived this tension if not for my best girlfriend, Elizabeth, who was also in the company and roomed with me on tours. She held me up emotionally and I drew my stability from her, depending on her great love and acceptance of me, as well as her generosity.

After dance rehearsals downtown in Soho, I would stop at the Fanelli Bar on Prince Street before getting on the subway to go home to Brooklyn. Fanelli's was a beautiful, old-fashioned bar dating back to 1847 with an exceptionally crafted carved wooden liquor cabinet, mirror, and bar; old-school silver tiles on the ceiling; and black and white floor tiling. Mostly, its patrons were men, from laborers to guys in business suits. But because I was socially shy, especially with men, I never talked to anyone, not even the bartender or any of the men seated on the stools next to me. "Just a Heineken," I would tell the bartender, and that was my only conversation. Later on, from the time I got back to my apartment in Brooklyn until I went to sleep, I would have a drink in my hand, on the table next to me, or nearby as I sat on the couch.

When Charley and I reconnected in 1976, he moved into my Brooklyn apartment and we got married. He also was drinking and drugging, so my use didn't seem to bother him or be a problem. And it felt normal to me: after all, wasn't that what my boyfriend, my dad, and my brothers had done at home?

In that Brooklyn apartment, I would add to my alcoholic haze by smoking pot or hashish. This would effectively obliterate any emotions I might be having, which I misconstrued as relaxation. My brother Robert conveniently sent me hashish from Amsterdam, in the Netherlands, where he lived. He made candles for a living there, and he would send me hashish hidden inside the candles. They easily got through customs. Of course, even though I worked hard to extricate the hashish from the wax, smoking hashish imbued with particles of wax (as well as smoking pot), was probably the worst thing I could do for my asthma.

I could tell that my drug and alcohol use was catching up to me. One night I woke up in my bathroom, collapsed on the floor, my forehead resting on the cool porcelain rim of the toilet bowl, and I didn't know how I had gotten there. Sometimes when I would do my body meditation for dancing, I would end up having uncontrollable tremors. My synapses were so overstimulated by drugs that they released their tension through twitches and tremors that felt like bolting fragments of lightning. This shocked and scared me.

My weight continued to be a problem for me as well. In the dance company, all the female dancers were very thin, if not skeletal, and I was the "fat one." But even though I had enormous incentive to lose weight, I would eat a pint of Haagen-Dazs ice cream before bed each night or I'd watch TV with a big bag of potato chips by my side. And I knew exactly which coffee shops had those enormous chocolate chip cookies with extra chips. But it wasn't really about the food; it was about stuffing down my feelings. When I first stopped overeating, I was surprised to learn that there was such a thing as taking a walk without the destination being about food—all my walks until then had been about stopping at a 7/11 or a coffee shop. I was also surprised that you could have a conversation with a friend without there being food or alcohol on the table between you. And after a while, I realized that eating so much sugar and junk food actually coincided with my asthma worsening.

In Europe, while touring with the Trisha Brown Dance Company, I had a perfect storm. The ingredients for my illness were all there: the tour was hard and stressful, it was taking place in the fall (my worst time of year), and I had no emotional resilience. As the tour progressed, I gradually got sicker and sicker with asthma and bronchitis. I kept increasing my dosage of medicine, but my illness persisted. One of my fellow dancers told me they could smell the medicine in my sweat when we danced.

Finally, one morning over breakfast at an old hotel in Graz, Austria, Trisha Brown leaned toward me and looked me in the eye. I could feel her love as well as her frustration. "What shall we do? This isn't working, Judith," she told me. "Your meds are not helping, and you are getting worse. I'm worried about you.

I'm not the one who should really make this decision, but since you are not making it, I will. I think you should stop dancing for a while and give yourself time to heal."

Trisha was fifteen years older than me, a beautiful, talented woman whom I deeply admired. Her fame attested to her genius, but she also was a woman of integrity, humor, and earthy humanity. In a motherly way, with compassion, she told me that I had to stop dancing for the last part of the tour even though it meant I would miss the last four performances. There would be four dancers instead of five. This was a terrible situation, for it meant I had become an unreliable member of the troupe. How could I live that down? Though Trisha communicated in a very kindly way, she inferred that the inconsistency between the demands of professional dancing and the way I was treating my body could not continue. She added, "You have to learn how to take care of yourself better." She wanted me to see her doctor when we got back to New York—Dr. Cassell, an Upper West Side physician with a stellar reputation. With a crushing sense of failure, I watched the last shows of our tour from the sidelines and came home demoralized. Thankfully, the troupe took a long break before rehearsals started again in the winter. I hadn't been fired, but finally I knew that something had to be done about my health.

At Christmastime, during my break from work, Charley and I went to visit his family. I was still dealing with severe asthma but because I'd had a little rest from work and I was out from under the stress of touring, my breathing was slightly better. Then, on Christmas Eve, in our motel room in the middle of the night, I had a vision—or was it a waking dream? In the doorway stood the classic figure of the Grim Reaper. He was cloaked in a black garment with a hood. There was no face, only a dark emptiness inside his hood. He carried a scythe. I knew if he touched me I would die—and that it wasn't out of the question, after my autumn of illness, that death might take me. I started to fight the image away. Entangled in sheets and blankets, I kicked and screamed. My husband woke up frightened, and asked me what was the matter. I fought until the image vanished. Afterwards, Charley held me in his arms. "You're okay, you're okay," he said, trying to soothe me. But I did not feel okay. I was terrified. I shook for the rest of the night, and the next day, while his family was opening presents, I felt distant and disengaged.

Oh my god, I was going to die. What should I do, I wondered. When we returned to Brooklyn after the holidays, I looked at the whole mess of my life: would it lead me to an early death? From asthma? From drugs? I was so afraid that I decided I would do anything to understand myself better and try to heal.

Moving Toward a Change

I went to Overeaters Anonymous (OA) first, where it was suggested that I limit or stop my alcohol use. Because I could not let go of drinking, I realized that I needed help with my drinking and drug use as well as my overeating. I entered the Alcohol Anonymous (AA) program in 1977 when I was twenty-six years old. At that time, the twelve-step program was almost unknown except as a program for hardcore alcoholics and street bums. Going to an AA meeting in Manhattan in 1977 felt like stepping back to the 1950s. The meetings mostly consisted of older white men sitting around drinking coffee and chain-smoking in church basements. What an aberrant sight I must have been to them—a young girl desperately asking for help. But it was the beginning of the surge of popularity for twelve-step programs. We who had been hippies and drug addicts were at the end of our overindulgent ropes and were coming to "the program" to change. OA was in its infancy and just crawling away from the idea that it was a diet club. But I went to both programs, persevered, and found the only hope that I could see to change my life. I began to experience transformative healing.

That first year without drugs, alcohol, and overeating, I felt quite insane. Take away the cover-up and what is left? Confusion and emotional distress. Although I had been going to Zen temples since 1973, I had found very little emotional and psychological support in that community—in fact, quite the opposite. We were told to "just let go" of our emotional issues and sit silently together. In many ways, for a person from a disturbed and violent family, it was heaven to be told to be quiet and unattached to people. But in other ways, that simply wasn't enough to address my whole person, including my psychological needs.

In the beginning of my recovery, it was important that I had a lot of support right away, and I got that through going to meetings. The start of my program life was engrossing and fierce. I went to a meeting every day. I signed on with a sponsor. I had a quite rigorous morning schedule. I woke up at 4:30 a.m. as in the Zen tradition and did my Zen routine. I sat zazen for forty minutes in the back of Charley's and my apartment on the corner of Clinton Street and Atlantic Avenue. The backroom's window looked out onto an airshaft between our building and the next one and was about three feet from the windows of the apartment across from ours. There was some external light, but not much. Each morning as I meditated, I could hear my next-door neighbor, who I assumed was an alcoholic, vomiting out his toxicity. This devastating melody of addiction was a truly wonderful accompaniment to my determination to stop using. After zazen, because I had memorized the Zen morning service, I was able to chant it in its entirety while walking the six blocks from our apartment to the New York Harbor, where I greeted the Statue of Liberty in the morning light of sunrise. It was a beautiful and transcendent start to the day.

I joke sometimes that, back then, Jesus and Buddha were wrestling for my soul and the Torah was silent. On the way home from the Statue of Liberty, I stopped at a Catholic church and attended Mass because that is what my sponsor did. I guess I didn't understand that mentorship was not about copying; nevertheless, I earnestly would have done anything to find healing. With this rigor, no wonder I could keep sober and abstain from overeating each day. I was in a great upheaval of spirituality. Sometimes in the afternoon, after rehearsal and my subway ride, instead of drinking, I would walk to another church near my apartment and say the rosary in a gorgeously lit small chapel to the side of the main church which was dedicated to Mother Mary and held what seemed like a thousand candles, all lit in offering and prayer.

In the end though, being a Jew, I just could not surrender to Jesus. In retrospect, I wish I could have simply chosen Judaism and allowed myself to be rooted in my own ancestry and the strange and often overwhelming role of Jews in society. But I could not find a foothold in my relationship with Judaism or locate the deep source of spirit within what I judged as the social confusion and values of synagogues in the aftermath of the Holocaust. My family history did not support a spiritual attraction to Judaism either, even though I had witnessed, over and over, my grandpa *davening* in the back seat of the car—rocking his whole body forward and back, side to side, while singing the prayers. But although Grandpa prayed, he always said he did not believe in God. No one in my Jewish childhood had noticed that I was a deeply spiritual child and needed guidance. I was gravely disappointed in my childhood congregation, my

Hebrew school, and my Bat Mitzvah, and all of those elements, at the beginning stages of my recovery, seemed just too difficult to overcome. In the end, I took refuge in Buddhism.

Resolutely Pursuing Health

In the aftermath of the dance tour, taking up Trisha's advice, I went to see her doctor. Dr. Cassell put me in the slot he called "the last appointment of the day," which usually started at around 9:00 p.m, and sometimes lasted until 10:00 or even 11:00, and was his experimental hypnosis appointment. Dr. Cassell was researching the role of emotions and psychology in his patients' chronic physical illnesses, taking an approach that was very progressive in the medical establishment in the 1970s. He told me that asthma might have multiple causes, and one cause might have to do with my psychology. His insightful care and attention really helped me begin my path to self-empowerment and change. During our hypnosis sessions, we often used the imagery of me sitting on a throne in control of my kingdom. Dr. Cassell was all about self-empowerment. He prepared a little three-by-seven-inch zippered leather kit for me which included three hypodermic needles, alcohol swipes, and a bottle of adrenaline to manage my nut allergies and severe reactions. This new strategy relieved my chronic fear of having an asthmatic or anaphylactic attack. (This was in the days before the invention of EpiPens.) Voila! I would never have to go to the emergency room again. No more emergencies; I could take care of myself. Empowerment!

After the first three rigorous months of my recovery program, I went to a sesshin—a seven-day meditation retreat—at Dai Bosatsu Zendo in the Catskills, north of New York City. By then, I had actively dismantled very strongly held behaviors and, with a lot of exertion, stopped my addictive substances. I had begun to look face-to-face into the center of my neuroses. When I entered this particular sesshin, my ferocious determination and intentions ripened into a spiritual awareness.

Located deep in the woods, Dai Bosatsu Zendo monastery's design is strongly influenced by Japanese temple architecture. The zendo, or meditation room, is a long, large room featuring two parallel raised platforms covered with straw tatami mats and seating cushions. Meditators face each other from opposite sides of the room or face the wall. A huge golden Buddha stands at one end of the meditation hall, which is surrounded by a corridor for walking meditation. All the retreatants wore black robes, and the whole atmosphere was solemn and intensely focused. In one of the moments during the retreat, I was looking around the room at other people, my mind soft and distracted, and what seemed like almost instantaneously, a zendo monitor came behind me and yanked my head back to center. Oh! No kidding around—concentrate! The intentional power of my first three months of program matched the zeal of this particular style of Zen. I didn't even mind the shouting or receiving the awakening stick, a long stick used by the monitors who gave us two hits on each shoulder. "Wake up! Wake up! Keep going! Keep going!" After a few days of this blazing fury of spiritual determination, something changed in me. I felt open and free for the first time in my life. My mind was very quiet with a new kind of spacious clarity. "Oh my I am Buddha, too," I thought, just like I had been reading. "I am more than my story." There was one moment in particular, as I stood looking into the bathroom mirror at Dai Bosatsu Monastery, when my eyes seemed fathomless. They were dark and went on forever and there was nothing inside my skull—just the universe. The universe is within me. Wow! A revelation.

Zen and Twelve-Step Entwined

Does one insight shift years of ingrained behavior? I have to report that it does not. These eye-opening experiences shift our understanding, but we have a lot of work to do on our repetitive, harmful behaviors. Major changes do not happen overnight. To deal with my destructive life patterns, I found three systems of support and inquiry—Zen, twelve-step recovery, and psychotherapy—and I have used those systems throughout my life.

Zen certainly investigates what it is to be a human and, along with that, the deepest levels of spirituality. It shines a light on how we are all connected to the whole of life in all its complexity and profundity. The Buddhist outlook gave me a container for holding the depth and difficulties of being a human. I learned that the meaning of life is in the living, that the present moment *is* the meaning.

The basis of twelve-step programs is that to heal, one needs to address the physical, emotional, and spiritual aspects of one's life. This fundamental triangle forms an unshakable stability for transformation, which added a new dimension to my understanding of what I needed to have happen in order to have a strong spiritual life. Zen helped me find a foundation of clarity and wisdom, while twelve-step programs and psychotherapy supported that foundation and taught me how to address and "clean up" my karma.

The twelve "steps" are a skeletal structure for spiritual life that can be found in any religious tradition. What I got from twelve-step programs and psychotherapy, which I didn't get from Zen, was an active way of working with the stories of my past and my psychological distress. I was able to pinpoint the stories of what things had happened in my life to bring me to my devastated situation and find ways to repair these issues. Psychotherapy fits into the recovery path in its similarity to the fourth and fifth steps. Step 4 is self-examination, while step 5 is sharing your story with another human being. These steps create a vessel for healing. Step 5 insists that we have a witness for our growth and that we stay connected with people.

I had searched for self-examination and amends-making steps in Zen. But even though in the daily Zen service we say, "May I atone for it all," I would not actually have known how to do that without the practicality of the twelve-step program. And if I had not also engaged in psychotherapy, I would never have gotten the depth of self-knowledge that could lead me to what I have become today.

It seemed to me that, in some ways, Zen dismissed my history. I was told to "just let go" of my story or disidentify with my history and work from the world of interbeing. Of course, in hindsight I see that unraveling our karmic story was not ignored by Buddhist teaching and, in fact, constituted the deepest of teachings, but in my early understanding of the Path I didn't realize that. I compartmentalized my personal karma almost in opposition to freedom. Until recently, I did not see my Zen community directly working with karma or our psychological problems. (This, to me, is why an alarming number of sanghas have blown up from ethical problems and power issues.)

For a few decades, I used my obsession with concentration and meditation as another method to avoid facing my problems. I didn't realize this at the time because in many ways meditation can also bring forth our unconscious issues. But meditation can be used as a substitute for an addiction and become another compulsive, intoxicating behavior—we can just go to the mountaintop, be quiet, and pacify our inner voices. But what I thought was "concentration" was really just a repression-of-thought method, which didn't seem to help me in the long run. I might be calm at sesshin, but as soon as I got home, I was a wreck once again.

The difficulties of practicing within a family setting produced in me a feeling that there was a hole in my early interpretation of Zen practice. That hole was in my heart and emotional body. I learned a great deal from Zen training about how to take precious care of objects. I learned how to cut a carrot, which is a root, in a different way than I would rip apart a piece of lettuce, which is a leaf. I learned how to clean an oil lamp without leaving a trace of fingerprints. I learned how to kneel down and wash the floor, perfectly. And yet, I didn't learn so much about taking care of human relationships.

I can perhaps trace this back to Zen's Japanese cultural tradition. Although the Japanese are a deeply emotional people, they do not address emotions and relationships as directly and expressively as do Westerners. I am not saying these cultural differences are bad or that one culture is better than another. But not understanding these differences created a problem for me in my own misperception of practice. It took decades for Tomoe-san, Katagiri Roshi's wife, to Westernize herself enough to receive a hug or hear "I love you" directly. These days, she might even initiate the hug or look you in the eye and say something about what your relationship means to her. But she still giggles with her hand over her mouth. We Americans smile at that. When she goes to Japan, her directness is an anomaly there, and she tells me that she doesn't really fit into either Japanese or American culture.

I struggled with what seemed like a lack of emotional integration in the style of Buddhism that I had learned, but as I began teaching, I discovered practices emphasized in the other Buddhist traditions that would help fill that emotional hole. I searched for teachings that would reinforce the healing practice of psychological self-examination and found the *Abhidharma*, texts from as early as third century BCE offering a highly technical systemization of the mind, sometimes called Buddhist psychology. Interestingly though, in my early years as a Buddhist, Katagiri Roshi told me not to study the *Abhidharma*, but to turn my attention instead to silence and understanding emptiness, so it was not until much later in my Zen life that I looked closely at the teachings in the *Abhidharma*.

I also appreciated the expansive teachings of the Four Divine Abodes and loving-kindness practices that came from the Vipassana Buddhist community. I began including these in my own practice and my teaching, emphasizing mindfulness of emotions, which was barely taught in my early Zen years. From the Tibetan Buddhists, I also learned a lot about dismantling karma and used "interrupting habit patterns" combined with the twelve steps, to great value. I found that the Tibetan Buddhist work corresponded best with my healing work and helped me with transforming my behaviors and making amends. In the '80s and '90s, while settled in Minneapolis, I organized a weekly study group that featured listening to the Tibetan-Buddhist teacher Pema Chodron's audiotapes, which taught me the traditional practices of *Tonglen* and the *Lojong* slogans. These teachings changed my approach entirely. Tonglen is a method of meditation that rides on the breath. On the inhalation, you breathe in and accept the poisons and suffering of the world. Because of this, you allow your heart to be broken. Through this torn-open heart, you can touch the larger perspective of life, feel the suffering of all beings, and find Buddha's heart within yourself. Then, on the exhalation, your expanded heart sends out love, compassion, and healing. This practice seemed to fill in the hole in my emotional body. In addition, the Lojong slogans provided instructions for spirituality in my daily life.

The psychological work of twelve-step programs and psychotherapy seem essential—and yet, if you *only* do twelve-step and psychotherapy, you won't necessarily get the depth of understanding that you need to truly transform your life in an unforced way. We cannot recover by psychology alone. This is acknowledged in the twelve-step world by the steps that work with the higher power and grace. Step 11 is called *conscious contact with God as you understand God.* This much larger sense of life was immeasurably enhanced by my Zen practice. I have a different understanding of a higher power than that which is taught in the Abrahamic religions of Christianity, Judaism, and Islam. My higher power is not anthropomorphized—it's not even a "higher" power. The energies of life in and outside myself, above and below me, pervade the whole universe and its functioning is available at any moment. One of the most important aspects of my meditation, is opening my heart to feeling the constant support of the earth, the sky, my body, DNA, the stars and dark space between them—everything. So much is supporting me that I usually don't acknowledge; by consciously leaning on that support, I can rest.

Even with all my critique of Buddhism, I did learn in the end how to hold the paradox of understanding our stories psychologically and also letting go of our stories within a deeper perspective on life. I was able to learn from Buddhism what it means to "let go" and how to, indeed, disidentify with my personal stories without bypassing my emotional history. Buddhism teaches us that our personal chronicles are not unique, nor are they owned by a "self." This detachment helps us let go of our entrenched narrative. The history of our life is part of who we are, but we are also much larger than our stories. In order to let go of our *dis-ease*, we need this vast view of life and humanity.

I have also learned about sangha and the development of community from Zen and twelve-step. The one body moving together of all of the participants in a Zen sesshin is a very rare experience in Western society. Sesshin participants embody a collective intimacy of group movement: Everyone bows at the same time, stands at the same time, moves at the same time, eats in a certain way at the same time, and is fed the same food. At first, it is often very awkward for Americans to be corralled into this surrender of individualism in order to experience an unconditional collectivism and an acceptance of human behavior "just as it is" without any overlay of meaning. Zen students sometimes go kicking and screaming in resistance to the strict schedule and discipline. However, unconditional surrender to the schedule and forms of sesshin oftentimes saved and comforted me. The very highly choreographed, collective structure of Zen buoyed me up in the middle of intense emotions or when my life seemed to be falling apart. I could just sit back and be supported by the schedule and the community. I was upheld by being a member of the larger group energy. It was like a collective wordless embrace.

But there was always something missing in the nonresidential or nonmonastic Zen sanghas of which I have been a part. This "something" I filled in with the twelve-step community, which offered deep emotional and practical support. As Jon Kabat-Zinn writes in the foreword to Dr. Judson Brewer's *The Craving Mind*: "Perhaps we feel so wounded that we cannot even entertain the possibility of our own essential completeness without a lot of support." I found this to be true for me. External support allows us to find our internal strength. In twelve-step, I could telephone someone from my group anytime, even in the middle of the night. I could stay overnight at someone else's house when I couldn't manage my life on my own. Helping other people in the small and large necessities of life was built into the twelve-step system.

But I was disappointed when I tried to bring this level of emotional support to my Zen communities. Clouds in Water Zen Center tried often, creating groups with catchy names like "the Bodhisattva Brigade," or "Hearts and Hands," or jokingly, "the women's auxiliary that includes men." We tried different ways of organizing mutual care, but it never seemed to work very well for the long term. We didn't know enough about each other's actual lives and stories to be invested in concrete help. Somehow, this type of giving was pigeonholed into our scheduled life, instead of flowing out of our deep understanding of generosity. Or else people considered the Zen community to be something they participated in once or twice a week. Mistakenly, our conclusion, it appeared to me, was that our Zen lives were about quietism and our own self-nurturance. Even though the Bodhisattva ideal of helping others has been studied and has been the topic of many lectures, I didn't see it actually manifested when a sangha member's parent died or someone had an illness. Perhaps I'm exaggerating or missing the individual acts of kindness people do inside a sangha, but I've been in Zen for over fifty years, and I think what I'm saying has some truth to it. In my life, I realized early on that I needed several systems of support in order for my healing to be sustained within a backdrop of love. For me, twelve-step recovery and Zen needed each other to be whole.

Sun-face Buddha, Moon-face Buddha

Koans in Zen practice are ancient stories that enter our brain and mythos and stay there, churning, waiting for understanding, sometimes for decades. They have become my spiritual friends and guides. Over the years, on various occasions, I have taken them out and had a dialogue with them. Sometimes my understanding of them grows into becoming a spiritual comfort. Here is a koan from the eighth-century Zen Master Mazu, which is found in the Blue Cliff Record, Case No. 3, and the Book of Serenity, Case No. 36, which opens up my understanding of: "Oh my, I am a Buddha" and informs my attitude toward illness:

Master Ma Is Unwell

Great Master Ma was unwell. The temple superintendent (the Ino) asked him, "Teacher, how has your venerable health been in recent days?"

Master Ma said, "Sun-face Buddha, Moon-face Buddha."

The Sun-face Buddha and the Moon-face Buddha are metaphors which were first introduced in the Buddha Name Scripture. According to that scripture, the Sun-face Buddha is eternal and lives in the world for eighteen hundred years, implying eternity—entirety of time and space. The Moon-face Buddha is one day of life, a twenty-four-hour period. Moon-face Buddha is our ordinary life and the different elements that interweave with each other to make our historic or karmic self. Master Ma's answer combines both the absolute and relative point of view. He was free enough to respond from either side of the coin because he knew they were actually one coin. He could say, on the one hand, "I feel fine, I am Buddha," meaning "I have completely accepted this illness and my life." He also could have answered from the moon-faced point of view, "I feel lousy and I'm sick. Why don't you bring me a cup of tea and my medicine?" Master Ma did not dismiss the situation of his human life and its difficulties. He saw equality between the sun and the moon, night and day, sickness and health. He understood that both points of view are essentially, and in actuality, not separate.

This koan is about the integration of what appear to be opposites: the spiritual dimension and the mundane, material aspect of life. These two sides of life, the sacred and the profane, I have come to understand, are one dynamic whole and are not compartmentalized as we sometimes think. These two sides are magnetically charged poles, not able to be separated, that mutually benefit each other. I liken this to the healing that came to me from my amalgamation of Zen and the twelve-step recovery processes. Zen enlivened my spiritual understanding of the reciprocity between the spiritual and the ordinary, while twelve-step dealt with my tangible, emotional blockages.

I have an aversion now to spiritual teachings that get stuck in the "transcendent" sun-faced Buddha's point of view. I look for teachings in Buddhism that support my more feminist point of view—that the messy quality of ordinary life, even the troublesome parts of illness or having a family, are all elements of life that are bound to each other like the spinning parts of an atom.

When I looked in the mirror that day at the sesshin, I met the sun-faced Buddha! I felt the sun-faced Buddha's arms wrapped around my moon-faced Buddha's difficulties with gentleness and compassion. This gave me great fortitude to continue. This experience gave me a possible way of soothing myself without chemicals or unhealthy habits. I had had my first spiritual awakening.

Cortisone or No Cortisone

After about eight months into my recovery program, Charley and I moved from Brooklyn back to Chicago where my parents lived, so that he could change jobs. I planned to continue my dance career as a soloist in Chicago. At that point in my recovery, I had begun to notice a pattern with my asthma that showed that it wasn't just all physical or chemical and I had started going to a psychosomatic psychiatrist. I didn't want to see that there was a pattern with my asthma, but the more I looked, the more I saw. Self-awareness is often painful awareness. My asthma, perhaps always, got worse when I was under stress. I had learned as a child to manipulate the environment by getting sick. I learned that if I had an asthma attack, the environment would "magically" transform and I would become the center of attention. When I look back on it now, I see this recurring pattern predictably timed to avoid things I was afraid of or what I perceived to be aversive environments.

My mother was gravely concerned when she saw how bad my asthma had become. She did her style of research and found a doctor who was reportedly "the best asthma doctor in Chicago." But when I became his patient, I saw that the reason he was called the "best" was that he very liberally put chronic asthmatics like me on high dosages of daily cortisone, which reduces inflammation. Taking cortisone by mouth consistently has many dangers: eventually the adrenal glands stop being able to make cortisone naturally, which necessitates taking the artificial form of this hormone by pill for the rest of your life.

At around the same time, I went to a lecture by a naturopath who said cortisone was more addictive than heroin. Oh dear. I was very confused about how I should proceed.

The dilemma of whether or not to take cortisone finally came to a peak during the Rohatsu sesshin in 1978. Rohatsu is the sesshin in December when, all over the world, Zen sanghas celebrate Buddha's enlightenment by meditating all day and sometimes all night. During this sesshin, when I took all my pills, including the cortisone, in the morning, I could, thanks to the heightened body sensation that comes with meditation, actually feel my body's reaction to the pills. I felt a strong, relentless draining of my energy out of my left adrenal gland. It hurt a lot and thoroughly exhausted me. This debilitation increased the urgency of my questions about the effects of my medication and participating in sesshins on my asthma. Did I have to choose between cortisone and doing intense meditation? I got very scared. But at this particular sesshin, my reaction was so intense, and my awareness had such a clear specificity, that I was sure the effect was caused by my medicine. I felt that I couldn't continue doing both. This problem, which was now predominant in my awareness, amped up everything I was trying to do with healing and recovery. Sesshin felt vitally important to me and I did not want to give it up.

In the winter of 1979, I went back to the "best asthma doctor in Chicago" and told him I was going to stop taking cortisone. Of course, I knew well enough that you should taper off the cortisone dosage and give your body a long time to remember how to function without the synthetic drug. The doctor erupted. I watched his face turn waxen and red. He leaned into me, his face practically touching my nose and started yelling at me. "I'm writing in your chart that you are going off cortisone against my advice. I am releasing you from my care. You are not my patient anymore!" He looked me right in the eye, and got even closer, shouting, "You are going to end up in the emergency room, begging for me to treat you."

Wow, I thought, who is this guy? And who does he *think* he is? At that moment, I realized that taking charge of my body was a very political statement. Of course, this was in 1979. I was emboldened by the book *Our Bodies, Ourselves,* authored by the Boston Women's Health Collective, which revolutionized how women saw the male medical industry and how we regarded our own bodies and our own sexuality. The medical establishment's patriarchy was embodied in this doctor. It was outside the norm that a woman might have something to say, might take control of her own body, and might go against the medical establishment's authority and what they perceived to be their faultless advice. In that moment when the "best asthma doctor in Chicago" shouted at me, I truly understood the feminist slogan "the personal is political." My break with my doctor affected my whole being and was a political action.

Within a month after I stopped taking cortisone, I was very sick again. I wrote to Katagiri Roshi, "What should I do? I can't and won't give up sesshin." He wrote me back right away in his disjointed English. "Don't be stuck on either side, do or do not. You do what is appropriate to the situation." My husband and I decided that I should go back on cortisone. It was easy to get a prescription from another doctor. I certainly wasn't going to beg. This was in May. Looking back, what appears to be important is that I let go of my *strongly held opinions for or against* and surrendered to what I felt was the right decision in that specific moment, and then, "whatever happens, happens."

Asthma's Release

In September 1979, I did go to sesshin in spite of my fears. It was the most difficult sesshin I have experienced in my Zen life. I had a cold and asthma. I was sneezing, coughing, wheezing, and crying, and all that sound was a disruption in the zendo at every turn. My zabuton, the rectangular sitting cushion, was littered with used, wadded-up Kleenexes. I felt like a disaster being enacted in front of everyone in the meditation hall. The other practitioners, of course, were accepting and kind to my bumbling, noisy self—at least on the surface. But I was going through what Katagiri Roshi called "psychic vomiting," and what my mind was throwing up was very revealing of my inner congestion. I was going over practically every memory I had of my mother. Hours of memories. Hours of crying. All the things I felt I didn't get from my mother. All the things I was unable to give her. My mind was insistent and unstoppable. Anger, love, jealousy, competition—what a wild mind! My brain was running films of certain scenes with her over and over; my mind was uncontrollable. In recalling this now, I believe that in this sesshin my body and mind were pulling out the karmic root of my asthma, which was associated with my complicated relationship to my mother. Though I called it a terrible sesshin, it was actually a very fortunate and blessed digestion of my confused inner life and allowed me to transition into something new.

The time and space of sesshin is where major shifts of energy and perspective can occur. The times between sesshins are when, through work and attention, we can till and fertilize the soil of our life by effort. We turn the dharma wheel. Sometimes, if I have paid significant attention to my problem areas in between sesshins, I can enter into the stillness and quiet of sesshin and in that silence, something greater than myself, some interconnected energetic functioning, enters me, releases me, and unravels "my karmic knots." This healing energy is spontaneous and intuitive and does not come from my willpower. The dharma wheel turns me.

I have had many such healing moments in sesshin over the years. They are lasting, but as I have said, also require attention in between the deep subtle energy states. Sometimes these healings have a vision that go along with this karmic unraveling in my body. These imagined visualizations that occur during zazen have a purpose and give me some affirmation that I am going in the right direction.

One vision I have about unwinding the karmic gnarls in my body and mind goes like this: I am sitting in the zendo and my body is completely porous and transparent, revealing a body of energy. Then these elongated, blue, forearms come down from the sky with hands that have very thin, long, delicate fingers like a surgeon's. These fingers enter my diaphanous body and slowly, sensitively, and skillfully untangle the hard, karmic knots present in my body and mind. I don't do anything. My hands stay receptive and inactive in the hand mudra. These dense masses in my body appear impermeable but as the fingers untwist the threads of story, a great relief and release occurs.

These healings happen by teetering back and forth in a dance between body and spirit. If one side forges ahead in opening to a release, it necessitates taking time and being patient for the other side to catch up. Sometimes the body opens first and the spirit or energetic system needs time to rewire itself; other times, it's vice versa. Often a release that happens in sesshin takes several months to digest in one's day-to-day life. The spirit moves in an instant. The material world moves much more slowly. Dismantling one's house is a gradual and difficult undertaking because that house is built on old stubborn habits and needs time to construct a larger shelter to hold a more generous spirit. I notice that often, if someone has had a big revelation through meditation in a sesshin, the next year or so of their life is about dismantling certain structures in their day-to-day life, like changing jobs, getting a divorce, moving, etc. When hermit crabs have outgrown their shell, they abandon it. They crawl, unprotected and vulnerable, on the ground until they find another larger shell that has room for their expanded self and for the growth to come. Then they install themselves in that larger home and a new chapter of their development begins.

It seems that that time, December 1979, unlike in the previous spring, my healing was led by my body, not by concepts in my head. In the previous spring of my healing crisis, my intellectual mental perspective told me that I needed to get off cortisone and that I was ready to heal. That hadn't happened, as I had gotten sick again. But right before Christmas, after the sesshin about my relationship with my mother, I felt like something was going on in my body that I couldn't identify. Although I hadn't been able to take away the cortisone in May, it now felt like my body, not my mind, was expelling it, detoxing. I felt a racing and fluttering sensation that had no corresponding thought. I lost my appetite, which was very unusual for me. It felt like my asthma medicine and the cortisone were coming out of my pores, my mouth, through my urethra and bowels. I had never felt anything like this before. I again smelled like medicine. The disease and the medicine wanted out of me. Did I believe in that feeling? I decided to try to get off my medicine again. Was the time ripe to stop taking it? Had that past fall sesshin about Mom released something?

I knew I needed a lot of support to go off cortisone, so I decided to do acupuncture, which I had never tried before. I found a practitioner named Dr. Moon, which seemed poignant to me because I loved the moon. He seemed like he knew what he was doing. He was Korean and worked in downtown Chicago, a short walk from my house, in one of the nondescript gray office buildings in the loop. He spoke broken English, had no secretary, and worked out of only a few treatment rooms. At first I was scared. I had never done anything like this before and I hated needles. But I was determined. I would lie down, sometimes on my stomach and other times on my back, while Dr. Moon put needles in assorted points on my body. Then he would leave me to rest with the needles situated and heat lamps on me for warmth and I would listen to recordings of soft bamboo flute music from Korea. I went twice a week to Dr. Moon for about three months while I tapered off all my asthma medicine. Both my husband and I smile when we remember Dr. Moon. After every treatment, he would smile and pronounce, "Fixed!" and we would laugh. But in some ways, he was right.

May I say something shocking? *I have never taken asthma medicine again.*

I bow down to that statement. *I have never taken asthma medicine again.*

* * *

With great acknowledgment of the mystery of healing and adding to that, my intense effort, I learned that it is possible for our habits and karma to change. Karma is a continuum of habit loops with a strong momentum. We have the capacity to break this propulsion up by repeatedly interrupting the forward drive of our patterns. This great change does not occur in large-scale conceptualization of what we *wish* to happen. It happens in the small day-to-day, moment-to-moment experiences of mindfulness, of interrupting our patterns with a mustard-seed-sized resolution to express a spiritual characteristic in that very moment, however minute. "Small interruptions, many times a day" is an instruction from Dr. Judson Brewer, a mindfulness teacher and neuropsychiatrist. Pema Chodron teaches, "The more you practice your habits, the stronger they get; the more you interrupt them, the weaker the momentum of the habit gets." This transformation requires both the fierceness of persistence and the gentleness of self-acceptance and self-compassion.

Three years after my asthma lifted, I had a conjunction of two very devastating events which changed the course of my life. Malissa, my dear friend and mentor, whom I write about in a later chapter on racial injustice, died in May of 1982, and I grieved her deeply. A month later, I experienced a street rape in the alley next to my dance studio, which I write about in a later chapter on sexuality. This nexus of events stopped me in my tracks and put a wrench into my carefully constructed life plans. What should I do with my life falling apart? I made a decision. Katagiri Roshi had been telling me to change my life trajectory by just three degrees by moving toward a Buddhist life. It would be a very small adjustment, he said, but as that adjustment played out, it would expand over the course of the next years, and that new direction would become a larger and larger piece of the spectrum of my life. I had wanted to become a priest, and so I decided, since my whole life seemed to be in ruin and the structure of my psyche seemed to have fallen down, why shouldn't I just rebuild my life going towards priesthood?

I stopped dancing on a dime. I couldn't really go back to my studio anyway because it was the scene of the assault. Within a month, I was registered in acupuncture school. It seemed to me that being a Chinese healer would align with the tone of priesthood, and after having success using acupuncture to support healing my asthma, I just took a leap. After completing the training, I became an Oriental Doctor with an acupuncture practice, and then Charley and I moved back to Minneapolis so I could be near Katagiri Roshi.

Not Done Yet

Even though my asthma did not come back, my relationship with asthma and cortisone continued. Do the deeper, personal koans just follow us around? I felt haunted, for no matter what I did, the issue of asthma and cortisone still hung around me. My first son, Nicolas, was born in 1991 with very severe asthma. Though not unexpected, hereditarily speaking, here was asthma again in my life. I was confronted with all the same issues, but now for my beloved child. I remember the first time Nicolas ended up in the hospital—maybe he was about a year and a half old. We were all in bed, in the middle of the night, and no matter how much medicine I gave him, Nic was wheezing so badly that I decided to phone the doctor on call. While I was talking to the doctor, he heard my son wheezing from across the room. "Is that him?" he asked. "You better get to the hospital right away!" And then I heard Nic's sweet little toddler voice say, "I need to go to the hospital." We bundled him up and took him there, and he was admitted for three days.

I called my mother. "Mom, it's happening again." She cried and she commiserated, understanding a mother's suffering around all the decisions and all the patience needed to be with a sick child. I remember rocking Nicolas in his hospital room in this big green, plastic chair that transformed into a parent's sleeping lounger. I kept Nic on my lap because I couldn't bear to leave him in the hospital crib that looked like a prison cell. It even had bars that covered the top so children couldn't crawl out. With his little oxygen tubes in his nose and the IV in his arm pumping in cortisone, I rocked and slept with him in my arms the whole time he was in the hospital. Despite all my inner turmoil over cortisone, it gave life, again.

My struggle with asthma and how to handle medication now took the form of decisions around my son's health. Here again, I would learn an important and deep lesson—not to hold on to my opinions too tightly. My mothering had started out by being very controlling. A voice in me said, "Let's be a perfect holistic mother." My concepts of "good parenting" and "good health" were quite stuck on the side of unrelentingly purist and alternative healthcare values. This very tenacious perfectionism was really quite contrary to the fluidity of mind that Zen, in the end, promotes. You would think I would have learned this well enough with my own healing, but sometimes we need to learn the same lessons over and over until we really incorporate them. This persistent rejection of all the more normal Western options of care was quickly interrupted by the severity of Nic's illness. So I learned again to let go of my stubbornly held opinions, to deal with the reality of what's needed right in front of me, and to have a flexible mind—especially because now I was not the only one making medical choices. My husband had his own opinions too. In the midst of our differences and the pain of watching our little one suffer with illness, could my husband and I be stable and together, as we made health choices cooperatively for our son?

As I write, my son, now in his late twenties, is starting his own adventure in healing. He is investigating how he, specifically, needs to heal himself with diet, supplements, and psychotherapy. I hope for him a healing, but as I well know, there is no guarantee.

Healing from the Inside to the Outside

I increasingly wonder if my own story of personal healing could have any correlations to the world outside myself? I fear the crashing and burning of our social order. Can the faith I have experienced and garnered personally in healing extend out to some kind of hope for the world to repair its many wounds?

I find myself seeking to balance the suffering I see everywhere around me with the beauty of life that is also present. The miracle of life is always here with its beauty and goodness, and I can connect with it even in the midst of difficulties. This is why it's important to have a daily spiritual practice. I hear in my head the voice of one of my students, Gentle Dragon. She, more than anyone I know, is an activist. She has dedicated her life to institutional, systemic change. But she also acknowledges her need for the depth of Buddhist practice to sustain her as she faces the suffering of the world. I can still see her face in our meetings together, saying, "I could never do what I'm doing if I didn't know the deep concentration and release of zazen." She very deliberately puts aside time to go to the monastery for meditation practice.

As Joan Sutherland, a Zen teacher in New Mexico, writes: "Let us forgive the world for being the world. Let us allow all things to be forgiven, to be blessed, just for a moment. Even just for the duration of a cup of tea." By "forgiving," I don't mean that we deny or allow bad behavior. But on a deeper level, this forgiveness brings me to a penetrating understanding of life's inevitable sorrows and softens my whole being into compassion. Forgiveness is an organic and intuitive release that happens after you have deeply digested the consequences of a hurt. Forgiveness is an unforced gift that happens spontaneously near the end of a healing process. There is a great release when we put all our stories of hurt and betrayal into the larger context of human life and the life of samsara.

You are a part of me and I am a part of you. Thich Nhat Hanh says, "There are no solitary beings. We do not exist independently. We *inter-be*. Everything relies on everything else in the cosmos in order to manifest. Thanks to impermanence, we have a chance to transform our inheritance in a beautiful direction." My connection to this unity can give me the fortitude to meet the pain of the world and act for transformation and change. Then, somehow, I enter the landscape of the Sun-face Buddha, and with a deep yearning, attempt to help heal the world through the most skillful moon-face expression of interconnection that I know.

Touching My Head to the Ground

I have lived now for forty years without asthma and I don't even think about it. Instead of dying in my twenties, I have grown to be a woman I never in my wildest imagination could have dreamed up.

I have kept my marriage together. I have had two children and have had the great opening-the-heart practice and challenge of parenting. I have had the engrossing and passionate opportunity to teach the dharma. I am still capable of learning and growth and, surprising myself, growth seems never-ending. In spite of the fact that I say I have had many difficulties in my life, I have also had so many, innumerable blessings. And so, I am moved to bow.

* * *

One morning I go early to the zendo and find no one there. I have deliberately come early for solitude. I changed into my Buddha robes, the amalgam of the present and all the history that has come before me. To the world, I wear the brown robe of the teacher: Buddha's robe, a patchworked wrap that is hand-sewn according to very strict guidelines. The model for that robe came from India, where Buddha told his attendant to sew robes for his community that look like the rice fields that give nourishment to all people. The next robe, worn beneath the teacher's robe, is a Chinese-style black robe representing the body of the Buddha as it traveled through China. Underneath that is a Japanese kimono and shirt which are directly tied to my teacher's homeland. Under that I wear American under-wear for the here and now. I hold a teaching staff which is a foot-long, wooden stick in the shape of a fiddlehead. For me, this staff represents my entire community's centeredness and fortitude, the unifying rhythm of doing and nondoing, and our willingness to meet life as it is. It is the symbol of the sun-face Buddha and the moon-face Buddha merged in one moment, and the human being's uprightness to receive that unity. I dress up in the history of my lineage.

I walk slowly into the darkened, silent zendo. As I move through this familiar space, I feel my body start to settle, breathe more deeply, and begin to relax. I light the single candle on the altar, walk around to the back of the *raiban* (the altar's rectangular cushion), and begin to bow. My hands come together in prayer, my knees touch the floor, I bring my fore-head to the ground, palms lifting up toward the heavens. My palms hold all my effort, practice, and longings. I stay down for several long, slow breaths, allowing my ever-present anxiety to be absorbed by the earth. By placing my forehead on the earth, I allow myself to release the angst of my frontal cortex, which tries to think, strategize, and control everything. I allow myself to feel the medicine of the whole earth and I relax. I thank everything. Gratitude and humility have become my deepest and most consistent practices.

Chapter Four

"WASH YOUR BOWL"

The day-to-day activities in the household of the Buddha-ancestors is our house, our life and our activity. This doing and not doing is imbued thoroughly with the total dynamic functioning of moment-to-moment reality. Nothing is left out and there can be great peace and ease in this understanding.

—Dogen Zenji

I am always rushing about, trying to accomplish things. Even studying mindfulness all these years has not slowed me down all that much. I often find my habitual pattern of going for a product and a good result taking over my mind. The balance and teaching of *doing and nondoing* seems quite hard to manifest in my deeply grooved and patterned consciousness.

I remember an encounter that I had with Tomoe Katagiri, Roshi's widow, who has become a teacher for many of us in her own quiet way. One day Sosan, my sister-teacher at Clouds in Water Zen Center, and I went to Tomoe-san's house to prepare for a *Jukai*, or Buddhist initiation ceremony. Part of the ceremony involves each participant getting a Buddhist name; at the time, we were giving the Buddhist names in Japanese with an English translation. For that Jukai, we had twenty-three names to choose. I gathered up all the many lists of names I had collected from previous Jukai ceremonies (my own and others) or from books, and thought, "Well, we can just look at these and give people names that have been previously used. That would be the fastest and most efficient way." I did not ask Tomoe-san what she thought of my plan. Twenty-three names was a lot of names! Along with all these lists of names, I brought along to Tomoe-san's house a bag bulging with English-to-Japanese dictionaries, and she and Sosan and I got to work.

But about half an hour into the session, Tomoe-san sat back in her chair, looked at me, and shook her head very gently. I knew well that her downcast eyes and the almost imperceptible side-to-side motion of her head communicated deep levels of meaning. I asked her, "What's wrong?" She replied, "I don't think using someone else's name is a good idea." Smiling, she continued. "We are, after all, naming baby Buddhas. Each name should be the teacher's deep wish for that baby Buddha's life."

Sosan and I were stopped in our tracks. Tomoe-san went on, "You should start with a wish for that person and then find the two characters that fit that wish, like we have done in the past." I replied with some frustration, "But Tomoe-san, I am trying to find an easier way that won't take so much time—for you and for us." She raised her eyebrows and tilted her head back. Clearly, she did not approve of my "easier way." Sosan and I sat in silence and took a breath. We understood that Tomoe-san's way truly honored and respected the process and the people being named. And so, we began again.

Breathe. What am I trying to do again? I ask myself that question often. How do you stay in the present moment, which is the only true moment? Fame and gain and projecting into the future are not our goals in a spiritual life. And so I start over, again.

* * *

There is a remarkably straightforward koan—"Wash your bowl"—that is a quintessential teaching of mindfulness and how to live in the present. My crowded mind finds it very hard to live in that way, but I keep coming back to these simple instructions from my favorite ancestor, Joshu (Zhoazhou in Chinese, 778–897), who was acclaimed for his language and nicknamed "Silver Tongue." Joshu's instructions are so simple and ordinary that they feel as if they are barely there. It is their nakedness that deeply instructs the barebones of Zen. This koan, "Wash your bowl," is one that I often use as the basis for mindfulness instruction.

Book of Serenity, Case No. 39:

> A monk asked Joshu, "I have just entered the monastery: please give me some guidance."
> Joshu said, "Have you had breakfast yet?"
> The monk said, "Yes I have eaten."
> Joshu continued, "Then go wash your bowl."

There is also a pointer that precedes the case:

> When food comes you open your mouth; when sleep comes you close your eyes. As you wash your face you find your nose, when you take off your shoes you feel your feet.

I smile at the beauty and simplicity of these instructions. This is the consummate prescription for presence and awareness in the present moment—so simple, but difficult to do. It reminds me of many slogans from twelve-step programs:

- "Do the next right thing."
- "One day at a time."
- "If there is nothing to do about the problem today, turn it over or let it go."

And from the koan liturgy (*Blue Cliff Record*, Case No. 14): "What is the next appropriate action?"

I am deeply grateful for these teachings. We do not have to look anywhere else but here, at what's in front of our nose, for practice. Being present and aware is very similar to improvisation, which I am very skilled at from my dancing life. But the simplicity and ease of doing this mindfulness is very hard to sustain. That is what Dogen calls *continuous practice*, and we often—or maybe I could even say *always*—fall short of this goal and end up in the land of automatic, numb behaviors and habitual responses.

It seems like my pattern of hurrying to get things done and finish my to-do list—check, check, check—corrodes the meaning of being present. Can I just be with what I'm doing now, and especially, can I be with my activity without my constant evaluation of good and bad, right and wrong, success and failure? Katagiri Roshi called "enlightenment" the ability to keep subject and object, or actor and activity, merged. The "I" of eating is merged with the object—the oatmeal for breakfast, for instance.

This type of teaching, in the realm of ordinary living and ordinary circumstances, provides some of the strongest education in mindfulness and sincerity that I have experienced. We usually learn this deeper layer of meaning in our activities from others, sometimes our teachers. Another story that has stayed with me involves Yasutani Roshi, a Japanese teacher who used to teach at Dai Bosatsu Zendo, which is where I practiced when I danced in New York City. Students had picked up Yasutani Roshi at the airport and were driving him to the monastery, which is in the Catskill Mountains. He was hungry and asked to have a meal on the road. He pointed to a McDonald's and said, "Let's eat there!" The students tried to discourage him subtly, covering up, perhaps, their disdain for fast-food joints. They pointed to other places where they could eat, but Yasutani Roshi insisted on eating at McDonalds. They stopped and pulled into the parking lot. He bought a cheeseburger, fries, and a chocolate shake, and preceded to sit on the bench outside in the fresh air and do *oryoki*, which is the formal Zen eating pattern that we do during retreats when we are served our meals at our meditation cushions. It's quite elaborate, like a Japanese tea ceremony. He folded the paper wrapping of the burger into a lotus placemat, he arranged the food—one, two, three—like his bowls in the zendo. He then ate with great care, relish, and joy—laughing and talking to his students.

These teachings have informed my understanding of mindfulness to a great degree. Continuous practice is taking our concentration and using it in life. It is definitely not stuck in the zendo (meditation hall). It is not bounded by circumstance or place. In formal practice, one learns this the best by being the *tenzo*, the cook at a Zen monastery or Zen center. That is a really difficult job that no one really wants. How do you keep a calm, loving atmosphere in the kitchen when you are under pressure to get the food—three meals a day plus a snack—out to the serving table on time? How do you meditate with pots and pans, knives, carrots, and rice kernels? How do you keep your cool with the other complaining cooks in the kitchen—or if someone cuts themselves, or loses their balance and steps into the large vat of honey? The latter actually happened to someone once when I was working in the kitchen at Hokyoji Zen Monastery in Minnesota. Honey not only covered the person's shoe but spread everywhere. All of us in the kitchen struggled to smother our laughter because noise from the kitchen traveled unhindered into the zendo. Ordinary mishaps can surprise us anywhere, anytime.

The tenzo position is the one least wanted by Zen students. Everyone would rather be in the quiet of the zendo. Everyone thinks that zazen is more important for enlightenment than cooking. But the tenzo position is a very important one. Being the tenzo is the middle gate between the zendo and our ordinary lives. It teaches us how to bring our concentration into activity, to learn how to take what we have learned in the zendo and bring it out into daily life. Based on a koan in *The Gateless Gate* collection, in a dialogue between Joshu and Nansen, Nansen teaches that *everyday mind is the Way*.

I have a beautiful memory of being the tenzo at Hokyoji. It serves as an example for me of the real beauty and poetry of Zen. Zen does not give outright instructions, but uses images, unfathomable stories, and poetry to lead us into understanding the intersection of the profound and the ordinary. I often was a tenzo at Hokyoji in the 1980s. At that time, Hokyoji had very primitive conditions: there was no electricity or insulation and the practitioners slept in tents. The kitchen was in a square, screened-in shed and for the early morning prep for breakfast, there was only one kerosene lantern hanging from the center of the ceiling. While preparing the oatmeal, fruit, and hot milk for breakfast in the dark, my mind settled down into very little thinking. My brain cleared and opened. My head filled simply with the birdsongs from outside, the swishing of my clothes as I stirred, the sound of the knife as it met the chopping board— nothing else. Ah, a moment of refreshment. Could I bring this tender, luminous feeling back home to my own kitchen? This is the great and difficult adventure of spiritual life.

* * *

When I first had children, I was forty years old and had already been practicing Zen formally for fifteen years. It was a shock to become a mother—to be engaged in the endless chores that went with taking care of infants, toddlers, and children. Could I surrender to this new reality, drawing upon my Zen training? It was like being a super-tenzo on steroids. When I first had my babies, I laughed and told all my friends, "Childrearing is just like going into the monastery. Everything you do is for the 'other,' and there is hardly a moment to think of yourself." But having very young children also meant that I wasn't able to practice formally, which I had previously used to stabilize myself. I barely had time to meditate. I learned to throw my *zafu*, my meditation cushion, down wherever and whenever my children were napping or watching cartoons, and finally, at the end of the day, with the dishes done, I would sit on the zafu and breathe for however long I could. I learned how to reconnect quickly with my sense of interdependence, the support of the earth and sky, and a mind that could let go of its thoughts. I was interrupted as often as I wasn't.

What is Zen practice under these new conditions? I began to investigate that question. What could I take from my Zen practice that could support what I was doing as a mother? Could a schedule help stabilize the family? I created a very sesshin-like schedule but with very different content: play, walks, meals, dishes, naps, diapers, all structured around a daily timetable. If the structure of the Zen schedule settled our minds in sesshin, I thought, couldn't it do the same for the children?

I relied heavily on walking meditation, which took place behind a stroller. I'd pack us all up with everything we needed and with the right outerwear for the weather and start walking around the block or to the park. I had memorized some Thich Nhat Hanh poems, mantras, and short sutras. As I slow-walked, step-by-step, I would recite the memorized prayers. If my child needed me, I immediately dropped what I was doing and scooted around to the front of the stroller to attend to the children's requests. As soon as I could, once all their needs were settled, I'd go back to pushing the stroller, walking and reciting. In this way, I would calm myself down and connect with the universe, which was so much larger than the small world of me and the children and what seemed like endless chores.

Most parents complain about night feedings. When I was nursing, this difficult night event rested on my shoulders. But I was able to make a turnaround with my complaining mind. In the deepest, darkest part of one night, while I sat rocking in my chair with my child to my breast, looking at the moonlight streaking through the window, I realized how extraordinarily peaceful and quiet the night feedings were. Oh, if I just focused on my breathing, calmed my mind, this *was* meditation. So I began to meditate like that, and then another insight happened: I realized that on my block alone, there were two other parents with small children who were also probably up at night, maybe even right then. I began to pray and commune with all the thousands of parents who were up with me at night, caring for their beloved children and surrendering their sleep. The night feedings became my favorite time of each day's twenty-four-hour period. They were quiet and deep and communal—my unique and treasured meditation.

My boys and I loved Richard Scarry's children's books. We read, over and over, his book *What People Do All Day*. There were pictures of construction workers, garbage men, nurses, grocery store clerks, plumbers, you name it. One day, while we were playing outside, I followed, with my three-year-old, a stream of water from the melting snow. What was this water and where was it going? We had just read about plumbing and sewers. I think it was because of mindfulness and improvisation that I gave my son the time to let this beautiful experience unfold. We followed the tiny stream down our driveway, which had a slight incline, until it joined the water in the street's gutter. Then we followed this little brook of water along the gutter, down the street, until at the corner, the water vanished down the sewer grate like a small waterfall. Oh, his bright eyes looked up at me.

"That's a sewer!" he said.

"Yes, my dear, that's a sewer."

"Where does the water go?"

"Down to the Mississippi River," I told him, whose park we had visited many times.

* * *

I tried to be prepared in advance for my children's needs. That attention to the details of process, I think, came from my Zen training. Like the *anja*, the personal attendant to the roshi who is always thinking about what the teacher might need next, I always had my "blue bag," as we called it, which was a large blue printed shoulder bag that was a post-diaper bag of tools for development and creation. In the blue bag was everything the children might need to entertain themselves, often refreshed with new and interesting additions: a large Ziploc bag of "guys," super heroes and monsters, Legos and Playmobile figures; books; puzzles; and an endless supply of drawing materials and snacks. My kids were entertained at restaurants, doctors' offices, friends' houses, wherever we went, by the contents of the blue bag. Was this bag born of my fear of having unruly kids with nothing to do? Or from my own aversion to boredom? At any rate, my kids have turned out to be extremely creative and self-directed.

My husband and I almost got divorced over "the little green army men." I did not want war play in my house—period! I was stubbornly opinionated. Charley, however, felt it was imperative that our sons learn and deal with the masculine archetype of the protective warrior and hero. Also for this purpose, he made a wrestling room in the basement with its floor covered with blue plastic tumbling mats.

In the meantime, one of my dharma sisters, who had followed the rule of no gun-play in her house, had an older elementary school son who was having psychological troubles, and she finally sent him to a child psychologist. She once, shaking her head, told me, with a baffled look on her face, "I am paying $100 an hour for a psychologist to play war with my son with superhero figurines."

So I softened. My husband was raising his sons in his way. I had to respect that. But I did have a mitigating idea. I bought myself a Playmobil ambulance—it became known as "Mom's toy"—and frequently, I got down on the floor with my sons and engaged in what I called "play meditation." I could concentrate on playing with my sons for thirty to forty-five minutes just like I was practicing zazen, and I would not allow other chores or problems to enter my mind. I played as nonjudgmentally as possible and did whatever they wanted to do. Often, I ended up being the ambulance driver amidst the fighting. Often, too, at the end of our fantasy play, my sons would pile up all the dead guys and we would have a funeral and think about the dead guys' loved ones left behind. In our play, we at least acknowledged the consequences of war.

For me, it was good to be an older parent because by forty years of age, Charley and I were much more settled than we had been in our early years of marriage. Our partnership was stronger and more traditional, and we both had been in therapy by then for many years so that some of our early wildness and neuroses had been addressed. I am always glad for that. The hard part of being an older parent is taking place in the present day with its reminders of mortality. Our children are in their late twenties and we are around 70. Will we get to meet our grandchildren if there are any? Will we get to see how our children's lives form and stabilize? Maybe, or maybe not.

Ironically, being a Zen teacher did not teach me, necessarily, about being a good parent psychologically. How do you learn to be a good parent when you yourself were not parented well? I thought I was doing such a good job at not allowing the karma of my past to bleed onto my own children. Perhaps that has been my hubris—thinking that I knew how to be a loving parent or that Zen practice would take care of the deeper psychological levels and life skills that I didn't have.

We reenact intergenerational trauma even when we are trying our hardest not to. I had learned as a child to skip over feelings and needs. Because my parents didn't know how to stay self-connected, and because I didn't know how to do that either, I was not able to give this wholesome, essential skill to my children. In fact, I often reinforced all the things I didn't want to reinforce with a judgmental, often shaming, response to my sons' actions—just as my mother and grandmother had done before me. These issues came from my own unresolved trauma. The consequences of the oppression of Irish Catholics from my husband's side and my Jewish trauma all combined into the mix of our childrearing to give our children an ancient, twisted karma that is rather formidable.

Sometimes, in the name of Zen practice and spirituality, when the going got rough with my kids, when I didn't know what to do or how to negotiate conflict, I would turn inward, be silent and do a practice on the spot of breathing in the pain and breathing out love, kindness, and understanding—in the car, in the living room, etc. That often centered me and perhaps even prevented me from some reactive and destructive outward behavior. But I now know that those silent prayers often left my children feeling abandoned and uncared for. The result of these meditations, then, had an impact that was exactly the opposite of what I had wanted to happen.

In the end, as I look back, I see that I didn't always have enough emotional bandwidth to handle the stresses of my work in a troubled sangha and the problems and needs of my children, both at the same time.

My role as a parent produces an enormous experience of joy, and yet when I recognize that I was not present enough with my children, I feel, simultaneously, the sorrow of loss. Is that the paradox of parenting? In the beginning, you have to develop a grave and deep attachment to the children for their safety. In the end, with such poignant irony, you have to let them go. This is an extremely fertile ground for receiving life the way it is, and the acceptance of both joy and sorrow. These days I am accepting both the good and the bad of my parenting and labeling myself a good-enough parent. But maybe it would be better still for me to just drop the evaluation altogether and resort to the nearly universal acceptance: "I did the best I could."

* * *

There is something indestructible about mindfulness. It leaps into the eternal while abiding in the present moment. It can help us distinguish between our swirling repetitive thoughts and feelings and what this present moment truly is. But mindfulness needs to be practiced. It isn't easy. It has to be practiced regularly, like weight training. Any kind of competency needs what seems like endless repetition. But it is the ongoing function of mindfulness that allows me to connect with the beauty of life, even in life's hardest moments.

Ryōkan Taigu (1758–1831), a Zen master and poet who lived much of his life as a hermit, wrote:

> Carrying firewood on my shoulder
> I walk in the green mountains along the bumpy path.
> I stop to rest under a tall pine;
> Sitting quietly, I listen to the spring song of the birds.

From the beginning of my practice, Ryōkan has instructed me on the walking of the genuine path of Zen in its simplicity. His poem conveys, simply and clearly, the rewards of mindfulness and "doing the next right thing." Its lucidity and beauty keeps me coming back to Zen.

Chapter Five
"DO NOT MISUSE SEXUALITY"

We are working with sexual passion and dancing with it all the time. It is better to have things out in the open than hidden away. If you have an active and engaging problem with your sexuality and face up to its challenges, you are certainly on the royal road to settling the great matter and realizing ultimate freedom.
—Roshi Reb Anderson

I never told anyone about the sexually abusive incidents in my childhood until I entered the twelve-step recovery program at age twenty-six. I never spoke of the secrets festering inside my aloneness. I didn't realize that this hidden shame could have been the source of much of my internal pain, drug and alcohol misuse, neurotic compulsions, and overeating. But those unattended-to secrets would block my ability to be present and inhibit my spiritual expansiveness for many years.

"Do not misuse sexuality" is one of Zen Buddhism's grave precepts. This particular precept acknowledges the enormous power of our sexual urges. That power is what makes sex exciting—and sometimes all-consuming. But our sexual drive can be misdirected. If there is a misuse of this primal energy, we can hurt others and ourselves, sometimes profoundly affecting the psyche of another or even our own.

The Original Wounding

My own experience of eroticism and sex began within my good Jewish upper middle-class family. I was vulnerable as a child. My parents' upbringing had not prepared them to protect me, and they probably did not have the word "abuse" in their vocabulary. They were doing so much more for me than their parents had done for them. Wasn't taking their daughter to live in the suburbs, giving her all that money could buy, protection enough?

My dad was the prototypical '50s man. Women were objects for his pleasure. His wife was his glorified secretary and maid, his daughter a fairytale princess with no emotions, and any female with a "good rack" was an object for his flirtations. I was often embarrassed and ashamed in restaurants by the way my father treated the waitresses after he'd had a few martinis. He would survey their bodies with his eyes, and if they met with his approval, he would make an outrageously vulgar comment in front of the whole family. Once, in the living room after dinner, when my brothers and I were all older, my father said that he could sexually satisfy my brother's wife better than my brother could. *Oh my god, what did he just say?* But by that time, I was old enough to stand up, tell him that his comment was absolutely unacceptable, and walk out of the room.

My eldest brother, the heir-apparent in our old-country Russian family hierarchy, was obsessed with pornography. The closet in the bathroom we shared was filled to overflowing with copies of *Playboy, Hustler,* and other magazines. I learned never to open the linen cabinet door because tall piles of girly magazines would pour out onto the bathroom floor. The images in these magazines confused me about my womanhood. These photographs built up in me a fear of showing my sexuality. If you fulfilled the "right" look, you became an object to be desired and then, devoured. And as an overweight Jewish girl with a big nose, I inherently knew I would never fulfill this vision of attractiveness in our society. No one was there to tell me this was pornography and male visual stimulation. No one was there to tell me that sexual satisfaction and real relationships were to be found somewhere else.

Even to this day, I feel paranoid in a small bathroom—its enclosed space still has the smell of fear for me. The little bathroom I shared with my brothers was dangerous. My female cousin recently concurred with me that she was afraid to use that bathroom in our house. Even though my childhood bathroom is long gone, as an adult, I find myself still affected. I am only comfortable in spacious bathrooms with big windows—or better yet, large women's locker rooms. I often leave the door connecting my bedroom and the bathroom ajar so as to have more open space. Such a lingering reaction from such a small thing. I wonder sometimes, did something else happen in the bathroom?

When I was an adult and told my mother, years after it happened, that Great-Uncle Lou had abused me sexually when I was in fourth grade, my mother's reply was: "Oh, he did that to everyone." Oh. *Oh, Mother.* She knew he had crossed sexual boundaries with "everyone," and yet she still left me overnight with Lou and my Aunt Manya when I was ten? What was she thinking? She wasn't thinking. In her experience, these things simply happened and you "moved on" and did the best you could. After all, in her Philadelphia childhood, she had lived across the alley from a brothel where the women hung out on the fire escape which she could see from her bedroom window. It was convenient for her to leave me overnight at Lou and Manya's house, and I don't think it crossed her mind to think of my safety. Yet, for me, that incident created my first concrete sexual wound. Thinking of this old man, with his ratty, squinted eyes and greedy hands all over me, putting his fingers up my vagina, makes me, even now, raise my tense shoulders, stick out my tongue as if to throw up, and shake my head in disgust.

There is a terrible paradox for children who are abused by someone who is a so-called "loving relative." You have an unconscious inkling that it is wrong, but you don't feel like you have the power to stop it. I didn't even tell anyone. Somehow, I knew that his touching me was wrong, but that telling someone wouldn't help me either. Whenever things went awry for whatever reason, my mother would either yell at me, make it my fault, or brush me off. I had learned that no one would care or come to my defense. Speaking the truth brought uncomfortable conflicts to our family and was not allowed. This began the regrettable amalgamation between my awakening sensuality and a contradictory feeling that sex was repugnant. This split reaction would follow me around in my body and mind for decades.

When the sexual boundaries in a family are loose, there are many opportunities for children's safety to fall through the cracks. Careless and unacceptable behaviors repeat themselves. The hardest experience for me to write about is the sexual molestation I received from our maid, Carrie, in seventh grade. She lived with us during my middle school years from about age eleven to fourteen. Because she was an African-American, the issues of race and class and servitude can't be skimmed over. Because of the gravity of these issues and my relationship to the Black women who raised me, I have written Chapter Seven on racial justice.

For the most part, the African-American maids were my surrogate mothers, and I bless them for bringing me up and introducing me to my understanding of spirituality. My earliest memory of the "maids" was Cora holding my hand and singing spirituals over my sickbed. Because I had asthma, I was often out of school and spent my time in bed or hanging out with Cora. I would hear her singing to Jesus while she was ironing, her melodic rich alto drifting up the basement stairs. It felt like those domestic workers knew how much this lonely little girl needed a hug and some attention. The African-American women brought love into my house and cared for me. I often say that I wouldn't have survived my childhood without their unconditional support.

As a young child my heart was open and I saw racism through innocent eyes. I saw how the maids were treated. They lived in the basement in a roughly renovated room with a very crude toilet stall. They worked from dawn until after dinner on meeting our needs and they never mentioned their own. They were told what to do with no consideration for the repercussions on them and they were, for the most part, silent. There was an obvious gap in economics and in the general level of respect. I saw but didn't know how to acknowledge our differences in economic and racial privilege. I truly loved these women, but that didn't actually affect the disparities. Occasionally, their children or grandchildren would come over. I would play with these children, of course, but I could see in their eyes their surprise at how I lived, how many toys I had, and how much I was pampered. When I was a tween, I understood a little bit more—I became aware of the civil rights movement in full swing and Martin Luther King Jr.'s assassination.

Throughout this time, Carrie and I had a lot of fun together. She would take me to the Riverview Park, an amusement park in downtown Chicago. I remember being so proud at thirteen that I was walking around with a Black woman. That showed I was not racist, I thought. Oh, how naive my white thirteen-year-old self was.

As well as being an energetic and entertaining caretaker, Carrie could also be mean and vindictive. One negative incident that sticks in my mind happened on the day I got my period. I was at an impressionable age, thirteen, awkward and uncomfortable in my own skin. My parents were traveling in Asia for business, far, far, away. Carrie was my sole caregiver and though she drove me to Gsells Pharmacy to get sanitary pads, when we got there, she said, "You go in and get them, here's some money." I begged her to buy them for me or at least come with me. Kids from school were working at the till and would see what I was buying. "No," she said, laughing at me. She just refused. I went in and bought my own napkins. I tried to hide my tears by looking out the passenger window on the way home. Carrie drove home with a smirk on her face, chuckling, with not one iota of sympathy for a young girl's embarrassment.

That is a small detail and not so bad. But the sexual impropriety she acted out with me had a long-lasting effect on my life.

Carrie was a very proud woman, which I can admire in spite of her at times upsetting behavior toward me. She was a physically strong woman with an attractive face. She was not religious or spiritual, like the housekeepers before her, but instead was rebellious and defiant in the way of the '60s civil rights and Black Power movements. Her resistance to her situation as the "maid," in the light of my family's prejudice and her lack of power in her role, was quite remarkable, and she was very assertive and subversive in her own way.

Breaking the subservient stereotype, Carrie was our first maid to own her own car, and she began showing up at the house with a white Cadillac, once wearing a mink stole and stiletto high heels. My dad's black Cadillac and her white Cadillac sat side by side in the U-driveway in front of the house. In 1964, two Cadillacs in our driveway was very impressive. Everyone would pass our house, as we were on the main scenic drive road, Sheridan Road, which was *the* road, running from Chicago to Lake Forest, hugging Lake Michigan's shore and passing through all the exclusive, wealthy, white suburbs. My parents liked the impression made by having two Cadillacs parked in front of the house.

At the family dinner table, questions were asked and jokes made about where Carrie got the money to buy the Cadillac and the mink stole. Was my family's reaction to her appearance just an expression of prejudice, or should they have questioned Carrie for the safety of us children? I wonder now if she was a prostitute on the side. Really, sometimes I just don't know what would have been "right" in the situation. Would firing her, based on this insinuation, have protected my thirteen-year-old self? Years later, my brother speculated in private whether she'd had it on with Uncle Lou. That wouldn't have surprised me—my two abusers getting together. Did she and my father have sex? I don't know. She knew about drugs and broken families, and she introduced me to forbidden sexuality by having sex with me, a thirteen-year-old, on the couch in the living room. I could also glean from her language and her actions that she was well familiar with what people caught in poverty and oppression had to do to get by.

As a young white girl, I experienced so many things beyond

my known environment—both the blessings of the Black Baptist women in my house and also a deep wounding from a person's criminal sexual activity with me. In my young white mind, I identified this range of involvements with Black people as qualities of Black culture—high and low. But now, in my learning about racism, I can see that I had a stereotypical reaction. These occurrences could have happened through any race, any gender, any human being. I see now that one of the basic seeds of racism is to see people as representatives of their race rather than as individuals.

* * *

My parents were often out of town on business, leaving Carrie to take care of me. One night—or was it many nights?—when I was in seventh grade and we were watching TV together in the living room, she invited me onto the couch with her to snuggle. That sounded good, just snuggling on the couch with my surrogate mother, feeling her close to me as we watched TV. When I told one of my dharma sisters, she asked, "Judith, didn't you know that was wrong? Why didn't you stop it?" But really, I didn't know how to assess or interpret what was happening to me. I was a confused thirteen-year-old, and Carrie was my authority figure. Would she do something wrong? The bodily sensations she aroused in me were actually a little bit interesting.

I didn't know what exactly Carrie was doing when she started to unbutton my blouse and kiss my neck. I didn't know what it meant that she was rubbing her hips on me and undulating her spine. Under the flicker of the TV lights and the background noise of a sitcom, she sucked on my little virgin nipples hard and the sensation went straight down to my private parts. I was so young, I couldn't even say "vagina" out loud, though I had learned about it in junior high health class that year. Her hands found their way down to my vagina and her fingers entered me while rubbing my clitoris. I knew about climaxing from having masturbated, but what happened with Carrie was more like a great disorientation, and it filled me with dread. The experience precipitated an unending period of confused feelings. Was sensual feeling wonderful or was it wrong?

After that happened, I was acutely uncomfortable with Carrie. I didn't want to be alone with her anymore even though the circumstances of my parents working left me alone with her quite often. Was there somewhere to go to get away? No. Sadly, I found that I had lost more than my innocence—I had also lost my friend and companion. I felt totally alone.

Through my relationship with Carrie, I learned about the underbelly of life and the dark side of sexuality. The hardest part for me was loving Carrie while realizing that she had harmed me—and maybe deliberately so. Or maybe unconsciously so. Or maybe sex was an addiction for her. The "why" may not be important or answerable. We will never know what is going through the minds of our abusers nor will we ever know how they may also have been personally victimized. I understand in hindsight that Carrie's actions were insidious collateral against the backdrop of generations of Black women being sexually used by white men. I am completely acknowledging the victimization brought on by the larger societal structures of racism. I see now the depth of the wounds Carrie held, and for that I can see my way to forgiving her for what she did to me. Perhaps her acting out was an unconscious expression of her own woundedness and rage.

All that being said, sex is a powerful energy and when

misused can create great harm in another person. That is what is important to me. That is why there is a Buddhist precept: Do not misuse sexuality.

This experience created lingering problems—a lifetime of consequences. It was at this moment of intrusion that my sexual desire awoke, and with it came a slow-motion fog of confused thinking. I knew that what happened between Carrie and me was wrong, but nevertheless, it was the very beginning of my realization of what sexual desire feels like.

There are many different reactions to sexual molestation. I shut down and became dissociated from feelings of sensual desire. But other people might do the opposite, becoming obsessed with or even addicted to sexual stimulation. Some learn to get approval through sexual promiscuity. If the sexual assault is kinky, violent, or sadomasochistic, sometimes victims actually lose their sense of choice over their own stimulation and act out the patterns learned in childhood for their whole life without a conscious choosing of that sexual expression. I do not judge anyone else's sexual life, but it upsets me when I think of victims losing their *choice* about their own bodies and sexuality. There can also be a lot of guilt if you were turned on by the sexual assault. Our bodies react when they are stimulated. And yet, many victims berate themselves and their bodies for having a sexual reaction to an unwanted sexual stimulation, which may lead them on a path of erotic confusion and perhaps even self-hate. This does not translate into a wholesome transition into mature sexuality; to the contrary, we are filled with reactivity, clinging to sexual stimulation, having aversion to it, or going numb.

As I began to explore my sensual feelings, as any thirteen-year-old should, I was now misdirected. I replicated the exact same situation of my abuse with my friend Lily. We were lying on the floor of her living room, snuggling together, her back to my front, watching TV. I just, almost like an automaton, unbuttoned her shirt and started touching her breast. Her very white, prim, maid saw us, and the next thing I knew, I was kicked out of the clique at school and had no friends. My view of myself as a popular girl disappeared, and I continued through high school as a loner. This expulsion was a huge consequence with a lot of psychological repercussions as I developed my personhood and identity as a teenager. My psyche was built around aloneness and self-reliance.

I told no one about my experience with Carrie. I began to be afraid of sex and boys. I did not consider myself a lesbian even though I'd had these experiences with females, and I can say as an adult that I am bisexual. In my teen years, I was a nonsexual, shutdown, overweight girl. I was cold and rigidly uptight. I dressed and tried to act like a hippie, but actually, I had no friends. I tried to give the impression that I was more sophisticated than everyone else so I didn't have to interact. I developed an extremely sarcastic tongue, and if any boy approached me, I could cut him down with one phrase or remark. I was completely alone, at school and in my house.

Young and Sexually Confused

At eighteen, I had my first boyfriend, Charley, who actually became my husband when I was twenty-five. This was a very important change and gift in my life. Finally, someone loved me, noticed, and accepted me, exactly as I was. I wasn't alone anymore.

That summer after my first year in college, Charley and I wanted to move to Colorado Springs together. I was to participate in a dance workshop at Colorado College. I told my mother this while we were in my bedroom on Sheridan Road, the house of my childhood. My mother was a woman whose full attention was on how she appeared. Her children were a reflection of who she was, and therefore, there was a great emphasis on us showing up "right." She always had perfectly coiffed hair, wore red nail polish, and dressed in the height of fashion. Even if she was dressed casually, she was wearing an "outfit." I almost never saw her relaxed. That afternoon she was sitting in the red corduroy stuffed chair in my bedroom. I was sitting on the floor. When it dawned on my mother that living together meant I was having sex with my boyfriend, she reacted in a catastrophic way. Her face became waxen and red, and she turned to me, yelling, "You're a whore, you're a whore!" I crawled on my hands and knees to my mother across my grandma's hand-me-down Persian rug, begging her to understand how important it was for me to have a boyfriend. But she only responded, "I'm going to tell your father, and he'll figure out what to do." She stomped out of the room and slammed the door. Her rage at me and her disappointment in me were very deep and clear. My parents forbade me to see Charley, so I proceeded then, for the first time in my life, to lie to my parents. I went to Colorado Springs with Charley but I didn't tell them any details. This whole episode, especially my parents' lack of support for me, was just one more reason on my long list of justifications to hate them.

But I was no good at sex with my dear boyfriend. I couldn't access my sexual desire and I couldn't have an orgasm with him. I just endured our lovemaking. And, as if I were in a Woody Allen film, my mother's huge, looming face would float in the corner of the room, watching me while we had sex. My whole body reacted to the stress of conflicting moral forces— my mother calling me a whore while my whole generation professed and practiced "free love"—combined with the personal aftermath of childhood sexual abuse. The physical ramifications of this inner conflict were strong. My asthma got worse and I was covered from head to toe with eczema. I took slimy mineral baths as a curative and went to the famous allergy clinic on the university campus, but the doctors there couldn't really resolve my physical symptoms, as the problem was mostly psychological.

I lived in the midst of the sexual revolution that had begun in the '60s and was now moving into the late '70s and early '80s. All sexual expressions were tolerated and even encouraged. This was before the AIDS epidemic. In the pretense of being a hippy, I was the first one to take off all my clothes at any somewhat private lake we visited and insinuate that anyone who didn't strip right away didn't deserve their hippie credentials. I did this even though my show of bravado didn't match my inner fears and dissociation—the deep inhibitions covered with a defensive and self-righteous attitude. This so-called freedom carried over into my willingness to go to dangerous places or engage in risky behaviors. In that sense, I continued to be quite unconscious.

My husband's heroes all were promiscuous, *walking on the wild side*. David Bowie's and Lou Reed's music played endlessly in our house. I knew Charley had a very strong energy, both in his art and in his sexuality. It was part of the reason I had been attracted to him. He had studied sexual freedom in high school. An influential book for him was Albert Ellis's *Sex Without Guilt*—a good book for a Catholic boy who was rebelling against the strictures of the Church. He also liked *The Harrod Experiment*, a novel about a group marriage experiment in college. Though I didn't have this information at the beginning of our relationship, I knew that he was full of sexual drive and that he liked the idea of sexual experimentation. How did he end up with me, I wonder?

Later, I think Charley and I got married in a kind of fog. We both were filled with unexamined contradictions. He secretly did not believe in fidelity but wanted to win the approval of his Catholic family by marrying me. Correspondingly, I was willing to ignore anything in order to keep my one and only relationship because I thought no other man would ever be interested in me. The subject of fidelity never came up for discussion. From my point of view, wasn't that what marriage was? But now in retrospect I see that Charley and I were not communicating about very important relational issues. I was filled with a fear of abandonment and he was quite used to lying to his family, all the way back to his childhood. In order to protect himself from having to deal with my jealous hysteria, he just stopped talking about our relationship issues. Obfuscating his activities seemed less difficult to him than dealing with me.

At that time I don't think that we were conscious enough or psychologically savvy enough to even imagine how we could change things. Colluding with his strategies, I went into denial and simply did not notice the signs of his extramarital sex. I got my life organized around being consumed by my work. I took my unconscious self into twelve-step recovery, which led eventually to psychotherapy. In the meantime, we lived parallel lives. One of the most difficult revelations for me was when I learned that my husband had kept meeting with one of his previous lovers even through the first years of our marriage. His omissions created a white elephant of secrecy that lived in our bedroom. All this cover-up hurt our bond, and our marriage lacked a deeper, more honest connection.

I remember the first time I found out that my husband, who was then my boyfriend, was cheating on me by having sex with our downstairs neighbor. I was young, maybe twenty. I was at a summer dance workshop in Washington, DC, when he wrote me a long letter telling me how terrific the sex was with our downstairs neighbor as if I would think that was great too. I don't think he even realized that I would be hurt. Was that *his* disconnect with sex and emotions? I, of course, had quite a different reaction. I was rattled to my core, as if a hand had gone inside my body, grasped my center of gravity below my belly button, and was vigorously and endlessly shaking my insides. After the dance workshop, back home, whenever I was alone, I would sit for hours in our green vinyl rocking chair, listening to Billie Holiday's deeply sorrowful lamentations. I cried all afternoon and into the evening, wailing away. My slightly misaligned rocking chair had a clump on one of its runners. With each rocking motion the runner came down hard with a bang on the floor. *Bang, bang, bang.* What had gone wrong? Did my downstairs neighbor hear the bang, bang, bang? I blamed myself and all my sexual inadequacies for what had happened. Charley was my first love. In the throes of his betrayal, in the middle of a screaming argument with him, totally shocking myself, I turned over the kitchen table and broke the lamp, which tumbled to the floor. Suddenly, we were both silent, and then he walked quietly out of the kitchen. He did, in the end, stop that particular relationship.

Turning It Around

This awful predicament of being closed off from the sensuality and physicality of my body was starting to affect how I felt about myself and my dearest held relationship. I began to want deeply to change and to experience sexual healing. The first thing I did in my sexual recovery was to go beyond masturbating and learn how to have an orgasm with a man. My husband patiently and lovingly helped me. What did I need? How should he move? He watched the movements of my self-loving. It was embarrassingly revealing and shockingly intimate, but it was my first attempt at communication and I was surprised and grateful to find him present for this in every way. I realized that despite his promiscuity he was still committed to me, and we began to work together on our problems.

Our experiments sometimes were exactly the opposite of what an abuse survivor should do to heal. Because I was still trying to please my husband, and because he was a sexual revolutionary, we tried to have an open marriage. At least he wasn't lying about extramarital sex anymore. I hid my hurt of jealousy, stuffing it farther and farther down with the rest of the poisonous sexual experiences of my childhood. My need for emotional connection was not acknowledged, especially not by me. I guess I didn't really know what I needed, except that I wanted to stay with Charley. We tried participating in orgies together, which was then euphemistically called "swinging." Swinging was a sexual game played by couples who wanted to have sex outside of marriage but with the acceptance of their partners. One big happy party, I say cynically. I guess it was a precursor of today's polyamory. Perhaps now, in the twenty-first century, there is enough support so that polyamory can be practiced with more consciousness. But I wasn't able to do it. I was completely jealous! Abuse survivor that I was, this type of sexual promiscuity only reinforced the disconnection between my emotions and sexuality. I taught myself how to have anonymous sex and learned to come with anyone. I thought at the time that this was a successful accomplishment and proved that I was an adequate partner. But rather than heal the empty spaces inside my wounded soul, this kind of sex only made me feel even more empty and less connected to Charley, the person I cared about most. I often said my soul felt like a piece of Swiss cheese with another huge hole made by each encounter.

Conveniently though, I was busy, which helped me ignore the disintegrating quality of my marriage. I was completely consumed by Zen training and my dance career. Being consumed by work is a coping mechanism that I have used my entire life. In this instance, work kept me from having to notice my feelings or the lack of connection between my husband and myself. In our parallel lives I was gone from home often, spending a lot of time at the monastery and touring with dance performances all around the world. I left my husband alone a lot, which provided him time to investigate his own life, his own sexuality, and take care of his own needs.

My father pulled me aside once when I had just come home from a two-month training period at Hokyoji Zen Monastery with Katagiri-Roshi, and whispered to me that it wasn't good for my marriage to leave my husband alone for so long. Well, Dad should know, right? I was aware, having heard through my cousin, who had heard it from my aunt, that my father had had extramarital affairs. But I didn't listen to him. My Zen practice period meant everything to me. My participation in those practice periods in my late twenties and early thirties very much influenced who I became. Focusing on Zen afforded me intensive time with Katagiri Roshi before he died and deepened my practice in a very profound way. Who's to say that it wasn't the right thing for me to do?

But I began to listen to what my husband was saying to me too. I endeavored to practice deep listening to his side of the story. He said that he felt betrayed or tricked by me. He had thought, because I had been a hippy, that I was fully committed to the sexual revolution too. He took me at face value with my defensive hippie mask in place, and so he thought I would want to go with him into the wild exploration of unbounded sexuality. He had been committed to this idea of sexual freedom since he was fourteen years old. He did not fulfill his family's fantasy that he, as the second son, would become a priest. It is a huge moment when a Catholic boy stops going to church and confession, and suspends his belief in Catholicism. Charley's rejection of his family's religion seems to me to have created a great schism in his psyche. His identity became deeply enmeshed with his strong sexual drive and breaking the societal rules of sexuality and marriage. And now, I had changed not only the bargaining chips but also my belief system. In the course of my adventure in healing, I had turned out not to be that brash red-headed uninhibited hippie girl he had first fallen in love with. When I finally did come to terms with my body and reassemble my sensuality, to the contrary, I became very shy and protective of myself. Charley was disappointed in me for becoming so conventional, so "straight." This put to the fore the question: Did he really want to stay with me in my changed state?

There was a moment when I realized that my husband considered my Zen practice tantamount to an extramarital affair. In his view, I had another lover he felt was more important to me than he was: Zen. In some ways, I would have to say he was right. Zen gave me my inner connection with my soul, my spirituality, and my deepest self. Now, I see the sense of self-reliance I valued back then more as a form of alienation and dissociation from people than as any spiritual understanding of the truth of interconnection. But at thirty years of age nothing could be more important to me than what I understood as enlightenment and my personal liberation from my suffering.

I can see now how the self-satisfaction I got from meditation could be construed as another lover. When my deeper bodily energies opened up, it was like having an orgasm. Who needed a husband? This is the kundalini energy that isn't talked about so much in Zen. I felt discouraged by the unspoken rules of Zen against speaking of chakras or the human body's elaborate system of prana or Qi or life force. Zen practitioners often feel—and in many ways, I think they are right—that these energies are a distraction to seeing the existential and greatest reality. But for me, *not* talking about what was happening in my body left me, again, feeling alone and misunderstood in the midst of the sangha. Once again, somehow, I was not supposed to acknowledge my body's energy.

Because I had spent so many hours developing my body as a dancer, feeling the inner energy seemed easy and like a gift. Every day, before and after rehearsal, I had lain on the floor and done a kind of slow-motion, micromovement meditation, feeling my body from the inside out. Hours of this kind of meditation made it easier for me to feel the Qi in my own body. After I left dancing as a career and became an acupuncturist I spent many hours feeling the Qi in other people's bodies. In Eastern Medicine, I learned that the sexual energy is viewed as energy coming from our ancestors—the energy of reproduction. Rather than dismissing this inner body dance and movement as an obstacle to freedom, I began to appreciate my experience as an opening into the enormous creativity and mystery of the world of form.

I have come to understand that the energy of creation—the Qi or subtle body energy and physical sexual energy—are the same energy. I did have another lover: me and the universe. But zazen didn't satisfy the needs of my human heart: connection, love, acceptance, and belonging. In the beginning of my spiritual life, the isolation and lack of relationship that I got in the silent meditative environment of the zendo seemed the only way to find some peace and individual release from my deep suffering. It was not until much later, as I matured, that I saw that Buddhism actually expressed the opposite. It posits that we are all deeply interconnected, that no one is an isolated unit, and that, in fact, the old idea of isolation needs to be completely reformed and reversed.

Charley and I realized that if we were to stay together, there would have to be a lot of compromises and surrender on each side. If I was asking my husband to give up extramarital affairs, what was I going to give up in return? Could I relinquish my love affair with Zen? Could the difficult-to-understand "detachment" in Buddhism somehow also include my deep-seated need for connection? I wondered if this paradoxical longing for both intimacy and transcendence could be reconciled by a more feminized view. In this case, where was the middle way? Even though it might be contradictory to the patriarchal structure of Buddhism, I wondered if, perhaps, I allowed my inherent woman wisdom to arise, it could balance and heal this oppositional and compartmentalized parts of my thinking. Could I say, as a woman, that sexuality, family, and belonging were completely interconnected with my spirituality?

With some trepidation, I began to state that Charley was the most important relationship in my life, above all others. "It doesn't matter if I'm lying or if I'm not sure," I thought. "My husband needs me to say, 'You are the most important thing in my life.' My own need for commitment in marriage, needs me to say that sentence." So I said it: "Our marriage is the most important thing in my life." From that starting point, our marriage started to change. Soon I realized I had done the right thing. Even though I still was quite committed to my Zen life, there was a shift. My Zen life began to include both things: my commitment to family and my commitment to understanding that there is something going on beyond the story of marriage, children, life, and death. I had to back up this new agreement with my family by occasionally making decisions that proved it. Sometimes I needed to choose my home life over formal Zen practice which my Zen zealot of my previous years would not have permitted. Sometimes I didn't go to sesshin. Sometimes I interrupted sesshin by going midweek to one of my son's high school orchestra concerts. Sometimes I bought matching furniture like a regular housewife for our living room. I realized that my understanding of continuous mindful practice was actually strengthened by learning what being centered means in the middle of the chaos of family life. I smile now because I'm still not very good at that. Finding equanimity and deep immediate presence in the face of the ups and downs of life is an unending challenge.

Now I don't blame Charley, as I used to, for all his sexual exploration and the hurt that I experienced in our early years together. I just accept and digest the hurt of my sexual story as my *dukkha* and own my part of the story. We began a slow recovery and discovery of what a marriage really was for us, for we two, very specific people with our unique issues. It wasn't a generalized compromise, it was a growing intimacy of revealing our needs to each other and trusting each other. I became committed to feeling a soul connection when I made love. I wanted to feel like I was making love and the person involved was making love back to me. Oddly, crazily, surprisingly, my husband turned towards me. He went to work on himself too. It seems to me that men's maturity also grows into an awareness of a deeper understanding of commitment and love. I guess, in the end, he loved me back. Miraculously, here we are, forty and some years later, still together.

Street Rape

In 1984, during this time of sexual exploration, in the midst of all my confusion about sexual boundaries, to add insult to injury, I was raped in the street in Chicago. This was strikingly timed. I had returned from a seven-day sesshin at Hokyoji Zen Monastery the day before, and my mind was completely wide open. My quiet mind was viewing *samsaric* life—the wandering-in-circles world—with its dissatisfactions and hurts, through the Buddha's eyes. I had an eagle's perspective, flying high above and watching the drama below. In this very expansive state of mind, I had experienced one of the lowest moments in human existence. My silent mind from the sesshin, in many ways, framed the entire experience of the venomous act of rape.

My dance studio was in a rough part of Chicago. I was dropping off some video equipment there, so I just parked the car in the alley. I ran up to deliver the equipment and when I returned, I was pushed from behind into my car. No one heard my screams, or if they did, no one responded. I was sandwiched in the front seat of the car between a man and a teenage boy. The young boy was the older man's nephew—information I picked up from their chattering back and forth. I surmised that this was the older man's teaching moment, instructing his nephew in how to rob people.

Oh, how I wished I had listened more to what you were supposed to do in assaults or that I had taken self-defense classes. I do have a lot of regret that I didn't try to do something. But I felt so powerless, and I was so scared. He kept saying "Don't you look at me, don't you look at me, or I'll kill you." If I tried to look up, he pushed my head down, chin to chest. Afterwards, when I was looking at the police books of suspects, I realized why he had said that—I couldn't identify him. After I had taken off my diamond wedding ring and given them my cash, he dropped his nephew off at his sister's apartment. He kept on driving to an abandoned lot and raped me in the back of the SUV with my skirt pulled over my head and eyes, so I still couldn't see him even. At one point, I was just lying there still, just letting him do it, and he said, "What's the matter with you, is this how white women fuck?" Oddly, he seemed to think that I was engaged with him in this sex act, that this rape was a form of sexual congress and not an expression of having power over someone else. I guess I wasn't in a place to laugh, but I just started wiggling and he climaxed.

When he finally left the car, he also pushed my face down to the seat, again avoiding my facial recognition, asking me, "Did I hurt your pride? Did I hurt your pride?" Through his tone of voice, I knew that this was not a benign question. It was a taunt. This deeply wounded Black man wanted to shame me. Having just come from sesshin, I had a still mind and could see beyond myself. Because of my eagle's-eye view from this quiescent state of mind, I was aware that perhaps these were internalized insults caused by the effects of racism and poverty and deeply embedded in this scenario. Was his aggression caused by living in and yet being continuously dismissed by a white world? In this situation, he could at least take charge and assume his power over me. He could easily wound me—a young white woman. Here again, I was having a lesson in the revolving door of victim/perpetrator. I could see quite clearly my rapist's life as a victim and realize that I, as a white, wealthy, privileged woman was also his perpetrator. I represented the white supremacist face of our society. Afterwards, I became almost obsessed with understanding the cycle of the victim turning into the perpetrator turning into the victim. Was there any true blame when we all have been victimized and trapped by the societal roles we play? There was no blame. There just was.

The rape had huge consequences in my life. This was another time when I felt completely shattered. Any identity or self that I had thought I knew now lay in shambles. My ideas of who I was shed off me. I felt completely naked of identity, almost a skeleton, and that my dance studio was contaminated and I couldn't go back there. Sadly for me, as I reconstructed my life, it did not include dancing. The pain of the assault and the grief of leaving dancing were all mixed up together. I wonder now if I ever really grieved or understood the enormous emotions around changing my identity and leaving my artistic life. I took advantage of this breech and decided to move toward my deep desire to become a priest. The rape was the catalyst for my changing my life, which eventually led to becoming a Zen teacher and leader.

It was a whole year before I felt anything near to "getting over" the rape—and in many ways, you never get over it. The fear that the worst can happen to me has never left me. It's created a fissure in my sense of personal safety, and I still carry that around with me always—walking down city streets, in dark parking garages at night, sitting alone on a park bench. I've learned to be hyperaware of my surroundings. But paradoxically, violence is often a catalyst for change. If everything is ruptured, you can rebuild in any direction. The terrible splintering that can happen in life is often the source of turning toward and desiring a deeper understanding of spirit.

The rape also meant the end of allowing myself to have anonymous sex. During the rape, I had thought, "This is no different than swinging. A stranger having sex with me." At that moment, in that predicament, it seemed to me that all of the sex I had had up until that point felt like rape, even sex with my husband. I have to say I am using the word "rape" in its widest sense here. It feels like rape when you are having sex but disconnected and dissociated from your body. The body might work, you may have even said "yes," but somehow it is not deep or true consent. You are not actually wholly present with the other person or with yourself. This sad statement is the profound consequence of early childhood abuse and the aftermath of being detached from my sensual and sexual energy. I was disempowered and disembodied. At the moment of the rape, I knew I wanted to change something deep within my own understanding of my sexuality and within my marriage.

Anna and Individuation

My husband and I began the journey of many years in individual therapy and then couples therapy. After several years of reconstructing our marriage, adjusting to monogamy, and doing therapy, we had two sons. A few months after the birth of my second son, when I was forty years old, my husband said a strange thing: he wanted to go to sex therapy. Oh god, I thought, a woman would never even suggest that, just having given birth. But Charley observed that two of our closest couple friends were on the verge of divorce and he wanted us to be proactive about having a full and wonderful marriage. Begrudgingly, I said yes. Who doesn't want to be proactive and fulfilled in one's marriage? Yet as I was nursing and had a newborn, jeez, what a crazy time to do sex therapy!

Anna, our new therapist, in some ways saved my life and the life of our marriage. Charley and I picked apart the history of our sexuality with each other and in front of each other. Anna guided us into revealing how we felt during the actual physical sexual act. I saw how uninhibited and strong Charley's sexuality was. Even though in many ways I was afraid of his vitality, I also admired it. I saw how fearful and closed off I still was in so many ways.

Anna counseled us in what an intimate relationship felt like psychologically and what it did not feel like. Coming from the less-than-nurturing examples of our parents' marriages and relationships, we found this to be new information. We learned about differentiation in marriage, which became our saving grace: that we are two separate people. We don't have to be the same, and actually we don't want to be. Our differences heighten our sexual attraction. Could I learn to hold the tension of disagreeing and the loneliness that arises when you don't insist that you and your partner have the same views on every-thing? We are not the same. Merging into one person actually hurts the differentiation and tension that is needed between partners to have good sex. Sex is the union and otherwise, we can be completely different. We agreed to a year of sex reedu-cation and the systematic use of sex exercises. Oh my! Really?!

At home, we had a toddler and an infant and a commitment to a once-a-week date. We had a babysitter but I felt uncom-fortable going to bed with Charley while this young woman and the kids were downstairs. Anna, naturally, had been trained in California, the original land of sexual freedom, and she had a set program of exercises. But how were we going to do our sex exercises in this situation? Because of my history of abuse and my feeling of inadequacy, I needed a very strong container to feel safe. How could we have a good, explorative sex life under the circumstances of no privacy? We tried going to hotels and motels, but that didn't feel right either and sometimes it just felt too seedy. What was a creative solution? Oddly, I also needed an office space at that time and so we merged the two needs. I needed time away from the kids for sex and also—I laugh here at what I'm about to say—a quiet place to do spiritual direction, for this was also the beginning of my Zen teacher life. My Zen group did not have a space of our own yet, and the community met on Sundays in the basement of the Unitarian Society. So I decided to rent a one-bedroom apartment, putting my office in the living room; in the bedroom, behind a closed door, we had a space for our marriage recovery. This was a big commitment and as it turned out, a useful one.

Anna's program started with avoiding intercourse for six months. Oh my god, would Charley go along with that? We started at the beginning, making out like teenagers. We did exercises designed to find out how and where we liked to be touched. It was the most intimate thing we both had ever done—scary and direct. Once we started making love again, our assignment was to write in our journals what we felt about the experience and read this writing to each other out loud. Sharing such self-revelations about how I felt about what we had just done—I couldn't imagine doing that, but somehow, we both were willing. This deepened our trust like never before. Slowly, slowly, as we did the exercises, I began to recover my senses and my body and my desire. Certain things we avoided. For a period of time, because of my initial abuse, I had flash-backs around my breasts and nipples. Recoiling when stimulated, I lost a primary erotic zone for decades, and during these experiments we agreed that Charley would not touch my breasts.

I was also encouraged to accept that we had different past realities. I always thought my view of the past and my values were the "right view" and my husband's history was Dionysian and, I concluded, "debauched" and therefore "wrong." This way of thinking, I now understand, is part of my own heavy mantle of judgments and self-righteousness. But as Charley and

I changed during therapy, I could hear and allow that he had good memories of swinging and his other explorations even though I hated that period of our marriage. He could say that we had always had a good marriage, at the same time as I could say that our early marriage was maladjusted and broken. We can have different views and understandings as long as there is a basis of respect and love.

We also learned how to fight. I was encouraged to say no, and not to compromise too quickly. I brought to consciousness my real feelings and needs. Through Anna's guidance, I learned how to hold my uncomfortable feelings when we were fighting. Sometimes that tension would exist for several days or even weeks. Before Anna's teaching, I never had kept my feelings in my own container and really experienced them. Instead, I had used any of my distractions to "not feel"—I could overeat, over-work, go shopping, read novels. Perhaps my repressed feelings surfaced in my critical and judgmental accusations. I learned through sex therapy to endure my terrible fears of abandon-ment. I didn't have to suppress my feelings or act them out, but just hold them and feel them. Charley and I learned to have a fight, make a compromise, and then go on.

My husband says, usually with a smile, that what he learned from Anna was that "understanding is overrated." Partnership does not mean that we will understand each other in every respect. We are our own universes and no one will ever get inside and know us thoroughly. But what we can do is demon-strate our love and respect even though we don't understand each other. Anna taught me that instead of getting all wacked out and defensive when Charley would say something I utterly disagreed with, I could say, "How curious" or "How interesting it is, that we are so different. What do you mean by that?"

There is a natural process of growth and change in these

long-term, lifelong relationships. Eventually, all of our individual maturation produces very different people than we were when we first started out. Now Charley and I sometimes have quite opposite points of view. As anyone who knows us can testify, we are very, very different now. Anna encouraged us to enjoy these differences: *Vive la difference!*

One day, while sitting on the couch in Anna's office, she turned to me after I had spoken and said, "Why would you continue to say that, when you know that presses Charley's button? A loving partner doesn't push their partner's sensitive button over and over." I laughed. That was an entirely new idea. In my family of origin, if you knew where someone's button was, you just hung out there and pressed it continually. Isn't that what buttons were for? To be pressed? Anna emphatically said no.

Sometimes I say that I learned diversity from my marriage. I learned tolerance and respect of differences right at home in my most intimate relationship. I don't have to understand everything, but I do have to learn to love as an action from the inside out.

Did Buddhism Help?

Many of my reasons for coming to Buddhism now seem to me to have been misguided. I was initially attracted to its silence. You could go to the zendo, the meditation hall, and not talk to anyone—in fact, you were encouraged not to have conversations. In hindsight, this culture of noncommunication and silence supported my underlying fear of relationships. The early Buddhist wanted to get off the wheel of life and death and leave human suffering behind—a "never-returner" is what the early Buddhists called the highest level of spirituality. I unconsciously incorporated this theology into my attitudes without questioning it. In my immature understanding, I saw Buddhism as an ascetic practice. Its teaching was that the human endeavors of sex, marriage, and children were fetters or bindings, chaining us to suffering. And this patriarchal interpretation left behind women, children, earth, procreation, messiness, blood, semen, mortgages, etc. Some Buddhist monks are admonished not to even touch a woman or be alone with a woman in the same room. Many of the nuns, over the centuries, were merely maids and cooks for the men. Many of the ancestors even went so far as to say that you couldn't get enlightened in a woman's body. And, as I have recently found, some of the youngest monks were used sexually by the older monks. Ah, another distressing example of the power of our unexamined sexual drive. Where do our bodies fit in? Where does that leave me as a woman entering the Buddha Way?

During these early years where I interpreted practice in a harsh and ascetic light, I had a vision during a sesshin that rotated me around 180 degrees. I was sitting still, and through the fierce intensity of my concentration, cracking open the world. My interpretation at that time was that I could use the sword of Manjushri (the Buddhist icon for transcendental wisdom) to cut every tie that I had to the world. These attachments I visualized as various tentacles coming out of my body like an octopus—some thin, easy to cut; others thicker, harder to sever. But there was one huge, maybe five-inch diameter tentacle, coming out of my heart and connecting to my husband, who was actually at home several miles away. So, I thought, for my liberation and for my devotion to Zen, and for detachment's sake, I began to hack away at this tentacle in my mind using Manjushri's large sword. The sword turned into a hatchet, hitting and hitting this cord that was attached to my husband. Finally, I broke open the wall of the cord, opening a slit at the point of the hacking. In my mind, I started to bleed. Red pumping blood spurted out over everything—my body, the cushion, my clothes, the wall in front of me. The blood was pumping out directly from my heart and moving over everything like waves gushing forth. All of a sudden, I realized that I was going to bleed to death. I was a person who never moved during a sitting and I was very proud of that. But during that sesshin, I, this person who usually was still and detached, moved both my hands to cover my heart, holding back the spurting blood. I pressed my hands into my chest and thought to myself, "This couldn't possibly be what they mean, to kill yourself and your loved ones. To allow yourself to die, pumping blood all over the zendo." I kept my hands to my heart for the rest of the period, pressing to stop the bleeding. I stood up and did walking meditation, still pressing my heart. I knew then that I had to rearrange my thinking. This concept surely was not what the ancestors meant—nor was it what I wanted.

In my search for understanding, I have been relieved to find koans from our female ancestors who might shed light on how to be with our life and our sexual energy in a different way. Can I find a woman's voice amidst the teaching? Through the efforts of many twentieth-century women scholars, you can find the stories of our female ancestors in several books.

Here is a women's koan that was included in the men's koan collection because it is so poignant and radical. It addresses the asceticism of detaching from our bodies, love, passion, and sexuality by some practitioners in Buddhist history.

The Withered Tree
(Or: The Old Woman Burns Down the Hermitage)
An old woman built a hermitage for a monk and supported him for twenty years. One day, to test the extent

of the monk's enlightenment and understanding, she sent a young, beautiful girl to the hut with orders to embrace him. When the girl embraced the monk and asked him, "How is this?" he replied stiffly, "A withered tree among frozen rocks; not a trace of warmth for three winters."

Hearing of the monk's response, the old woman grabbed a stick, went to the hermitage, beat the monk, and chased him out of the hut. She then put the hermitage to the torch and burned it to the ground.

Is our practice leading us to be a *withered tree among frozen rocks with not a trace of warmth left?* The old woman didn't think so. Are we trying to become a cold emotionless corpse? My understanding now is that Zen's true expression is not a withering of our perceptions but a movement toward and merging with the enormous creativity and energy in each moment. It is not about suppression at all. It is learning a compassionate and responsible response to the workings of a human life.

* * *

Ikkyu was a fifteenth-century Zen teacher who has been much written about. He was quite an iconoclastic influence in Zen. He is mainly noted as an artist, poet, calligrapher, and eccentric, but he also was the abbot of a monastery for a period. He is acknowledged as a great rule breaker and the epitome of the "transgress-the-rules" type of liberation. His response to the koan "The Withered Tree" follows:

"If a beautiful girl were to embrace this monk, my
withered willow branch would spring straight up."
This makes me laugh out loud!

The old woman burnt down the hermitage of ascetic cold-
ness. But how do we become an open vessel that is completely
responsive and connected to the present moment? How do the
walls of our egocentric defensiveness disappear? Our karma
and our traumas are held in our bodies entwined with our
mind and experiences—like a shroud wound round and round,
wrapping us up. This armoring is built up by a reaction to our
ordeals in the past and manifests as frozen, clenched places
in our bodies that we ignore or of which we are unconscious.
Zazen, Zen's concentrated sitting, offers a great vehicle for
noticing our constrictions and releasing them. This release
goes back and forth between body and mind. The more I open
psychologically, the more my body needs to open. And vice
versa. Sometimes one side has to catch up with the other—back
and forth, psychological and physical releases—a seesawing
flow of change and transformation.

Often, when we are in deep concentration in zazen, a vision
or an imaginative story arises. Sometimes it is a trauma from
the past that has been stimulated and the visions are more like
flashbacks. It is very important at this time to work with a good
teacher that is experienced in trauma healing. This trauma
education is not very common in Buddhist centers. But there
are different practices and changes in the schedule that can
help modulate the experience of releasing these traumatic
events. In these cases, our flashbacks, if worked with properly
and intelligently, can help release our suppressed tension and
offer some healing energy in the repair work.

Visions in meditation are also experienced in a place between the ordinary world of appearance and the world of extraordinary experience and can help the healing of our blocked energies. Something is trying to be communicated in these zazen-induced hallucinations. When some Zen teachers hear about these visions, they just laugh and hit the student with the kyosaku, the awakening stick, and say, "Makyo!" Or "Delusion." Or "Thinking." Or "Not this!" But for me, these visions are often an expression of the way my body/mind is releasing an internal trauma. So, I take care and observe these visions, without holding onto them but being grateful for signs of healing and for cues that can teach me how to continue to let go. Here is my recounting of one of the stories I have experienced while deep in concentration; this one came to me on the fourth day of a sesshin:

> Sitting quietly at Hokyoji with Katagiri Roshi at the helm of the ship of sesshin, I opened to this vision. There was a gigantic spear freestanding in front of me. The handle started about a foot above my head, came down at a slant, and then the arrowhead of the spear struck deeply into my womb. This experience was quite painful with a sense of heat and intense sensation right there at my womb. The spear stayed there, supported by nothing, for many hours. All of my energy was concentrated in my womb and there was nothing to be done about it. Four or five meditation periods later, after sitting with this strange powerful sensation in my womb and this unrelenting vision of being harpooned, I felt something change. Dwarfs, like those in Walt Disney's Snow White, started prancing up my vagina into my

womb. I was astonished. They told me to sit still so they could pound from the inside of my womb with their hammers and get the arrowhead out of my uterus. For another couple of sittings, they did just that. Pound, pound, pound. Finally, the spear toppled over and fell out. The dwarfs told me that I would heal now. They also told me that they would keep a guard, with one or two dwarfs always in my womb, so that this would never happen to me again.

Soon after this vision ended, the bell rang, signaling that it was time to chant the evening gatha or verse. I left the zendo, walked through the moonlight to my tent to go to sleep. Allowing this healing vision to continue, I lay in the soothing moonshine that peeked through my open tent door. I said the going-to-bed chant and realized that I did, indeed, have a clear and calm mind, free from my stories, just as the chant suggested.

I feel like this moment is an example of a vision that expressed a bodily release of frozen energy in my body. Wild as the vision was—a moment of discharge and celebration.

A Woman in a Zen World

I have always wanted to feel like a whole woman. Yet because of my commitment to being a Zen priest, I have often looked like a man with a short-clipped or shaven head, and I have not worn adornments like makeup or jewelry. I have, breaking the rules on rare occasions, found myself hiding my painted toenails under the *zabuton*, the square mat, while bowing. So silly, really. Why do I have to hide my "decorations"? From a female point of view, decorations are a celebration of life, attractiveness, and beauty. Instead, I have felt that I have had to conform to the Zen monastic rules which consider anything to do with personal beauty as a frivolous distraction. I have complied with black-monotone-everything-Zen. We even sing in a monotone. But I have come to understand that I can unabashedly be a woman and a deeply devoted Zen practitioner too. The support for this comes by penetrating into the koans of women practitioners in the eighth, twelfth, and fourteenth centuries.

One example is this koan from the twelfth-century nun Miaozong (1095–1170), "Miaozong's Dharma Interview" (from *The Hidden Lamp*):

> Before Miaozong became a nun, she used to visit Master Dahui Zonggao's monastery to study with him, and he gave her a room in the abbot's quarters. The senior monk, Wanan, did not approve.
>
> Dahui said to him, "Although she's a woman, she has outstanding merits."
>
> Wanan still disapproved, so Dahui urged him to have an interview with Miaozong.
>
> Wanan reluctantly agreed and requested an interview.
>
> Miaozong said, "Do you want a Dharma interview or a worldly interview?"
>
> "A Dharma interview," replied Wanan.
>
> Miaozong said, "Then send your attendants away."
>
> She went into the room first and after a few moments she called, "Please come in."
>
> When Wanan entered, he saw Miaozong lying naked on her back on the bed. He pointed at her genitals, saying, "What is this place?"

> Miaozong replied, "All the buddhas of the three worlds, the six patriarchs, and all great monks everywhere come out of this place."
>
> Wanan said, "And may I enter?"
>
> Miaozong replied, "Horses may cross; asses may not."
>
> Wanan was unable to reply. Miaozong declared: "I have met you, Senior Monk. The interview is over." She turned her back to him.
>
> Wanan left, ashamed.
>
> Later, Dahui said to him, "The old dragon has some wisdom, doesn't she?"

Every worldly experience is a dharma moment to one who can really see. "Dharma" and "worldly" arise together. And furthermore, Miaozong is not excluded from the dharma because she is a woman—actually, she's an old dragon with a lot of wisdom. She explodes into the scene by lying on the bed naked. Wanan is stopped in his tracks. Her nakedness goes straight to the point. She breaks the taboo of the hidden nature of sexuality in the monastery. He doesn't respond to the situation very well. He asks, "May I enter?" Because there is no relationship whatsoever between them, that's like asking, "Can I use you as a sex object or not?" She declines him as an ass, someone who doesn't see the whole world of interconnection and the source: *All the buddhas of the three worlds, the six patriarchs, and all great monks everywhere come from here.* He is still living in his compartmentalized mind. The source expression is everywhere and in everything. Does her presence really threaten the men's vow of celibacy, or does her presence teach it? Couldn't women's presence in the community be an opportunity rather than an obstruction for everyone to deal directly, and hopefully mindfully, with their own sexual urges?

Hoka Chris Fortin writes in her commentary on this koan in *The Hidden Lamp* (page 108).

> *Zen teaching had been traditionally conveyed through a predominantly male lineage, a lineage that I have entered and that I honor. But prior to entering the koan of Miaozong's Dharma interview, I had never before been consciously aware of how some part of me was subtly and perpetually changing from a woman's body into a man's body in order to fully engage with the teachings.*
>
> *We performed a skit of this koan on the opening evening of our retreat, and I volunteered to be Miaozong. I wore a flesh-colored full-body stocking, and I was deeply moved and even jolted by the experience of entering into Miaozong's skin and enacting her fearless and compassionate activity. Here was direct body-to-body, heart-to-heart transmission, across time and space, from a full-blooded woman who had no shame about her body, and who was a deeply realized practitioner, to me, now, a woman practitioner more than a thousand years later.*
>
> *As I lay on my back on the floor, my knees apart, calling out, "All beings everywhere come out of this place!" I became aware that this womb that bled rich red blood every month in my youth, and that had given birth to a son, was timeless, the womb of every woman. Miaozong's unbounded confidence in the pure Dharma body of practice, and her embodied faith in the sacredness of a woman's body, resonated through me like a dragon's roar.*

Wanan's first response was a self-referential question: "May I enter?" *May I enter what?* There are two corresponding metaphors. One is on the level of pure physical sexuality. *As a man, may I enter you sexually?* Well, at least he asked—it could have been worse. It could have been an overpowering sexual aggression. But on another level, it was the question of enlightenment. *Can I enter the source point?* The place where all the worlds and every being spring forth. The question suggests an exploration of who is in touch with that place, the source point? Do you need permission to enter the source point? What are our practices that allow us to be in touch with the source as we go through our everyday life? This deeper level is actually not related very directly with the anatomy of sexuality but rather with the intimacy of direct contact with the energies of life.

You either know direct contact or you fall down. "*Horses may cross, asses may not.*" In a single moment's response, we can take the road of the larger universal perspective of this source energy, free from our personal desire and the three poisonous minds. If we have this large mind, then we are a horse that is able to cross. A horse in a comparative world is considered more desirable than a donkey or ass. The horse is like a Porsche over a Ford Escort. Or, in a split second and with a distracted and automatic mind, we become an ass like every other ordinary person filled with self-centeredness. Liberation is like that, a moment-to-moment response.

Over the years, I have done many experiments to try to bring my female identity into the maleness of Zen practice. When I was still in my thirties, before I had kids and after I had started my intense life of therapy, I wanted to deeply acknowledge my womanhood even in the middle of a seven-day sesshin at Hokyoji Zen Community in southeastern Minnesota. I did not want to lose that part of myself again. How could I do that amid the very regulated structure of a male-made ritual? I didn't exactly know how to do that in the black robes of sitting with my head shorn and the feeling of detaching from my body, which I thought Buddhism encouraged. I decided to wear sexy black lace lingerie underneath my robes all through sesshin to keep in touch with my female sexuality. My little secret, underneath it all: I'm a woman! Surprise!

At that time, at Hokyoji, we all slept in tents. In the morning, when we got up, it was still black as night. I would walk from my tent to the showerhouse, where I had a little cubby to hang my clothes and towel while I washed my face and changed my clothes for zazen. I held all my clothes from the previous night in my arms as I walked, and I changed clothes in the shower room. One day I walked into the shower room and there was my black lace bra tied to the string that you pulled to turn on the light bulb hanging from the ceiling. I had dropped it in the field on my way to the tent and someone had found it and tied it to the light bulb string. That prompted a good laugh for me in the Noble Silence. So much for my secret identity as a sexy woman.

Women as Objects of Men's Desires

Since I started writing this book, the whole universe of sexual aggression in the twenty-first century has exploded throughout our culture and the media. The objectification of women as sexual objects still exists everywhere and is now being called out. "Ryonen Scars Her Face" is one of the first koans about women that I discovered as a young female practitioner in the book *Zen Flesh, Zen Bones: A Collection of Zen and Pre-Zen Writings* (compiled by Paul Reps and Nyogen Senzaki) in the "101 Zen Stories" section. This story is filled with the projections on women which, unfortunately, seem timeless. What did a woman in seventeenth-century Japan do in the face of these projections and exclusions? She made herself ugly in a dramatically violent and startling way.

When I first found this koan it affected me greatly. It is a rare women's koan in the primarily male collections. In many ways, when I first encountered it, it matched my ardent intent to study Buddhism. I felt like Ryonen. I would do anything to know the truth. I also felt like her because I was entering a male world, and even though I often felt like the odd woman out, I was following my unyielding determination to achieve liberation. But this koan is also a vivid statement of the sad truth of men's power over women. Ryonen, who had been a beautiful attendant to the empress, puts an iron to her face to make herself unattractive in order to be allowed into the monastery. It is significant that she burns her face with an iron, which is a tool of women's labor in the domestic arena. And she wrote her poem on the back of a mirror, a symbol of female vanity.

"Ryonen Scars Her Face"

As a young woman, Ryonen Genso was an attendant to the empress and was known for her beauty and intelligence. When the empress died, she felt the impermanence of life, and she decided to become a nun.

Ryonen traveled to the city of Edo in search of a Zen teacher. The first teacher refused her because of her beauty. Then she asked Master Hakuo Dotai, who also refused her. He could see her sincere intention, but he too said that her womanly appearance would cause problems for the monks in his monastery.

Afterward, she saw some women pressing fabric, and she took up a hot iron and held it against her face, scarring herself. Then she wrote this poem on the back of a small mirror:

> To serve my empress, I burned incense to perfume
> my exquisite clothes.
> Now, as a homeless mendicant, I burn my face to
> enter a Zen temple.
> The four seasons flow naturally like this,
> Who is this now in the midst of these changes?

Ryonen returned to Hakuo and gave Hakuo the poem. He immediately accepted her as a disciple. She became abbess of his temple when he died and later founded her own temple.

* * *

Many of us have had to make great sacrifices to follow the Buddhist Way. Sometimes the catalyst is violent. After a terrifying rape, stripped of my identity, lost and confused, I left my career behind and turned toward the priesthood. I was struggling to find a deeper meaning beneath the ongoing troubles of life. But I pray for a day that Ryonen doesn't have to burn her face. Is it possible to find out who we are "in the midst of these changes" without violence? In many stories, great turbulence seems to be a triggering point for searching for the Way. In my case, the rape pushed me. Crises are often the doorway out of Samsara and into a more profound understanding of life. I wonder, is this devastating entryway to spirituality archetypal or is it something that can be tempered or adjusted? But certainly, we no longer have to burn our faces.

The sexual objectification of women is still so prevalent, and sexual microaggression is a daily occurrence in our contemporary life. Even small sexual offenses often strongly affect women. One of the women practitioners at my temple told me that she was popular in high school—quite attractive and with a big bust. She said that now, as an older woman, she looks back and realizes that it was a regular occurrence for her to be groped by boys all throughout school. After saying this, she started to cry in our small teacher's meeting room. She still feels the effects of those violations. For her own healing, even after so many years have passed, she is having breast reduction surgery now. Coming from a lifetime of microaggressive reactions, she wants to do something that she believes would be a positive nurturance for the part of her psyche that still seems so wounded.

Recently, I heard another story through the tears of another older woman. Her brother had touched her breasts and lain on top of her frequently during her childhood, and when she told her mother about it, her mother said something like, "Boys will be boys." She says that her sexual responsiveness has been a problem her whole life. She kept repeating, "I forgive my brother now, but still, still it has deeply affected me."

A young woman in the high school sex education class that I teach at Clouds in Water Zen Center's youth practice program recently asked me, "Is there such a thing as too much self-expression? Can I dress like the music videos? My mom says this is asking for trouble."

We had begun our class discussion with the question of who is in charge of the boundaries in sex: the man or the woman? Is it up to the woman to slow down or stop sexual aggression, or are women completely powerless, which has been the case throughout history? This binary view of man and woman also brings up questions. If we add the modern upheaval surrounding gender roles and bring into the conversation the concept of fluid sexual identity, there are many different considerations to be had. But no matter how our examination of sexual identity proceeds, the hurtfulness of the misuse of sexual power is still relevant. Where in our culture do we educate our children about the power of sexuality and the principles which might mitigate that power as we try to convert egregious actions into life-affirming encounters?

* * *

Sexual misconduct has huge consequences, often a lifetime of repercussions. Sexual transgressions within spiritual communities also have deep and lasting impact. I write this chapter for this reason and because I am strongly lifting up the precept of "Don't misuse sexuality." I have been in two sanghas that have had sexual breaches by the teacher. After Katagiri Roshi's death, it came out that he had had sexual relationships with several women in the sangha. (This is discussed in detail in famed writing teacher Natalie Goldberg's memoir, *The Great Failure: A Bartender, A Monk, and My Unlikely Path to Truth*, published in 2005 by HarperOne.)

I think that Roshi's students in the 1970s and '80s put him up on a pedestal, and it was excruciating to take him off of it. How do you keep the wondrous Buddhist teaching you received from the teacher and still hold the teacher accountable for their actions? All teachers have this complicated duality of human failings and dharmic teaching. Can we hold both sides of our teachers? I had to readjust my understanding of teachers, for my intelligent discernment of conduct must remain fully intact, especially when interacting with leaders who are often charismatic.

To my great dismay, after I found out about Katagiri Roshi, sexual misconduct occurred again—with a male teacher in the very sangha I had helped to create, Clouds in Water Zen Center. Was I in denial for too long so that my sangha was going off course? I did leave, finally, but perhaps a little too late. Or perhaps I should have stayed and blown the sangha up by speaking my truth. I left two years before the community actually did explode. At Clouds in Water Zen Center I became what I have come to call "the cleanup teacher"; not surprisingly, the teachers who follow up after a scandal are women. A sangha that has suffered from power or sexual abuse issues, which often come hand in hand, needs a more horizontal and heart-centered teacher to heal. As the cleanup teacher, you can see intimately the consequences and decimation that these issues create—not only for the person abused, but for the whole sangha. Many people left Clouds in Water and never returned to Zen; in fact, many people never went back to belonging to any kind of spiritual community. If you were in the inner circle, your practice was affected for life. It took a decade to normalize the community, and perhaps these scars will always be present. It is because of experiences like this one that I now emphasize the Precepts, or Buddhist guidelines for behavior.

The Practice of Following the Precepts

The Precepts come under the practice of ethical conduct, *Sila.* "Receiving the Precepts" is a very important aspect of Zen practice. It is the central pole of the Zen ceremonies: Buddhist initiation (Jukai); priest ordination; and the last ceremony of transmission, which takes place at the end of one's training and at the beginning of being a Zen Teacher. Deeply embedded in the heart of each of these ceremonies are the Precepts, the guidelines for spiritual conduct in the world. One of these Precepts is: Do not misuse sexuality.

How do we discern what is healthy sexuality? We can use all the other Precepts as buttresses or supports to examine this one. All of the Precepts are interconnected. They are the guidelines that help us improvise our reactions to individual experiences; they are not, as fundamentalists would have us think, absolute truths. We are like the rose bush, which is supported by the trellis. The supported, growing plant does not follow the exact lines of the trellis wood. It is not black and white with rigid, unmovable rules. Our conduct should be appropriate to the situation. We weave in and out and all about the trellis, figuring out our responses with the help of the backbone of our behavioral guidelines.

Studying the Precepts in a cluster has proven to be a great help for my discernment process. For example, regarding the Precept on sexuality, we can use the other Precepts as a probe. Am I killing something with this action? Am I stealing something from another? Am I being honest? Do I put myself above and my partner below? Is this sex act coming out of anger? Through these types of questions, we can often be helped in discerning what is wholesome and what isn't.

Using the above questions arising out of the Precept structure, I can, in most circumstances, figure out what is helpful and what isn't, which is one interpretation of *prajna* or wisdom in Buddhism. But if the Precepts aren't emphasized or if people aren't taught how to really use them, then naturally they don't help. In my early training, the Precepts were there, but they took a secondary importance. If Buddhism is only interpreted as finding emptiness and quietism, then indeed, we will have sexual breeches in Buddhist centers and with individual people. Precept practice is at the core of learning how to be a kinder, more humane person; the Precepts are the core of all the ceremonies of transmission. I ask my Zen associates to please, please, use them.

A lot of times, I see that the guidance I'm seeking does exist in the Buddhist teaching but may not be emphasized in the way my twenty-first-century mind would like it to be. I have to find the teaching and then decode it to fit my modern needs. In Buddhist practice, our sexuality and our humanness is often denigrated or called dangerous to spirituality. But our practice, in my opinion, is to embrace the sacredness of sexuality simultaneously with the worldly difficulties produced by its power. It is not to eliminate desire but to see that the arising of our desires actually is the energy of life and occurs in the exact same place where practice occurs. This fourteenth-century koan from the collection *The Hidden Lamp* is a great example of what I am talking about:

"Eshun's Deep Thing"

Eshun was a nun at the monastery of Saijoji. The abbot of Saijoji wanted to send a message to the abbot of the great temple of Engakuji, which was known for its rough treatment of outsiders. None of the monks from Saijoji dared to go; only Eshun was willing to volunteer. When the Engakuji monks saw her walk through the main gate, one of them rushed forward, raised his robes to expose himself, and said: "This monk's thing is three feet long. How about it?"

Eshun calmly lifted her robes, spread her legs and said, "This nun's thing is infinitely deep." She dropped her robes and continued down the corridor, unaccosted.

Let's practice like that! Eshun is so bold and clear: She knows who she is and nothing stops her. We need quite a bit of confidence to speak freely and straightforwardly as Eshun has done. Our Buddhist centers and our Western culture need this candor to change. Nothing about our lives should be hidden or taboo. There is no problem that doesn't offer an opportunity to learn. Hiding in a mountain hut and letting go of life, which was an image from my youthful interpretation of Buddhism, is no longer my dream.

Women in Buddhism are making a difference. We can add certain attitudes that will change the priorities of Buddhist practice. We need to emphasize in our teachings how Buddhist practice can teach us to welcome all the "nows" that arise within the stories of our life. I yearn to get more versatile at accepting the present moment exactly as it is. Too much attachment to detachment doesn't work for me anymore; sometimes it takes me away and then, actually, that detachment becomes a rejection of the present moment. Our Buddhist spirituality includes our human failings and hurts. Nothing is excluded. If we continue to ignore and leave unexamined the religious belief structures built by centuries of men, then the women who have birthed the world will continue to lose out. Our voices will not be heard. Eshun's boldness is inspiring. She just holds up her womanliness and speaks from her connection and expression of infinite depth.

Chapter Six
INNER FORTITUDE

The Buddha told Kisa Gotami that he would bring her deceased and only child back to life if she could find white mustard seeds from a house that had not suffered from the loss of death. She desperately traveled around and could not find a single house without suffering.
—Gotami Sutra

In February 2015, I had a bad ski accident in Colorado. I was at Copper Mountain Ski Resort with a friend, Bill, on our last day of vacation. For the last run of the day Bill and I decided to go to a part of the ski hill we hadn't been to before, where there were more difficult runs. Even though we were tired, even though it was snowing slightly and it was hard to see, and even though Bill had a premonition we shouldn't do it, we went. The snow was inconsistent—icy in one place, smooth in another. The visibility was poor, and before I could even do any corrective measures, the edge of my ski caught and I went tumbling down the hill with my skis releasing and left scattered behind me. For a moment after I stopped rolling, I just sat there in the snow, stunned beneath the vast blue sky, looking at the snow-capped mountain tops in the distance, breathing in the cold air, trying to catch my breath. I surveyed my body. "Oh man," I thought, "this is bad!" Bill gathered my skis and came to help me get up on my feet; very slowly, he walked me to the side of the hill. I did not know then that I had fractured my humerus and badly twisted my knee and ankle, only that my shoulder was aching and I couldn't move my hand very well, and that limping along, even with help, was excruciating.

We waited for the ski patrol to arrive. As I sat, dazed, my mind began to come back on line, but it was accelerating into a mind of worry and future-thinking—I was imagining all the bad things that were in store for me. One thought, "I'll never ski again," upset me because I have loved skiing since I was fifteen years old. Thinking that I would never ski again, I cried. And then, god forbid, came the thought, "I'll never walk again." As I watched my mind spiral out of control, the Zen teacher in me kicked into gear. "Guard your mind, guard your mind!" she encouraged me. I began to use one of my practices, which is to envision the ferocious guardians seen in Buddhist mythic iconography at the gates of my mind, guarding the thoughts going in an out: huge, ugly he-men with bulging muscles and fangs; wrathful goddesses, wreathed in flames, their blazing eyes and lethal swords overseeing the stream of thoughts. Unwholesome thoughts, watch out! This is similar to the Buddha's instruction to separate into two baskets our wholesome thoughts and our useless ones. Guard the mind. Do not futurize.

Because we were so high up the mountain and the runs were so steep, no snowmobile could get to us. Instead, a very young, slight woman dressed in a ski patrol outfit showed up. "Oh my god," I thought, "is this petite creature going to take me down the hill?" The answer was yes. No one else came. She strapped me into a covered toboggan, slowly, slowly, as I could hardly move with all the pain. Then she zipped up the toboggan, completely, over my head. What? I was alone, in the darkness, trapped in a cocoon and about to travel down a mountain, and I couldn't see where we were going. My rescuer set out to snowplow her way down a very steep mountainside. The toboggan had two long poles, which she held onto as she started the business of pulling the sled behind her. As we began the descent, I was petrified and in pain. In response to this anguish, Byakuren, my inner Zen teacher, leaned into me and whispered, "Chant." I know many chants by heart: "*Gate, Gate, paragate, parasamgate,*" an emptiness chant from the Heart Sutra; Kuan Yin's compassion chants; Jizo bodhisattva chants; the chant of the Medicine Buddha. I began to sing and went through them all. My rescuer's snowplow held, run after run. She would yell out warnings to other skiers that an emergency vehicle was crossing their path. She asked Bill to call out warnings as well a little bit ahead of the toboggan.

For twenty minutes, I chanted down the mountain in my bumpy, cloistered darkness. I don't know why I was surprised by this, but by the time I had reached the base of the mountain and the emergency room, I felt quite calm. I had radically accepted that this was my new "now." I wanted to go to the emergency room as my best self and not as a crabby, complaining, angry, scared person. After all, I was sure that I wasn't the worst case they had seen that day. When my young ski patrol guardian unzipped the toboggan, she peered in, and with a huge smile, said, "Wow, I heard you singing all the way down, it gave me so much strength." I recognized once again, the blessings of Buddhist practice and its benefits to others.

Inner fortitude is a quality that I can, without question, acknowledge that Zen practice has fostered within me. I developed this internal endurance, year after year, sitting without moving, notwithstanding feeling physical or emotional pain while remaining still. What do you have to do with your body, your mind, and your heart to stay with these sensations of difficulty? We explore this continually in zazen. How do you remain steadfast in aversive conditions? Cultivation of determination sustains you when you have to do something that you really don't want to do—like following the rigorous schedule of a Zen retreat day after day, which can seem relentless, as if it goes on ad infinitum. Under these rigorous conditions, Zen students nurture a personal power that can withstand hardship—sometimes through surrender and sometimes through sheer tenacity.

This inner fortitude shows up in my life in so many ways and in unexpected places. It is the opposite of being fragile. It is an unexpected reward from sesshin practice. Many times in my life, when the going has gotten rough, my practiced response to hardship has given me a way through the darkness and grief. Step by step. Being present. Breathing. Welcoming the present moment as is. What we have practiced in formal Zen training starts to become our way of life. There are so many examples of this in my life, but giving birth particularly demonstrates what I have been describing.

Breathing, Concentrating, and Birthing

I have wondered many times over the years—but especially around the time of my own babies' deliveries—how do women give birth and stay with the pain without having been trained in sesshin? I smiled when the birthing coaches in our classes talked about staying with the breath and elongating the exhales or puffing the breath in short bursts. Oh, that's just like Zen! But in spite of my training, my first birth was not easy. It was in 1991, and I wanted and did have a natural birth without drugs, but the delivery was a long and tenuous trial by fire and my son ended up in the baby ICU. I had also wanted a homebirth, but I hadn't taken the chance, which, as it turned out, was a wise choice. Because of the sexual abuse in my past, opening up my sex chakra in the way that birth does was risky business. Who knew what was held in there energetically and needed to be released? Indeed, I was stuck in a blocked delivery. Many hours and several days went by with contractions but there was virtually no movement toward the magic eight-centimeters-dilated diameter scale for my cervix that would signal that my body was ready to start pushing.

But even though these were quite a grueling couple of days, I'd had a lot of experience with "grueling." My inner determination and power of concentration had been forged in the oven of sesshin. I also knew how to persevere in adverse conditions for days at a time—that is the residual benefit of not moving in zazen even if your back is hurting, your knees screaming or your foot fallen asleep. I have often taught my students about sitting in pain by using two fundamental instructions. One direction is to go straight into the pain with a minute examination of each sensation. Where is it? How does it change? Does it move around? Become completely absorbed in the details of that sensation. Or take the opposite guidance, which is to overlook the pain by switching your subtle curiosity and attention to your breathing. Become completely absorbed in the breath. When I am working with awareness of breathing, I do not allow my mind to leave the sensations of the breath for one second. That is the lifeline, for that one second of inattention could allow the mind to enter this breech and conjure up all kinds of debilitating thoughts. I also include the instruction to relax totally on the exhalation—with an emphasis on "totally." If I follow these points of practice, I feel like I can get through anything. There is not an iota of space for withdrawal or complaint. And this honed discipline of breathing did indeed get me through anything—the extraordinary and supreme challenge of giving birth. Even though I felt stuck at certain times, my backbone of concentration was absolutely useful and sustained me for the duration of the birthing process.

The night shift came on at the hospital and an angel/nurse appeared—very kind, very patient, and very knowledgeable. She took stock of the situation and said, "I think we should put you in a nice warm bath, close the door, and let you be alone." In this somewhat dilapidated hospital, she took me into the private bathroom that had an old-fashioned bathtub. She adjusted the temperature of the water, turned down the lights, and helped me into the bath. With my rotund stomach, I could barely fit into this old, deep tub; plus, I was stopping for contractions every minute or two. With her support, I slid into the warm water and felt myself start to relax.

But before I had left the hospital room for the bathtub, my midwife suggested that maybe it would be helpful to connect with an animal who could give me instructions on birthing as our animal bodies know exactly how to do this. In the isolation of the bathroom, I searched for my animal. Just a few months earlier my husband and I had gone on a last-hurrah vacation to Mendocino, a gorgeous ocean town on the Californian coast. One day we'd spent sitting on huge rocks at the ocean side surrounded by seals, some of them not even five feet away from us. These seals started to appear in the bathroom and share with me their wisdom on birthing. They told me, "When the contraction comes, be completely one hundred percent contracted, and when it goes away, float in the water like a seal." For an hour, I followed my seal friends' advice. I did not miss a breath or a contraction. My mind centered. The seals floated with me. They were encouraging me to contract. "It's hard, but completely natural," they said. "Don't worry." They taught me fearlessness as I allowed the intensity of the contractions squeezing in my lower belly and back. "Surrender entirely to that compression," they told me. My hands clutched into fists so hard that nail marks appeared on my palms. Each contraction was a complete head-to-toe clench. As the waves of each contraction ebbed, I envisioned my seal friends floating with me, totally relaxed on the surface of the water, even being playful. And then, repeat. When the door opened and the nurse came in to take me back to the bed, *voila!* I was at eight centimeters and I could push.

Zen's Controversial Strength

I have fielded innumerable questions from Western students about the "masochism" of Zen training. Why do we have to sit still when our bodies are screaming to move? This has been a big question for me too, especially as I see that other sects of Buddhism don't have a particular requirement demanding, "Do not move until the bell rings." They offer other styles of retreats that do not demand that you surrender to the strictness and precision of Zen's arduous monastic daily life. These rituals and schedules of Zen are tailor-made to break down your attachment to self-centered concerns. That is their purpose. When you come to a Zen retreat, you forfeit your personal comfort and rhythm and adhere to the schedule of the community. But, in hindsight, I am questioning this very covenant. At the same time that I praise Zen for instilling me with strength, I wonder if my Zen practice also reinforced my dissociation from my body. Did following the schedule support my tendency to ignore my own personal and psychological needs? I have spent many hours with these questions and I still don't know the answer. This investigation is so deep for me that as I write this book, I am neither teaching nor doing sesshin. What needs to happen now? Do we loosen up the protocol? I'm stymied about how to resolve my objections.

But there is another less cynical part of myself who also wants to speak up. That part of me wants to convey her deep gratitude for the strength I developed in practice. My personal forbearance was cultivated by the practice of not moving and following the sangha's schedule. The daily life in the monastery has taught me so much. I was fortunate to experience the harmony of a collection of diverse people moving as one body throughout the day, living together as a community, developing respect for each other, and giving care to our chores in the inevitable maintenance of human life. I remember work periods where I would pull out weeds from the pebbled paths for hours in the hot sun, day after day. This can be quite challenging and sweaty and tiring. Ironically, as soon as I would reach the end of one path, wanting to escape and be finished, I would look back behind me and see that I could just start all over again, from the beginning, on the very same walkway. Weeds continually grow and need to be removed. In these practices, you become starkly aware of the rhythm of life. In the quiet of the cloistered experience, you open to the miraculous, like sunrise and sunset, and you endure the monotonous, like doing the dishes after every meal. Through Zen, I learned how to take out and put back the tools I have used—not disrespecting them as I tend to do and leaving them helter-skelter on the table or the floor. Everything has its place. Zen emphasizes the small duties of life: cooking, cleaning, working, and studying. This focus has helped me find my inner stamina, which has come to my aid many times in my life. Katagiri Roshi used to call this quality *spiritual stability*. It has also taught me how to navigate the darkest times.

The Inescapable Darkness of Grief

A few times in my life I have experienced incapacitating grief, and the only solution seemed to be endurance. At these dreadful moments, all my "techniques" proved useless. No particular koan—too heady. No kind of breathing technique—I really couldn't even concentrate at all. I would feel distraught, and pressure in my chest, my puffy and swollen eyes, and the constant ache in my heart would not get released but instead would drag me down into melancholia like a heavy, immovable, black cloak. I would become almost catatonic, walking around the house aimlessly with nowhere to go for relief.

But in an indirect way, even though such situations are not addressed emotionally in koans or through the coolness and impersonal nature of the Zen schedule, it is the deeper layer of Zen, the existential layer, that gets me through these times. Through Buddhist insights and contemplations, I have become familiar with the rhythm of life—of birth and death—and I know that our circumstances are constantly changing. Life is impermanent, change is inevitable. In these moments, I have had enough fortitude and faith to allow myself and my fixed identity to die. I have come to believe, in a deep way, that when you die, you go through a transformation, and then you are reborn. And with that faith, I have allowed myself to let go of my identities and wait to see what happens to me next.

The last time I was in this grave circumstance of sorrow,

I leaned on the words of Sarah Blondin, a modern spiritual teacher, and listened again and again to her guided meditation "When We Must Endure." Here are some of her words:

> *In these times, we are like a deer hide, strung up and pulled taught between two branches, placed in the sun, the weather, there, to endure and then be made into something stronger, more malleable, everlasting. We understand that we are going through the time-consuming process of transformation from soft hide, useless unless cured by the sun and weather, undergoing change of form, in a chrysalis, born one thing and becoming another. They are places of great shift and change and rebirth, only a few of them in our lifetime, if we are so lucky. A major part of the learning is in the waiting. Allow yourself to be out of control. This is the time-consuming process of great transformation, and you will rise up again.*

During the last bereavement I had, there were some nights when I couldn't sleep and needed so desperately to cry. I remember Katagiri Roshi saying that if I didn't know what to do with myself, if I needed to bawl, I should sit in front of the altar in my house and let it rip. Heeding his advice, I sat in front of the altar in the candlelight and cried. And cried some more. Then I remembered all the times I had slept in the zendo during sesshin on two zabutons, wrapped up in my sleeping bag, and I decided, why not? I could do that again. I went to the basement and crawled around the suitcases and shelving units until I found the sleeping bags. I put out my zabutons parallel with my altar, placing the pillows and sleeping bag on top, and I crawled into my cocoon and closed my eyes, hoping to sleep.

My mind was uncomfortably blank, but still had a lot of energy in it. It was galvanized for action but with no clear solutions to take or a path to follow. My heart was continuously howling like a wolf who has just lost its mate—howling into the night but with no corresponding response. Acceptance of my loss was far from accomplished. Unable to find comfort, I imagined myself held in the arms of the Buddha and Avalokiteshvara (a most important bodhisattva who embodies great compassion). Envisioning myself rocked and held by great and loving beings. I wanted so badly to have my human suffering witnessed in the middle of that cold night while all the other human beings near me were fast asleep. Where could I find some consolation? *Hear my cries, oh great compassion beings!* And with this conjuring, I had a glimmer of being held by the universe, arriving somewhere far beyond my personal story, and I could feel this great, unconditional love surround me and calm me—a love that demanded nothing and did not judge. Holding this love to my burning heart, I finally, slowly and gently, fell asleep.

Chapter Seven

MALISSA AND THE LEGACY OF ENSLAVEMENT

It was a fine cry—loud and long—but it had no bottom
and it had no top,
just circles and circles of sorrow.
—Toni Morrison

I, a person of European-American descent, was raised by a succession of African American women. Their comfort and warmth was a saving grace in my childhood and teenage years. In the beginning, I saw these relationships only through my own eyes and the story of my own neediness. As I have grown older, I have begun to realize the truth of these women's lives—the devastation caused by systemic racism and its consequences. I see more clearly the forces that must have controlled the lives of these women I hold dear, and I recognize that I need to learn all I can about the conditions under which they had labored. They are all dead now, so there is no way I can repay them personally for the gentle caring they gave to the lonely child that I was or for the labor of cleaning house, cooking our meals, and serving my family. Can the debt of slavery ever be paid back? By money? By legislation? By not-for-profits? By what?

With these questions in my mind, I've set out to explore how my family's white privilege expressed itself and how I participated in that. This is a journey of questioning, of reexamining my upbringing in light of power and class and the environment created by the American infrastructure of racism. In a small measure, can I, as a white woman, bring forth my experience to investigate these issues and wrestle with these enormous questions? There is a howling in my soul as I tell these women's stories.

I do not want the Black women to whom I owe so much to be erased by white America. They worked eleven-hour days for very little wage. They raised America—both Black and white—and fed its workforce and cleaned its households. The women in my household supported me in every way, even by doing some of the chores that should have been mine. With embarrassment, I look back and see how spoiled I was. I had no chores and I didn't even have to clean up my own room. If these women held judgments about how I was being raised or felt anger at my entitlement, they remained silent in order to keep their jobs. Because of having full-time maids my entire childhood, I had no guidance in physically taking care of myself. That essential education I gained from Zen practice after I left my parents' house at eighteen. At the Zen center, I learned how to clean, cook, and do laundry—the ordinary, necessary chores of life—particularly supported by Katagiri Roshi's wife, Tomoe-san. This was an upside-down and surprise education. What I had thought was the extraordinary practice of Zen and meditation actually turned around and taught me the mundane day-to-day basics of life, training me to do these commonplace activities with care.

Among our housekeepers over the years, there was one who worked for us through my high school years and on until her death. Malissa was the woman with whom I shared the longest dependency and then a deep friendship. It was during her dying that I recognized the crux and complexity of the pain in our relationship and the grounds of poverty and racism in which it was planted. Through Malissa I began to see the enormity of the impact of racial injustice, which is so huge that it seems incomprehensible.

On the final day of Malissa's life, I sat on one side of her bed while her real daughter by birth sat on the other. Malissa had left her daughter in the South to be raised by her sister when she moved up to Chicago. The separation of families is just one of the signs and symptoms of oppression. The dislocation of family has occurred with the Indigenous People, throughout American slavery, and is currently happening with the immigrants at our borders. There is a theme of disconnection that runs through the discussion of American racism, revealing people disconnected from their history and their identity, and only allowed to have their identity shaped by whiteness. Even the idea of whiteness is a concept constructed to create another category of people as opposed to dark-skinned people. Before the concept of whiteness, people were identified by their ethnicity. We live in a perfect caste system that is bounded by skin color and class, and this system allows very little room for mobility. Even when Black people have achieved success as defined by white society, they still are considered to be exceptions. As one successful Black friend told me, "I am an anomaly even in my own family."

I was the child who had received most of Malissa's day-to-day care. Malissa had a fraught relationship with her daughter. I had also had a conflicted relationship with my mother. Malissa's daughter Alicia and I spent significant time together at Malissa's deathbed—a time filled with much emotion and discomfort and a dawning awareness of truths of which I had been totally unconscious or that I had ignored. Alicia and I tried together to soothe and calm Malissa in her dying, and this shared endeavor broke my heart.

On the day Malissa died, I knew I needed to seek healing and restitution; I needed to give back to Malissa in the deepest way I could. But what are healing and restitution? What are the actions of giving back? So many enormous, complex, and seemingly unanswerable questions are finally emerging in the evolution of our culture.

* * *

I have found in several research books a stunning statistic: In the 1950s, as high as 90 percent of Black women were employed as domestic workers. This work was the only job available to a Black woman, no matter her experience or intelligence, in an employment field that was completely prejudiced against African Americans. Many white children were brought up by Black domestic help. A many-faceted relationship develops between the domestic help and the employer. These Black women live in the same house as their white employers and raise white children together, but they are separated by race, class, and the employment power differential. In her article, "A Complex Bond: Southern Black Domestic Workers and Their White Employers," published in the magazine *Frontiers: A Journal of Women's Studies*, in 1987, Susan Tucker writes:

> What do you find when you examine the meaning of frequent contact between two groups of women separated by race and class and yet connected by long years of knowing one another? For within the entanglement

of race relations, economics, and power struggles based upon race and economics, there grew a complex bond of mutual dependence and mutual distrust, and sometimes, a guarded but nevertheless remembered affection.

I am wondering, in spite of all the obstacles and systemic economic and racial injustices surrounding our relationship, could the affection I shared with Malissa have been as genuine for her as it was for me? Our connection was looked upon as taboo and improbable, but it was definitely real for me. Given the circumstances, how could it also have been real for Malissa? After all, she was the hired help in a situation of built-in inequality, and our relationship existed in a world that at that time did not support authentic connection between the races. Within the norms of society, was Malissa as confused about her identity and her role as I was? Of course, I assume she had a conscious sense of disempowerment through racial injustice, but did she ever have a sense that this could change? Or that she could do or say something about it? I will never know.

In honoring this very important person in my life, I knew that not only must I investigate the seeds of racial injustice and their fruition in our culture but that I also need to explore my own reactions to it. I felt the need to pay back my debt to Malissa and to understand racial injustice, but how to do this? One of my efforts was to volunteer as a meditation teacher at a prison. Our group, the Unpolished Diamond Sangha, included a very diverse group of inmates, many of whom were African Americans.

Before each visit to the prison, I have to gather my strength and courage to face the anguish and bereavement of the men I meet. Do I have enough bandwidth to allow their despair to penetrate my heart and do I have enough depth to respond with openness, understanding, and compassion? This is a current and abiding challenge. And I recognize how scary and intimate it is for the inmates in my meditation group to allow themselves to close their eyes and sit in silence in that unsafe place, let alone check in and have a meaningful conversation. Establishing even a modicum of trust in this environment is rare.

After witnessing the degrading life in prison of these incarcerated inmates who are, in large part, people of color, I have yearned to do more. At the same time, I question my motivations for helping: Is it a white savior complex? My journey toward racial justice is a continuing source of humility as I question my automatic responses stemming from my position of privilege.

I have continued my exploration and service at Ujamaa Place, a not-for-profit organization that helps young Black men, ages eighteen to thirty, with a holistic approach to healing the trauma that has been inflicted upon them by our society stemming from racial injustice and poverty. Ujamaa Place's mission is to offer a transformative empowering experience that teaches young African American men how to navigate inequality, poverty, and a criminal justice system which, unfortunately, perpetuates recidivism.

As I work in these institutions, I am offered many opportunities to face my own twisted racial consciousness. Do I think I am entitled to be a leader or to know more about organizational development than others? Do I unconsciously believe that I have the right to be in a central position on a board of directors? Small gestures sometimes expose my racialized consciousness. I once brought in a poster of beautiful, fashionable Black women, thinking it was important to recognize

Black beauty—and to my embarrassment, of course, all the men already knew that Black women are gorgeous. My small prejudice was unmasked. Such exposures reveal and teach me the horrible, obvious consequences of structural racism and the history of enslavement and its successor, mass incarceration. Having more transparency about racism has pained my heart and opened my mind.

My exploration has also taken me to Malissa's hometown of Greenville, Mississippi; to Africa's slave castles in Ghana; to the Legacy Museum in Montgomery, Alabama; and to the National Memorial for Peace and Justice, also in Montgomery, which emphasizes America's history of lynching and racial terror. One of the ways I have conducted my own spiritual growth is to place my body in different environments and geographies to receive the teaching of these places—often without words and through my body's visceral experience. These experiences form the matrix through which my understanding of my personal history with Malissa is opening and, I hope, transforming.

PART ONE: MALISSA'S STORY

Perhaps Malissa and I bonded because we were both steeped in sadness. She—very obviously, it seemed to me—had known hardship. She barely conversed, and in her appearance, she expressed a very deep silence. Did that silence reflect her strategy to live among white people who held all the power and also held the purse strings? She did her job without comment. She worked quietly, almost as if she wasn't even there. I never heard my mother reprimand her for a job not done or not done right. She shared very little of her past. She retreated to her room when the work was done. Malissa lived her life absorbed in the white space of my family and our house. She never interrupted it. She held her cards close to her chest and was very hard to read, except on the rare occasions when she opened up to me. In a rare moment of intimate expression, one day, she leaned over and said, "You have no idea what my life and my childhood were like. You can't imagine the suffering I have endured." What I perceived as her voicelessness and attitude of having been beaten down was devastating to me as someone who loved her. But this perception, whether true or not, began to build my growing awareness of the devastation that can happen with oppression. I really did have no idea.

Malissa and I had a cautious and tentative relationship at first. But because we were alone in the house together a lot and because of my very obvious neediness, we forged a connection. She was there for me in the many situations when my parents were not. She noticed me and listened to my many complaints about my (very privileged) life. She seemed too reticent to hug me, but if I were crying she would lean over and touch me, placing the tips of her fingers on my arm or at the top of my head. For a lonely and alienated teenager, just that touch was an enormous, caring gift. How little I expected of love, coming from a family of sporadic and superficial connection. When Malissa did smile or talk, I experienced her as incredibly sweet, giving me glimpses into a person and a life I would never really know or understand. Malissa's truths were hidden by silence, mine were hidden by defensiveness.

When I came home after school, Malissa would give me a snack and take a little break, sitting with me at the kitchen table. Afterwards, I would practice my cheerleading in the cramped quarters between the table and the kitchen counters while she sat at the table doing small chores like peeling potatoes. I was an atom whirling around in a confined space, yelling, dancing, jumping in Cs and Xs. No one else spoke so encouragingly to me, smiling and telling me things like "You dance so well" or "You are a great cheerleader" or "Hey, you look great in that dress" or "I like your hairdo." Such simple moments. Malissa's face would soften with a gentle smile and she would say, "Oh, you did that so well!" because I was starving for affection and notice, Malissa's little phrases and her affectionate eyes looking into mine helped lighten my heavy heart. I devoured her small encouragements.

I took my high school rejections—not making the cheerleading squad or being kicked out of the clique—quite dramatically, but I always knew I could find solace with Malissa at home. She would be in front of the sink washing dishes or sitting, tired and slightly slumped over, at the kitchen table. She would listen to my teenage tears, watch me sitting there sobbing, bent over the table with my forehead propped on my crossed arms, and was always sympathetic to my strangely disordered and entitled fifteen-year-old values. "It'll be all right," she would say as she touched my forearm, offering me her small bashful smile. Once in a while, we would actually laugh together, and she would hold her hand across her mouth to hide her dentures.

Malissa was not much taller than me but she was stouter. She didn't seem fat but she did have a little paunch that could be seen from the side beneath her aprons, which were always clean and ironed. She particularly liked the brightly colored, embroidered aprons my mother brought back for her from Spain, which she wore over her gray or white uniforms. For a long time I didn't realize she was wearing a wig; I simply assumed that her straight black hair was her own. The wig ran curved around and just past her ears, and always looked sleek. Sometimes she wore a bit of red lipstick.

Although Malissa could be almost invisible if she wanted to

be, she never was unnoticeable to me. I often searched for her all through the house. Sometimes, I would hear her in her bedroom, which was off to one side of the kitchen, where her TV was usually tuned to a game show or a Black gospel program with gorgeous singing, and I would stand outside her door to listen.

For quite a long time, Malissa had not had a home of her own and the room off the kitchen in our house was her base. I did not know until much later that she actually owned a house, bought with her sister, in her hometown of Greenville, Mississippi. Malissa came north in the Great Migration, when six million African Americans moved to northern cities to escape the dangerous conditions down South and establish new lives. Malissa's line of migration followed the movement from the Mississippi Delta to Chicago. Greenville was a historic area for cotton plantations and its population was 76 percent African American, with 30 percent of them living below the poverty line. On weekends, Malissa often took the train down to Chicago, where she would stay with one of the friends and relatives who had come north with her to find domestic work that often paid three times as much as they would have made back home. Once, as we talked at the kitchen table, she leaned over to me and, giggling quietly, told me, "Oh yeah, I have so much money, I can send some down South."

When I was in high school my brothers went off to college, leaving the house empty, and my mother went back to work with my father in his company, thinking that we kids were grown and didn't need her anymore. I suppose that I was too afraid to make any connections or real friends. I took the stance of being a hippie so I could hide my loneliness and live in a make-believe world, pretending to be better than everyone else. I liked to present myself as a wild and radical loner and had a few outfits that fit my role. One of my brothers had brought me a handwoven serape when he visited Mexico to study Spanish. It had a V-neck and looked sort of like a macramé hanging. I wore that serape over a gray flannel culotte dress with black lace stockings and black boots with little heels—old-school shoes, like my grandmother might have worn. I also liked to wear Farmer John-style blue-jean overalls paired with what I called my "Gertrude Stein" sweater—a gray and brown herringbone-knitted cardigan with a deep neck and buttons. I also wore the largest, most complicated, dangling earrings I could find. I had a one-of-a-kind beaded macramé necklace, which had clumps of beads dangling along the sides that culminated right above my belly button in a tiny, knotted bag that held a gray stone that my friend who made the necklace for me had picked up in the forests of Northern Minnesota.

Besides the exotic outfits, what I liked most about the hippie world was the influence of Eastern religions. I adopted a macrobiotic Japanese vegetarian diet, which was popular then among members of the hippie counterculture, and followed it as much as I could, even though I was still usually an undisciplined, compulsive overeater. I bought a lot of literature on macrobiotic diets along with products like tamari, tahini, seaweed, and umeboshi plum paste and would spread them all out on the kitchen table to show Malissa. She became a willing student, preparing a separate macrobiotic dinner for me each night, even in the face of my father's and mother's scornful disapproval and exasperation. For my sake, Malissa learned how to cook brown rice, tofu, and vegetables nizuki. She would quietly, proudly, and almost rebelliously serve me this meal at the formal dinner table while she served everyone else meat and potatoes from a silver tray.

Radical Politics

During my middle-school and high-school years, a lot was going on in the outer world to reveal and address the need for racial justice. I was in seventh grade when the Civil Rights Act of 1964 was passed. We had just gotten a new color console TV. The 6:00 and the 10:00 news shows were always on, with male newscaster's voices, which provided a white interpretation of racial violence, blending with the other sounds of the house. The nature of the violence of that era shocked the nation. Or perhaps I should say, it shocked my family and my community. I know there were also communities of white people who were not only not shocked but also rooting for the police, feeling that "those negroes deserved it." In 1965, when I was in eighth grade, my family and I watched on TV the Black men and women being beaten by police in the nonviolent Selma-to-Montgomery march to support Black voting rights, and Malissa watched with us, standing in the back of the living room. She was particularly silent in the face of the social unrest we saw on TV and wouldn't talk about it even with me. The policemen wore riot gear with gas masks. Today, such images are commonplace, but back then, clips of the police beating protestors with billy clubs and dragging them into police vans stunned the world and seared my heart. I watched, crying, with my hands over my mouth. How could this be happening? The deep, melodic yet strident voice of Martin Luther King became a soundtrack in my mind for liberation and justice.

White Jews were still active in the civil rights movement, and rabbis marched to Montgomery, Alabama. As a young Jewish girl, I felt pride in my heart in realizing I could become a woman committed to liberation. But the Black-Jewish alliance quickly deteriorated. As the Black Power Movement grew, Black activists very naturally withdrew from their association with whites to establish their own self-determination and sense of empowerment. Jewish activists had to find a different way to offer support. It took another fifty years for us to arrive at the current question of what appropriate action and support by white-bodied allies actually looks like.

Was there any understanding within the Jewish community at that time of the fact that, even though we were Jews with thousands of years of oppression, we were still benefiting from white privilege in America? How did the accessibility of higher education and connection to wealth affect the power differential? Although Jewish oppression and its consequences are still an issue, some Jews do not understand that any assimilation we have experienced has been based on our whiteness. Gradually, my youthful fantasy that Blacks and Jews were fighting together against persecution crumbled. To add to that, even to this day, the Ku Klux Klan and white Supremacist movements present in their manifestos a deep, abiding anti-Semitism. We are, still, somehow in this together.

Some members of the Black community's negative views of Jews add to the anti-Semitic backlash. I believe that this prejudice was born out of Black people's day-to-day experiences in the ghettos and at work. In the Black community, Jews often showed up as greedy landlords, shopkeepers, and business owners, making money off the Black community and giving back almost nothing. There were many Black maids in Jewish households who experienced racial prejudice from the Jewish community firsthand. At home, in our kitchen, I am sure that our Black domestic help could hear my family and relatives using the Yiddish word "schvartze" to refer to a Black person in a derogatory way.

I can see today that it is as damaging to live under the illusion that there is a connection and friendship between Blacks and Jews through the commonality of oppression as it once was to believe the fantasy that Black hired help somehow loved their white families. This notion is upside-down and not helpful. I have discovered over the years that my interracial relationships are one-on-one and are not based on some generalized "idea." Rather, they are born of individuals with mutual respect for each other—yet who acknowledge, simultaneously, the ramifications of systemic racism.

Throughout my youth, I watched as successive Black Liberation movements were scrutinized and dismantled, sometimes violently, by the American government. For instance, in 1956, when I was five years old, J. Edgar Hoover centralized his disruption of domestic political groups in a secret FBI operation called COINTELPRO (COunterINTELligencePROgram). He is reported to have said that the mission of this FBI group was to "expose, disrupt, misdirect, or otherwise neutralize Black Nationalist groups." Members of the Black Panther Party and activists such as Martin Luther King, W. E. B. Du Bois, Malcolm X, and Angela Davis, among many others, were all watched and "disrupted." Even as late as 2008, Nelson Mandela was included on the CIA's terrorist list. In 1956, J. Edgar Hoover declared, "In the light of Martin Luther King's powerful demagogic speech ... we must mark him now if we have not done so before, as the most dangerous Negro of the future in this nation from the standpoint of communism, the Negro, and national security."

In the context of this history, it is something of a wonder to me today that the Black Lives Matter movement can survive at all. As Bryan Stevenson of the Legacy Museum in Montgomery states, "This history of arresting demonstrators is the beginning of the criminalization of protest." The white world incarcerates people not because of their crimes but because they participated in protests against the white-power authorities, challenging capitalism and white supremacy. This stance is what lies behind the high-level of incarceration of Black people.

At the dinner table in the late '60s we discussed whether my father should hire a bodyguard. Right after Martin Luther King's assassination in 1968, we saw on TV images of race riots in Chicago, where we lived, as well as in all the major cities of America. Even now, white people do not question the fact that the white media labeled these events "riots" without any under-lying acknowledgement of the systemic white violence which was begetting these outbursts of deep anger and frustration. Through the TV came images of streets in flames and the chaos of looting along with the sounds of wailing sirens. My father owned a plastic manufacturing company in Chicago on the corner of Superior and Orleans streets, close to the downtown area (which now houses art galleries and expensive loft apart-ments). Most of my father's workers were African Americans, and he feared that his Black employees would rally their forces and attack him in a factory uprising or as he walked to his car one night in the parking lot. My dad was afraid of this even though the actual rioting was taking place miles away. In the end, he did not hire a bodyguard and he never faced an immi-nent threat. But I was still afraid. I remember, when I was in middle school, looking out a window of my house and wonder-ing if there would be a march down our street, Sheridan Road? Was I in danger? The whole world seemed to be falling apart and in flames. Everyone, regardless of race, was afraid.

As I entered the University of Michigan in 1969, Students for a Democratic Society (SDS) was very active on campus, encouraging violent protest, and in Ann Arbor, SDS was centered at the experimental college where my husband Charley, who was my boyfriend at the time, and I were living. Bernardine Dohrn of the Weather Underground, which was founded in Ann Arbor on the University of Michigan's campus, proclaimed, "We've known that our job is to lead white kids into armed revolution." I was told by SDS that they would teach me how to use a pistol and even give me one so that I could shoot my father in the head for owning a manufacturing company—the dirty capitalist pig!

On my campus, many protests took place against the Viet Nam war and in support of BAM, the Black Action Movement, including huge marches involving thousands of students. On the edges of the marches would be my SDS acquaintances, including Charley's and my friend Kenny, a Jewish boy from New Jersey, breaking windows with baseball bats—supposedly radicalizing through violence the mostly young, white, middle- and upper-class students. Often the rallies took place at 1:00 p.m., and I would head to my dance class instead, but I would encourage or even pressure Charley, who didn't have a class at that time, to participate. One day, as thousands of students were marching towards city hall, Charley and I were in the front lines with SDS, but when we turned the last corner, we encountered a line of police in riot gear, holding the leashes of growling dogs. As untrained student protestors, we members of SDS were horrified and we ran back toward the university, scattering into the side streets and the campus squares. This was so different from what I saw on TV. The well-trained Black protestors in Birmingham held the line and did not run away, and neither did the three thousand young Black marchers in the Children's Crusade in Birmingham, which was publicized all over the world, who faced firehoses and attack dogs.

Hundreds of those children were arrested and detained, but they did not turn away.

* * *

The first time I brought Charley home to meet my parents, my father took us for a tour of the factory. After seeing the air-conditioned offices, we went through the door to the factory floor and were hit with a blast of the heat that penetrated the space, even with the windows wide open. As we passed through each room, the rhythmic sounds of the machines enveloped us. All the workers, most of whom were African American, watched my father and his entourage. The head of the factory was Polish, so there was also a small number of Polish workers. The foremen, who were both Black and white, had informal relationships with my father, and warmly shook hands with my dad and us as we were introduced as the boss's daughter and her boyfriend. Afterwards, Charley and I sat at the kitchen table at home drinking tea and schmoozing with Malissa, telling her about touring the factory and how ashamed and uncomfortable we were to be with the capitalists. Her eyes squinted, her eyebrows pulled together, and her head tilted away from us as she listened. I wondered, did she not understand what we were talking about? Or was something else going on? She had a grimace on her face and was shaking her head. Was the usually shy Malissa angry with us? I didn't know if she was protecting my parents or angry at my lack of appreciation for my entitlement. Maybe it was too scary for her to express any kind of protest to the social order. "You are lucky to be with the bosses!" she told us. "All those people have work because of your dad."

These encounters with political protest, sometimes touching the edges of violence, deeply scared me. Some events in which we participated, like protesting the capitalism of the university store, seem kind of ridiculous now. But I remember how terrified I was during the March on Washington to end the Viet Nam War in the fall of 1969. Charley and I had ridden in the back of a van with no seats overnight from Ann Arbor to Washington, DC, and that night, before the march, we slept on the floor of a church. The next day, we ran through the streets, the fog of tear gas stinging our eyes. I saw people being beaten by the police and lying in the middle of the street. In my already traumatized emotional life, I could not tolerate this new fear. I recoiled, confused about what I should be doing to bring about change. I was petrified.

* * *

Does hatred beget hatred, and violence beget violence, as both Buddhism and the nonviolent revolutionaries say? Angela Davis tells us, more recently, that change occurs when a mass collective group forms to demand it. It is not individual but collective. These days, I want to add my voice to the larger movement, which I hope will come from deep compassion instead of hatred and violence.

But in the early '70s, I was overwhelmed by the world. I was rich, white, and smart. I was in a position to achieve probably anything I wanted to do. But this was true only if my emotionally challenged self could hold it together in the face of my own internalized craziness. Racially speaking, I was comfortable in the freedom of my whiteness and my resources. I wonder if I even thought about that? In my privilege, I could afford to be blind. I turned away from politics to focus on developing my dance career and spent all my energy becoming a high-caliber New York City dancer. The heartbreak of racial injustice, however, sat as glowing coals in the chambers of my heart. I'm ashamed to admit that these coals sat inside myself for far too long a time.

The Triangle

A painful spot in my heart is the triangle that existed between my mother, Malissa, and me. It produced jealousy, competitiveness, and exclusion, and it hurt all of us. I didn't want to give up on my relationship to Malissa to ease my mother's pain. This pain had a direct cause—while I did not get the love and emotional support that I thought I needed to receive from my mother, I suppose the reverse was also true. My mother never received from her daughter what she needed or wanted either; for her, the relationship was never what she imagined it should be. I received from my mother a lot of "shoulds"—criticism and expressions of disappointment in me. Malissa was in a position to accept me without conditions because she wasn't "the real mother." And maybe she wasn't really invested in the daughter of her bosses either. But of course, she also couldn't afford to jeopardize her relationship with my mother, her boss, by bringing tension into my mother's relationship with me.

This sad triangulation is a source of great pain. Nobody wins. It is natural that the connection is strongest with the more active caregivers. The sense of familial belonging gets twisted and the deep need for mutual bonding in families gets lost, as Susan Tucker notes in her article:

> A recurrent sentence in the interviews with white women was, "she was closer to me than my own mother." This was probably accurate; in homes that employed

full-time help, Black women domestics were the more active caregivers. They were the ones who were there in day-to-day emergencies. They were often the ones who told girl children about menstruation, about sex, about relationships with men because they were often with these children at crucial times in their lives.

For me, the truth that *I was closer to the maid than my own mother* still produces a lot of pain; I can feel it in my chest. Such anguish. My family and my class were disconnected from what true family means and disassociated from the deep yearning for familial closeness. I received love and attention not from my parents but from the hired help. The maids also were separated from their families. I witnessed, with the eyes of an innocent but observant child, the grievous and agonizing social inequities of our time as I watched the maids interact with my family and white society.

Toni Morrison's novel *The Bluest Eye* describes in harrowing detail the other side of the coin: the emotions of the maids and their complex reaction to whiteness. One bit of dialogue in the book, stated by a housekeeper, explodes off the page: "White people are so dirty, they don't know how to clean. They can't even wipe their own behinds and I know because I wash their underwear." When I read this, I had a startling and horrifying flashback to Carrie, the maid of my middle-school years, who was the only member of my family's domestic staff who would break the rule of keeping silent. One day, in a complete state of umbrage, she found me downstairs and yanked me upstairs to my bedroom where she pointed to some underwear on the floor of my room and erupted, "You can clean your own damn bloody underwear!" I picked up the underwear and she grabbed both of my wrists and pulled me into the bathroom. Shouting out the instructions, she taught me how to wash it in the bathroom sink using cold water and soap.

It pains me so to write this, but at the time I didn't know how to take care of myself. I hadn't even been taught how to wash my own bloody underpants. I was so humiliated. I had no mentor. I felt absolutely devastated to have done something so bad and to have insulted Carrie. But now I have compassion for that thirteen-year-old. And I have compassion for Carrie—I see the pain of that grown woman so filled with fury! The burden of her controlled anger and her long-enduring racial indignation burst out of her on many occasions, not the least of which resulted in her sexually accosting me. At thirteen years old, from my point of view, all I could feel was a house full of rage— my father's, my mother's, Carrie's—no matter where I turned.

Was my mother what was known back then as a "good white woman employer?" What a terrible question—so condescending and patronizing. It reflects all the mess of not-so-hidden codes contained in this aspect of racism. Yet that is what was happening at that time. My mother paid her employees well, including benefits and vacations, and she took care of them legally. She did care and felt connected to her employees, like some but not all white employers. But she was oblivious to the need to act on the racial issues in the society, even though they were blatantly obvious. Her particular group of white suburban women did not engage in activism and were most probably afraid of this type of social change. This self-absorbed and protective white consciousness is still prevalent today and is what undoing racism workshops and many recent books are trying to address—the complacency and defensiveness of those of us in the dominant culture.

Malissa and my mom seemed very close, especially after I

left the house. They lived with my dad for seventeen more years after the children were gone. Besides cleaning, Malissa acted as my mom's personal assistant, running errands, answering phone calls, preparing for dinner parties, and supporting the perfectionism my mother insisted upon for her business guests. All the maids employed were personally trained by my mother and ended up being excellent Jewish cooks. It seemed like Malissa always knew what my mother wanted before my mom said anything. She knew the smallest intimacies of my mother's life, like where to put all my mother's possessions down to the tiniest detail—where each object belonged in a drawer or part of the closet. She knew exactly where my mom kept her makeup. On occasion, when my mother was sick, Malissa would massage her feet.

The two of them did a lot of activities side by side. Malissa had a closet full of fine clothes and so did my mother, though of course my mother's closet was larger and her clothes were costlier. Malissa looked quite fashionable on Sundays when she went to church, often wearing a fitted suit with a small hat, a string of pearls, short-heeled shoes and shiny stockings that reflected the light off her dark skin. A pocket-book with a silver chain dangled from her forearm. My mother and Malissa shared a love of fine things and shopping—they would show each other their purchases and delighted together in the details of each buy. However, my mother observed certain boundaries and restraint as the employer, especially because she was often admonished by my father not to get too close to the hired help. When the familial yelling and discord would begin at the dinner table or in front of the TV in the living room, Malissa would sneak into her bedroom if she could and stay out of sight. She told me once that occasionally, after a party, she would help my mom put my drunk father to bed.

I, on the other hand, showed no such restraint. I fell in love with Malissa even though this was very taboo. Malissa still resides so deep in my heart that there is no mistaking that emotion for me. When I'm asked in a Buddhist guided lovingkindness meditation to find a seed of kindness in my life, I go to my memories of Malissa.

* * *

On rare occasions, at night mainly, when Malissa would invite me into her room, I would sneak a glimpse of her without her teeth, which rested in a glass by her bed, and without her wig, which graced the white Styrofoam mannequin head on her dresser. There was a sweet smell, maybe of talcum powder, as I walked into her room. She wore a stocking tightly fitted over her head with the small knot as a bauble right in the middle of her forehead. She would never allow just anyone to catch her off guard like this. At all other times, she wore her wig and, it seemed, would have been embarrassed by anyone seeing her natural, short-cropped hair. But I always liked seeing her without her wig. In those moments, I thought she seemed deeply surprised that I accepted her, stripped of what she felt were the necessities of decorum in a white world.

Only rarely did Malissa give us any information about her life. Once she told me that as a child she had worked long and strenuous hours picking cotton, barefoot under the scorching sun, and with bleeding fingertips. Her hands were bulked up, disproportionate in size to her small stature. She said that as a child picking cotton, getting through the burrs was a real ordeal. At first her hands had been scratched and bleeding, then she developed the calluses and toughened skin that I noticed, for this evidence of her childhood labor never went away. She had once been married and I knew she had a daughter my age. Where was this daughter? "Down South," was all she would say.

Where was her daughter? This situation seems to be an example of the centuries-old negligence of the upper class, who demanded that servants take care of their children. As upper-class parents left their own children feeling unloved but well cared for, the servants' children were left without that same watchful protection. Susan Tucker notes:

> As symbolic and surrogate mothers to whites, many of the maids felt intensely the irony and sadness of their lives—that to support their own children, they had to mother other women's children. They also felt intensely the luxury white women had (and often refused) of being able to choose to care for their own children; "You'd be there just taking good care of their children and yours were probably just somewhere running wild." One woman described the drowning of her own son while she was at work, minding white children.

This passage breaks my heart. I got the attention that Malissa's daughter did not get. I got Malissa's proximity and presence.

Even though affection might have grown between white and Black women in these settings, this did not affect the racial prejudice and injustice of society. There was a code of silence in which neither side brought up the issue of race. It was dangerous for a Black domestic to bring up racial injustice if she wanted to keep her job and not appear "uppity." One Black woman in Susan Tucker's interviews said, "You just flat didn't mention anything. You acted—even in the 1960s—like you were pleased with everything—*pleased.*"

In our household, Malissa's and my relationship really aggravated and hurt my mother. By the end of Malissa's life, my mother was extremely jealous of our friendship. Why did I take Malissa out for lunch and not her? It was painful evidence of the lack of connection between my mother and me. It became an extension of the hurt that my mom and I felt that we couldn't get what we wanted from each other. My father, shaking his head, would say, "You and your mother, like oil and water."

Malissa and Hospice

Charley and I moved back to Chicago in 1978 and lived in one of the first artist's lofts on Hubbard Street. My parents and Malissa lived about a mile away. My parents had long since moved from my childhood house in Highland Park and had a condo above the Water Tower Place and the Ritz Carlton Hotel. Malissa still had a bedroom and private bath in their new apartment. I would see her quite often but of course our involvement with each other was much less now that I was married and also somewhat estranged from my parents. But I still felt a very strong connection with her.

One day, when my parents were on their biannual trip to Asia on business, I got a call, out of the blue, from Malissa. She said that she had gone to the hospital with one of her headaches and that they had admitted her. They thought it was cancer. And so, her cancer journey began. Malissa was alone in the house and needed an ally. I was young, maybe around twenty-nine; I had never been the responsible advocate for someone in the hospital. Although Malissa had no schooling to speak of, she had enough street smarts to know she needed a white advocate in the hospital for better treatment. Did I think that Malissa couldn't understand what was happening to her? Did I think that she didn't understand the power differential when she wanted a white woman advocate? Where do we get this collective white projection that Black people are dumb? It is an assumption reinforced over and over by the media, our conversations, and our interpretation of history. This concealed or not-so-concealed judgement is rarely brought to the surface of white consciousness. But even given all this racial conditioning, a bossy, strong, outspoken, Jewish woman who could demand respect and conscientiousness, probably would work well for Malissa's benefit. I went quickly to the hospital, but I didn't know quite what I should do there. I began to panic. I called everyone frantically—my aunts and uncles and my older brothers—could they help? They all said, "Oh, it's too bad that Norma and Mike are away, so I guess it's in your hands." For now, I was it. The doctors said Malissa had three months to live. Did she realize this? Had they told her what they told me? I tried to handle the situation the way my mother would, and did what I had watched her do many times in hospitals in the past. I harangued the doctors for information. I checked up on the nurses to make sure Malissa got proper care. I went to the hospital dutifully every day. She was so happy to see me and so grateful to have someone else to talk to the doctors for her, or simply be the second ear. At that time, I recall feeling conflicted about pulling myself away from my dancing rehearsals and giving her this time and attention, but I felt it as a heart obligation that I wanted to show up for her. It was certainly disheartening to see that she needed me—a white woman providing power and protection—to get the same care and attention that others routinely received.

When my mother came back from Asia, she took over as the "responsible party" again and my role faded slightly into the background. Malissa came home from the hospital and continued to live in my parent's apartment, which was luckily across the street from the hospital, and my mom cared for Malissa as she went through her treatments.

The way Malissa handled her dying was to bring her religious beliefs to the foreground. She never missed church now. She had her Bible and read it with her thick glasses on while sitting in her armchair in her room. She talked to me in religious terms, which she had not done before. I saw her, in her enduring and quiet way, meet the challenge of cancer. One day after working in my dance studio, I went across the street to the Hispanic jewelry store and bought her a beautiful gold cross, usually used for a necklace, and took it to the hospital. It was the size you could hold in your hand, and every day when I visited, there it was, in her hand. I felt that in the materialistic, nonspiritual world of my parent's household, this was a gesture of commonality, a sign of recognition that Malissa and I shared a spiritual life. I hoped that I was acknowledging that prayer and her God connection would help her through this.

This was the beginning of 1982. The guru Ram Dass and Buddhist teachers Stephen Levine and Joan Halifax had just begun exploring the role and characteristics of spiritual help in hospice caregiving. A little later on, in 1987, Frank Ostaseski started the Zen Hospice Project for AIDS patients in San Francisco. These teachers all talked about the benefit of going with someone, side by side, to their death. This gave the person who was dying companionship in the lonely journey to death. But these teachers also talked about the spiritual benefits for the person befriending and traveling with the dying. There is a tremendous amount to learn about living and dying by being intimate with the process of letting go of life. Inspired by these leaders, I decided I would be Malissa's hospice buddy. I don't think I told her this outright, but inside, I committed myself to going with her all the way to the end. I tried to carve out some space in our visits for her to be able to talk about her feelings so she wouldn't keep it all inside. Though I was often unsuccessful with such a very quiet person, I didn't insist, but I offered the opportunity.

The extreme difficulties of chemotherapy began. In the eighties, I think chemo was even cruder than it is today and the effects were very hard to endure. Malissa lost her hair. She vomited. Her body completely surrendered to the trauma of the treatment. Her walk slowed, and even to go down the elevator and across the street to sit with me in the park left her exhausted and needing to lie down. Once she let me hold her forehead as she threw up. My mom, of course, knew much more about her deteriorating condition.

Malissa worked very minimally now, when she could. My father, condescending and angry that my mom was giving her care and time, would grumble that he was paying Malissa for my mother to take care of her. Why should my mother nurse the hired help? "Why are we paying someone for doing nothing?" He had already lived through my mom's mother dying in the house, did he also have to live through the maid's death too? He would make cryptic remarks about Malissa being lazy, but my mother held firm and insisted that she was going to take care of her. There was a cold silence after my parents argued; usually my mother placated my father but not on this subject. Malissa withdrew into an even more silent, internal space when she was around the house or in the face of my father's rejection of her. My mother, for all her faults and imperfections, just held fast to her yes to caregiving. Mom would give Dad a look if he went on about it, and for the most part, that look would shut him up. I wonder now, as I look back, if my mother's caregiving was patronizing or lovingly generous, or both. There was no clearcut answer in this mixed-up situation with racism and class so deeply imbedded in the structure.

I often went over to read to Malissa from her Bible when it became hard for her to read. The whites of her eyes had turned a dark, dull, yellow. She liked my reading to her a lot. She would rest in a stuffed armchair in my parent's living room as I read. It was a quiet, beautiful space, really. My parents usually weren't home because they were working. The windows of their fifty-first floor apartment looked out over Lake Michigan, the Chicago skyline, and the enormous vast blue sky. I didn't know the Bible at all, but Malissa would lean over and find the stories or psalms she wanted me to read. Then she would relax, hold the cross I had given her, sometimes by her heart, and close her eyes or look out the window. Occasionally, a tear slid down her cheek. Several times, I sang her the twenty-third psalm in a melody that I had composed.

I took Malissa out for dinner or lunch sometimes and Charley and I began to promise her that we would take her fishing. She said that would have to wait until spring because it would be easy for her to catch a cold when she was doing chemotherapy. In my heart, I wondered, would she still be there in the spring?

One Sunday, Malissa took Charley and me to her church on Chicago's Southside. It was a storefront with painted purple wood slats across the windows. Inside, although it was winter, somehow the heat had been turned off, so we all sat bundled in our coats. I wondered what she was thinking, bringing white people to her church. But it seemed, by the soft and smiling look on her face, that she was proud of us. She knew I was excited to experience a type of spirituality that was different from mine. I held her hand tightly, and she introduced us all around as her friends.

Malissa had told me that she was mad at her church and her pastor. She didn't think they did enough for her when she "took sick." The pastor hadn't come to see her in the hospital. The last time she had gone to church, the pastor had promised to pray over her and then had forgotten about it. Though Malissa had saved up a lot of money, she told me she would never give it to him. And yet she still went to his service. She needed church.

The service was highly ritualized with a very disciplined air. There were guard-like ushers, men and women, positioned at the doors and along the back wall. Each wore white gloves and stood very erect with one arm across the waist parallel to the floor and another gloved hand, fisted, held behind his or her back. The choir entered as the gospel music swelled. There were many musicians—electric guitars, tambourine, and a piano— at the front of the church on the podium. Right in front was a small boy, maybe eight years old, playing a trap drum set that was so big it almost hid him from view. The choir walked toward their positions on the risers behind the altar with the smallest children first, holding their arms in that special way and proceeding down the two aisles, swaying from side to side, tapping a foot with each step as they moved. I sang and clapped along with a smile on my face and joy in my heart. The pain and the joy of life came roaring through the room. These were the soaring cries of voices going up to God.

The pastor began to get in touch with the Holy Spirit moving through him. As he worked himself up, the men in the community surrounded him as if to ground him to the earth so that he could really lose control and freely express the spirit. Now that I have been to Africa, I look back on this memory with more appreciation and understanding. I am gratified to see that there is still a connection between the extraordinary mystic space of spirituality in American Black communities and their ancestors in Africa. It seems that American Black spiritual communities' experiences of being taken over by the spirit come from a root with the motherland that has not been cut. I knew mystic realities through Buddhist meditation and could relate to these moments of spontaneous spiritual union. Connections to ancestors can ground people in their own humanity and identity. For me, this grounding is very rich, for I can connect with my Eastern European, Jewish, and now, Buddhist ancestors. This feeling of connection to our ancestors seems to give power and enhance the mystery and the healing of spirituality. I imagine that some Black Americans who are religious may experience the spirit world as part of their interconnection to the mysticism of Africa.

During the service, Malissa and I held hands tightly. A couple of times, I turned my head to watch her and saw a tear in her eye as my own tears were running down my cheeks. We both knew that the shadow of death was crossing our path.

One thing Malissa and I shared was our lung issues. She had lung cancer and I, at the time, was right in the middle of my search for a way to heal my asthma. There was a certain point in the service where people who wanted to be healed went up to the podium and were prayed over. Malissa and I looked at each other. Would we do it—go up there together? Did I have the courage to be that obviously visible? Malissa took my hand and we walked up the aisle together towards the singing. We knelt down side by side and we looked up to God and asked to be healed. The pastor put his hands on each of our shoulders and began to talk-sing or even shout, praying for us. His assistants surrounded the three of us and held the ground for this small circle where divine spirit could manifest itself. My adrenaline was rushing so hard, I thought I might keel over. But I squeezed Malissa's hand and stayed upright on my knees. After a couple of minutes, which felt like much longer, we headed back to our seats. Charley had a huge smile on his face, but his eyes held a little anxiety—were we all right?

Malissa lived for three years after her diagnosis. She had a very strong will to live. My mother bore most of the responsibility of caring for her. I'm not sure if my mother saw that as a loving gift or a burden. My father continued to complain about the situation. Charley and I never did take Malissa fishing, which I regret to this day.

I talked to an older friend of mine about my relationship to Malissa in the winter before she died. My friend asked, "Have you told her everything you want to before she dies?" With this prompting, I asked Malissa out for dinner on a weekend when my parents were out of town. I didn't want to arouse my mother's jealousy and increase the triangular tension. Malissa was getting worse. Her skin had darkened. I wonder if this darkening of her skin from chemo might have made it even harder to negotiate the white space of the world or even her own community? She was so thin now that her flesh hung off the bones of her face, and her walk was noticeably slower. She hung onto my elbow and didn't let go. We often stopped for her to catch her breath. Over dinner, I told her I loved her and thanked her for taking care of me when I was so lonely during high school. I expected Malissa to retreat from this emotional directness. I thought she would be too shy to talk about her emotions and her death. But as usual, she seemed to know exactly what I was doing and she surprised me. She was right there! She said how much she loved me. "Judy, I love you. You have helped me so much in these last years. We have had a long good spell. It was a pleasure to raise you." And she smiled her biggest, most expressive smile. What more could be said? We finished dinner and went home.

Malissa's Death

Malissa decided to go South to her hometown of Greenville, Mississippi, while my parents were on another business trip to Asia. One Monday morning, I got a call from her at 4:00 a.m. and she told me that her family had taken her to the hospital. She had started to have convulsions in her arm that she couldn't stop. And so, the story ended the way it had begun, with my parents in Asia, and me being the family's connection to Malissa in the most extreme times. I wondered how much longer I should wait to go down to Mississippi. But during our first phone calls, she seemed well enough, talking to me on the phone; the doctors were not indicating rapid changes, and everyone was glad she was in Greenville with her family. I called her every day, but I knew by the following Friday that things were bad. She fumbled with the phone and sounded very far away, as if she were talking to the wrong end of the handheld phone. Hearing from the sound of her voice that she didn't want to talk too much and feeling her death draw close, I decided to go immediately down to Greenville. I canceled the dinner party we were going to host the next day and got on a plane, praying that Malissa would wait for me. Her sister and her daughter Alicia picked me up at the airport. Malissa's *real* daughter was beautiful, tall, well dressed, and intelligent. Why would I have ever imagined otherwise? Ah, it was another small sign of my own habituated prejudice. How were such projections built up? How can such views become so ingrained and tenacious? Meeting Malissa's sister and daughter at the airport, I realized that I was entering unknown territory. Soon I knew that I was entering another triangle; this one was between Malissa, her birth daughter, and me—her daughter by proximity.

When we arrived at the hospital, I saw that our sweet Malissa had waited for me and was propped up in her bed. We talked and joked and laughed a little, with our love for each other very evident—to the shock of her family, I thought. The nurse told me that Malissa had really been suffering since Friday. After about an hour of conversation, Malissa allowed herself to transition and she began the journey toward her ultimate letting go. She began to withdraw from the conversation and be absorbed in her pain. I felt like a midwife at a *deathing*. I had been lucky to be present at a few births and a few deaths as a spiritual helper so I could see the progression Malissa was making, as well as notice the similarities between the processes of giving birth and surrendering to death. Going toward the gate—whether of birth or death—is very difficult and profound. At the gate of death, it's very hard to let go of a body and a life. Malissa spent the next four hours lying down and sitting up, trying to get comfortable. I stroked her back, wet her brow with a cool compress, wiped the sweat off her forehead, rubbed her back. "Maybe if I walked around, that would help?" she asked. She was fighting for life and resisting surrendering. She fought death and clung to me, and I nursed her, for we had ultimately exchanged roles. I said to her in a whisper over and over, "It's time now, Malissa, don't fight it so; it's time now, Malissa. You can let go."

I took turns with Alicia to comfort Malissa. At one point Alicia and I went down to the cafeteria together for a break. A heartbreaking story about her relationship with Malissa emerged while we got to know each other. We had been together for a little while by then and perhaps there was some small, very small expression of trust beginning to develop. I wasn't very hungry in the midst of the tension of the circumstances, so I just sipped my tea while Alicia began to tell me parts of her story. She talked softly and leaned in toward me to escape the cacophony of sound in the cafeteria. Malissa had not told either me or my mom the full story about her daughter. "My mother refused to acknowledge my first child, who was born before my husband and I were married," Alicia told me. "This was very hard for me, very hard for me." She paused. "She and your mom would send presents to my children who were born after my marriage but they would leave Kayla out of it, as if she didn't exist." She slowly shook her head from side to side. She looked up at me with her eyebrows raised, shrugging her shoulders, shaking her head, and holding her hands up in the air, palms turned up. Malissa could not or would not reconcile herself with the fact that her daughter had been an unwed mother, not even after Alicia married. Oh, Malissa! Though I was hearing just the infinitesimal details of this story, I felt heartbroken.

So there actually was a third grandchild. Malissa had held this secret close inside. I wondered if my mother or I could have helped her in some way if we had known her sorrow around this. Oh I wished I could have helped ease this pain. But what more was I capable of?

Now, in the cafeteria, Alicia continued her story, surprising me, "Two days ago, in this very hospital," she smiled, "I gave birth to my fourth child, a daughter." She hesitated, "I named her Malissa," she said, and she started to cry. I touched Alicia's arm, just with my fingertips, the way Malissa used to touch me. This announcement hit me in the gut. This beautiful woman, hardly showing her fatigue or self-concern after childbirth, was sitting by her dying, estranged mother's bed. Here we all were in the painful swirling mess of samsara.

From this new vantage point, I had to see the whole situation differently. Malissa was not an idealized mother figure pitted against my own flawed mother. Malissa, too, was a flawed person. And now, years later, I realize that I am a flawed mother too. This new awareness of my faults as a mother has brought forth a deep searing pain in my heart. Many mothers experience this pain of their own fault, of their differences with their children, perhaps also of estrangement. Some of our beliefs, and what we don't understand about life, get passed down, often destructively, to our children. Through generation after generation, the hurt and trauma of humanity moves down the line. We are all flawed individuals and we are produced by a universe of collective conditions that create our problems. I have found that in order to have some peace or self-acceptance, it's greatly important to have a larger view. We must hold ourselves in a huge network of interconnection of causes and conditions so that we can see more clearly the truth of our histories. We must understand history.

We are all very, very, flawed—and yet there are causes for our faults and still, alongside our flaws, there can be love and reconciliation. We can allow both love and hurt to exist simultaneously. It seemed to me that Alicia still loved her mom. Of course, I have no idea what her true experience was, and I had very little information to understand the dynamics of her relationship with her mother. But healing I sensed in Alicia and experienced myself seemed to come from our spirituality, not from our self-centered perspectives. Perhaps naming her new daughter after her mother was a gesture of forgiveness and understanding by Alicia.

Finally, in the end, the nurses gave Malissa something to sedate her and obliterate the pain. Alicia, one of her cousins, and I sat very quietly in Malissa's room, with me on the right side of the bed and Alicia on the left. That silent moment was scalded into my heart and has remained there for my life so far. I had a kind of pure love, without resentments, for the Malissa I had known. But Alicia, seated across from me, had had a very, very, different experience. Their relationship had been filled with abandonment and missteps and, I guessed, a lot of resentment and anger—the kind of sentiments I felt for my own mother. I was in the role of the white privileged woman who had received most of Malissa's attention, and I was set at odds with her own beloved daughter she had left down South. I wanted to explore and understand this karma, for it was the karma of mothers and daughters but also the repercussions of oppression, racial and ethnic injustice, and slavery. It broke my heart, and that broken heart still wants to heal and to find some restitution in this world. I want to offer what little I can to the healing of the world and to repay my debt. Without the older Black women in my life, I don't think I would have survived my childhood. Without Malissa, I would have felt unloved. How could I repay that? I am engaged in racial justice work to honor them. Such an insignificant repayment in relationship to what I consider the enormity of their generosity.

At one point, Alicia, whose profession was nursing and who knew about all the machines that were operating by the side of the bed, leaned over and put her head on her mother's chest. She lay there for a long time and then began to cry, and I knew it was over. There was no longer any rhythm in the working of the oxygen gear, only a continuous hiss. I stood up and asked everyone to hold hands and then I, the white Jewish Buddhist girl, closed Malissa's eyes, made the sign of the cross over her body, and said the Lord's Prayer and the twenty-third psalm, which everyone joined in prayer. Then we cleaned up, gathered her things, and left.

The Aftermath

Malissa knew me well. She knew that I would want to experience staying at her family's house, and she had arranged it with her sister, who had promised her that I could stay at their house and sleep in her bed. Sometimes I got the feeling that I was the only white person who had ever entered their house, and perhaps that was true. This seemed so topsy-turvy. Malissa had lived much of her life as the only Black person in a white environment, and there I was, just for a day, in the reverse position.

Malissa and her sister owned the house together, but other relatives lived there too. Each room in this small house was someone's residence. Malissa's brother lived in one room, Malissa's sister and her husband lived in another, and two nieces and a baby lived in the third. I stayed in the living room, which was where Malissa's bed was. I was intrigued to see that the extended family really still existed and to discover that it was not uncommon there to be raised by an aunt or for many generations to live in one house. Malissa's daughter, though, lived in her own house with her nuclear family a few blocks away. I immediately loved Malissa's sister Deloris. She was in a wheelchair, but even in her difficulties, she was still the center of the household and the archetypal matriarch. She reigned over the household from her wheelchair in the middle of the kitchen.

It was a whole new world for me and I think my presence in the house was kind of a shock for everyone. I ate whatever they served—including grits for breakfast with greens and cornbread—and I was eager to learn about their lives. I knew Malissa would have laughed and loved this—me visiting her world. In the morning, the littlest niece took me for a walk through the neighborhood. It was a gorgeous morning in May 1982—warm and sunny with the balmy air wafting freely and the curtains of the opened windows of the houses all billowing in the wind. Laundry undulated slowly on the clotheslines and the large gardens overflowed with flowers and the starts of vegetable plants. As it was Sunday, gospel music and preaching from radios or TVs floated through the air out of every house we passed. This little niece was all eyes on me with nonstop conversation and questions: How long had I known Malissa? Had I flown down? What were airplanes like? Was I married? Did I have children? That house over there was her friend's house. This house coming up was her cousin's. "I hate that woman," she grumbled pointing her finger at one of the houses. The people we passed would look up, startled at first, and then wave, smile, and laugh. This little one knew where every dog in the neighborhood lived and how to avoid them. I savored my walk with her. It felt like I was being invited into the heart of the Black South.

Malissa's funeral was set for the upcoming Thursday. That was four days away. I wondered if I should stay down South until the funeral took place. I wanted to observe the way of life there, like a cultural anthropologist. But what did that mean: cultural anthropologist? Did my desire land me in the "good" category—was it a positive thing that I was interested and curious and could benefit from studying another culture? But I am ashamed to use that wording now because it is such a strong acknowledgment that I had placed my Black acquaintances in the category of "other" and something that was to be studied. Is the term "cultural anthropologist" belittling in its very essence? The anthropologist is above those she studies. I became aware of my own propensity to "other" people and to create a distance between me and my new friends. I quietly considered the circumstances: We were all deeply grieving the loss of our loved one, and my presence added another tension to an already unsettled household. So I made the decision to fly back up to Chicago and return for the funeral with my mother, who would be coming back from her trip on Tuesday.

The Funeral

As soon as my mother returned from Asia we made plans to fly down South for the funeral. In the Jewish culture, everyone goes to a funeral, so I was surprised when my husband and father chose to stay home. I felt angry at them and thought they were being disrespectful to Malissa. My mother told me on the plane that she was glad they hadn't come. If Dad had been around, she said, she couldn't really have an authentic emotional experience, so for her it was better this way. My mother traveled with a briefcase full of Malissa's legal documents— her will and bank statements. She told me that Malissa had not been planning to leave her daughter any money in her will. *Oh, Malissa.* But my mother, even before she knew the story of the illegitimate child, had convinced Malissa that was not a good choice. My mother had encouraged Malissa to soften her heart and leave her daughter some of the money she had saved and the additional income produced by her profit-sharing account in my parent's business. My mom had been expressing her own spiritual understanding that in death, one has to be more forgiving and generous. Fortunately, Malissa had taken my mom's advice and changed her will. My mom told me all this on the plane, and I told her about Malissa's unacknowledged grandchild. She was deeply shocked that Malissa had drawn a line and never shared this. As we flew down to Mississippi together, I knew that with my mother entering the scene, my role would change and definitely lessen. Now I would be the daughter of the boss-lady.

Everyone gathered at Malissa's house, where my mother and I were treated as honored guests, and we rode with Malissa's sister and her daughter in the black limousine behind the hearse. At the church we were escorted to the front row where the family sat. Malissa's pastor, the one she didn't like from Chicago, had come down to do the service. Mom and I, knowing about her relationship to the pastor, chuckled a little at this. But it seemed really important to me that the Chicago congregation had sent him down, for I knew that Malissa would have been glad that such a fuss was finally being made over her. The ritual in the Mississippi church was that row by row everyone passed by the coffin for a last goodbye. It was a very organized procession, guided by the white-gloved ushers. The choir's singing began to soar as people said their last goodbyes. Some passed by slowly, some knelt and prayed, some touched the coffin with a bowed head. All of a sudden, my mother wrenched herself out of the pew to run up to the casket and kiss Malissa. She started to cry, and everyone sat stunned and silent. The white boss-lady needed a "nurse," which was what it turned out that they called the white-gloved ushers. One of them came up to me and said, "Go, go be with your mother." I jumped up, but Mom was almost finished by then and I escorted her back to our seats. We realized later that the front-row relatives would go up one by one to say goodbye. Mom passed her turn. When my turn came, I went up by myself to the casket and leaned over to kiss Malissa's heart. I whispered, "You know that I truly love you, Malissa"—my final goodbye.

I often still cry about Malissa. It happens when I hear gospel music or when I see people fishing in urban lakes. My inheritance was Malissa's Bible, her most treasured possession.

Malissa will never leave me, never, even though she came into my life as the hired help. She was both mother and friend to me when I needed her most.

PART TWO: THE LEGACY OF ENSLAVEMENT

My love for Malissa and my growing awareness, surrounding her death in 1982, of the overwhelming presence of racism in our society, including how I participate in it, sent me on a long journey. Mostly it has been an inner journey, but also, outwardly, I have traveled to some of the places in the world that most intensely embody suffering from racial injustice. A place can instruct us as much as, if not better than, any lecturer or book. Nothing teaches us more than immersion into the felt-sense experience of historic places. These travels can provide a focused pause in our busy lives, bringing to the forefront traumas that we need to digest and discharge, especially if we want to escape the fate of reenacting them.

My travels took me to Ghana, Africa, and its slave castles, and to the Legacy Museum in Montgomery, Alabama. But to begin my exploration, I started with my local community, entering institutions in my own backyard. After going to many workshops on racism that were attended mostly by white people, I decided that I needed to throw myself into situations where I was in the racial minority, outside my comfort zone. But in talking to the inmates at the prison where I went to volunteer, I learned that there is a fine line between being a white do-gooder—a type that all the inmates hold in disdain—and someone who wants a mutually beneficial relationship. The so-called charitable stance of the do-gooder still reinforces the position of white supremacy. The "near enemy" of compassion in the Buddhist teaching is pity, which puts you above the person you are trying to help. When I began to serve on the board of Ujamaa Place in the Twin Cities, a white board member repeatedly said, "We talk about the theory of transformation *for the men*, but what I have learned is being at Ujamaa has transformed *me*."

Incarceration

The first time I went to the prison to teach meditation and stress-reduction, I practically had to hold my friend Cal's hand as we walked up to the door. Cal was a Buddhist who had taught university courses and meditation in the prisons for a long time. It took him several years of persuasion to get me to come with him. I was afraid of the pain I would encounter there. Approaching the big solid metal doors of the prison, I felt my heartbeat accelerating while my lips locked in a tight grimace and my hands clenched. Was I strong enough to bear witness to the inmates' pain and hold their feelings and my own reactive emotions in compassion? I really didn't know. I say now that I have gotten used to the frustrating process of applications, background checks, metal detectors, and all the bureaucratic rules one has to navigate to enter the prison. But even though perhaps this is true, still, on Tuesdays when I go there, I gather up all my resources, breathe deeply, and overcome my dread of the harshness of the prison environment by encouraging myself to be present for the men I serve and to be available for new, unfamiliar but burgeoning relationships. From the start, the men have seemed always to surprise and inspire me, and eventually they became my teachers. Of course, these are self-selected inmates. Most of the men who come to our meetings don't do so to become Buddhists but simply to sit in silence every Tuesday afternoon and experience a small escape from the prison's noisy, threatening chaos—and perhaps to have a conversation that addresses their humanity.

Some of the men have chosen to participate in *Jukai*, Buddhist initiations. This ceremony includes taking vows to refrain from exactly those behaviors that got them in prison in the first place: no killing, no stealing, no selling drugs, no lying, and no misusing sexuality. Some of the men actually become Buddhists and receive lineage papers and a handsewn prayer shawl, more like a bib, which is the small Buddhist robe for lay practitioners.

The Christian chaplain at the prison has told the group of us who facilitate the Unpolished Diamond sangha, how deeply moved he is by the silent Zen Tea Ceremony for Buddha's enlightenment day that we enact in December. The Buddhist volunteer facilitators serve tea and a cookie to each participant individually and formally, bowing in several moments before each man in silence. Individually, and with care, we honor the dignity of every participant, which is something that is really rare in the prison environment—the chaplain likens our bows to Christ washing the feet of his disciples. We also offer the Buddha's birthday celebration in the spring. Each participant pours tea over a baby Buddha statue. This represents honoring both the historic Buddha as well as, most importantly, the potential for each of us to become a Buddha—both the whole person we already are and the person we can aspire to be.

When I go into the prison and look around at my mostly people-of-color class, I am so dismayed. Most of these men, many of them African American, did not have a chance to succeed in life without ending up in prison. Both poverty and racism determined their fate. Racist housing, economic policies and practices, and the trauma of our educational system to people of color help shaped their backgrounds. All of these systemic conditions set them up for crime and drugs. Add to that a racialized court system that rushes to convict dark-skinned people, and the situation seems almost hopeless except that people can be very strong and resilient, and I have seen evidence of that in many of the prisoners I serve. We cannot afford to fall into the hopelessness that produces inaction.

In prison, there is some attention paid to remedial education but not nearly enough, in my opinion. Very little is done to teach these men the skills that they absolutely do need in order to reenter society and not return to jail. I can hear the voice of Scout, one of our longstanding members. He is a lifer who has come to the Buddhism circle since the beginning of the sangha, which is at least twenty years old now, and is one of our leaders. He once asked his fellow group members to come up to him whenever they see him clenching his fists getting ready for a fight, and whisper "mindfulness" to remind him to change his attitude. He always tells people that they can prepare a tool belt of skills and that his tools are the eight-fold path, the Buddha's instructions for achieving spiritual centeredness.

As the doors clang behind me when I leave the prison, I am always extremely exhausted from dealing with the heavy, obvious suffering of the people inside. But I also leave feeling gratitude for the many joys and freedoms of my life. My heart is raw and open to the pain of the world, and my hope is that our sangha offers a little bit of love and healing within this austere and violent environment. And through it I achieve a deeper level of acceptance of what small problems I do have, which are nowhere near as bad as incarceration.

Ujamaa Place

After going into the prison to teach meditation and Buddhism for fifteen years, I began to want to do something more. How could I really help these men transform their lives and support them in becoming stable and contented men connected to society? I found Ujamaa Place, an organization based in St. Paul, Minnesota, that supports African American men in a holistic Afrocentric manner, employing what they call their transformation theory. I teach meditation in their health and wellness program, and I'm on its board of directors. This organization helps any young Black man who wants to grow. Many of Ujamaa Place's clients have already been incarcerated or are homeless, unemployed, or in crisis. Some of them are trying to leave gangs or get off drugs. Some had almost no parental support from an early age and feel traumatized by their schools. Success is slow and often seemingly impossible. And yet the organization's staff and its clients persevere, and many of these young Black men change their lives.

At Ujamaa Place, young men enter into a family-oriented brotherhood where men mentor men and work through an interconnected system of stabilization: housing, employment, behavior, health and wellness, criminal justice advocacy, and education. Off-site housing is offered and most of the men come in daily or after work to attend classes or meet with their coach. Three meals a day are served. Most of the men participate for several years, but once a Ujamaa man, always a Ujamaa man.

At lunch on Wednesdays, there is a "power hour" featuring a speaker. As I set up for meditation classes, I sometimes hear a booming voice and then laughter from down the hall. Or I'll witness a young man changing a baby's diaper in the community room, surrounded by a lot of baby paraphernalia, like a stroller and a diaper bag, enjoying the giggles of his child. Or I might see a man with his pants pushed down to his knees being asked to pull them up.

At one recent meditation class there was one man who had meditated before and who I knew liked it, but the other three participants were absolutely brand new to Ujamaa. It might even have been their first day there. During the course of the meditation, all three of the new men walked out. Oh dear. But afterwards, the mental health counselor who joins me in my classes just shrugged his shoulders. You never know when something you say might impact one of the men and/or come into play later in his life.

But these occasionally discouraging experiences are countered by inspired moments. At a recent benefit concert, some of the men approached me and, smiling, told me they still meditate. After I had led a guided meditation for protection and loving-kindness for self, a thin boy who comes often but always sits somewhat nervously and quietly in class participated in the discussion and said, "I never really understood 'self-love' until this exercise. In order to do this visualization, I had to first find my soul and then bring it into my body so they could be together." At the same class, another man who was lying on the floor in relaxation pose, lifted his head, looked up into my eyes, and said, "Thank you so much for coming. This is better than any anger management classes, which I have only understood in my head. But this, I am feeling in my body."

Two years ago, we took a small group of men to Clouds in Water Zen Center to have a new and broadening experience and to see the zendo, a room devoted to meditation. One man walked into the zendo and said, "Wow, I can feel it. It's so quiet in here, so peaceful." Just recently that same man came back to meditation class and told me that often when his life is very tumultuous, he closes his eyes and imagines himself in the quiet of that zendo. He looked so sincere as he told me, "That's what I want in my life."

Working in this environment, I am learning to live through the embarrassment of my racial ignorance being exposed. The awkward moments when this happens are teaching me to be humble, to apologize for my blindness and my sense of superiority, and to restart and continue on. I do this in the environment of acceptance that has been cultivated throughout Ujamaa Place. All of the men have been taken into an atmosphere of love and support, and so have I.

Pilgrimage to Ghana

During the summer of 2018, Ujamaa took two clients, two board members (I among them), three staff members, and two community activists to Ghana on a Black History and Return to Africa tour especially focused on both the history of slavery and Ghanaian culture. We had planned on bringing more Ujamaa men along, but there were so many obstacles in their way for getting passports that only two out of ten men received authorization to travel. If a man was on parole, had overdue child support payments, or no home address, or maybe even just too many parking tickets, he could not get a passport. What a shame that was, because the two men who went had a quite extraordinary life-changing experience. The trip marked their first time traveling out-of-the-state, being on an airplane, having a passport, and maybe even taking a vacation—not to mention that it was also their experience of being a Black man in an all-Black society.

For different reasons, my journey was equally powerful and

enlightening. As I am often the only white person at Ujamaa and was the only white person on the tour, I had the chance to feel skin-color racialization in my own body and bones. I wish every white American could have this education in reverse racial awareness. This provided the chance for an unusual exploration into understanding my privilege and yet also my need to belong. Could I allow myself to belong to this group? Could they allow me to be part of them?

My total in-the-body racial education began the minute I sat down in the waiting room for Accra, Ghana, at JFK Airport. The room vibrated with boisterous families dressed in head wraps and beautiful colored, boldly printed fabrics, all of them jammed together on too few seats in a sea of Black faces. There was a festive spirit of going home. Cross talk and laughter filled the room, and it was very unlike the all-white, silent waiting area across the wide walkway. Interestingly, I mentioned this to Monique, one of the staff members on the tour, and she said, "Oh yes, I sat down and felt totally at home. Being here, in the racial majority, has made me deeply relaxed and at peace." My fellow travelers also seemed to experience a deep sense of relief that in this environment they could truly, authentically be themselves. My companions dropped their mantle of protection against the suspicion and ill-will that follows them around constantly in our American environment. This was a visible transformation. What happiness! And perhaps, I hoped, a signal of healing.

In her foreword to Ato Ashun's 2018 book *Elimina: The Castles and the Slave Trade*, Dr. Rose Walls, resident director of the University of California Education Abroad Program and senior lecturer at University of Ghana-Legon, addresses the implication for African Americans of making a return to Africa:

After ten generations of my family being in the USA, my small nuclear family dared to break the cycle and returned to Africa, making Ghana our home. This transition has been filled with many challenges, much learning, growth and joy beyond measure. Ghana is a beautiful and imperfect place like most of the world. But here in Ghana, I have this one simple joy fulfilled almost every day. I walk into a room unapologetically Black and I am surrounded by a group of people who usually expect nothing but the best of me. I am not considered dangerous, a thief or "less than" due to the colour of my skin. Many will perhaps not understand this, but most Africans living in a country where they are the minority certainly will.

I cannot imagine having this constant level of scrutiny and "otherness" as my daily experience, but that is what happens with dark-skinned people in American society. In Ghana, over just a few weeks, I learned a tiny amount about living skin-deep in an illusory world of "others."

Ghanaians have little or no experience of contemporary racial prejudice as it exists in present-day America because they live in an all-Black society. Of course, they still appear, to my eyes, to have deep, damaging scars of colonialism. But the young people we met often were enthusiastic about going to America because in Ghana it is seen as a place of opportunity for education and jobs. My traveling mates had to explain to them that the so-called land of opportunity wasn't actually like that, because there are glass ceilings for Black people in America. The young Ghanaians' eyes stretched wide in astonishment and disbelief as they learned about Western racism.

While traveling, I heard a very revealing conversation about the tensions between Africans and African Americans. One of the Ghanaian men had traveled to the United States because he had a job with the YMCA. He said that when he went to America, he never was around Black people and never went into Black neighborhoods. His white coworkers told him that the Black neighborhoods were unsafe; when he did meet African Americans, they were often unwelcoming to him because he was an African. He was surprised and disappointed by this. The very sensitive discussion that ensued among my colleagues about the tensions in America between African Americans and Africans revealed how much more complex all the issues are, beyond the obvious commonality of the color of their skin.

Besides having gained a heightened awareness from being a white American in Ghana, I also sometimes became conscious of class. One day our group went to the Royal Senchi Hotel, a luxury resort. I found it odd that on that day I felt the most different from the rest of the group. Perhaps my psychological and class separation from my traveling friends had brought to the surface my own mental-health issues, or perhaps I was experiencing the felt-recognition of the shadows and ghosts associated with growing up in the owning class, which was represented by the extravagance of a luxury hotel. I did not feel grateful at all for the affluence and entitlement of my childhood—and accompanying that, I felt like I was reexperiencing the emotional poverty of my growing up years.

By the time I was a tween, I felt a level of dissociation from people that, until recently, I didn't realize goes so deep or would be so long-lasting. I think some of this estrangement stems from the psychological problems of wealth. Behind the Royal Senchi Hotel's perfect and hedonistic façade are the hidden problems of my class: broken homes, hostility, addiction, and abuse. Within all the abundance, you can become very jaded and lonely; if it keeps up, eventually nothing seems to make you happy and your enjoyment of all the luxuries stops. I come from a class that can afford anything (and more), but for whom love, attention, and relationship may be missing. What does a young child understand about all of this? I was hurt in the midst of material abundance.

I remember my whole family—my parents, my two brothers, and me—going to Puerto Rico for our first luxury vacation at a resort very much like the Royal Senchi Hotel. I was perhaps twelve. My father was very proud that he could finally afford to take his entire family on a fancy vacation. But that vacation was so fraught with fighting, aspersion, and familial torment that my father said, "I am never taking this family on vacation again!" And he kept his promise: I don't think we ever did go on a vacation like that together again.

At the Royal Senchi Hotel, the pool reminded me of my family's country club. There was beauty all around me, but I never felt like I belonged. No matter how much I tried—to wear the right clothes, to put on makeup, to lighten up my personality—I felt rejected in my youth, especially sitting around the country club's pool, feeling a little zaftig, hiding my plumpness with cover-ups.

But as it turned out, maybe because I liked my fellow-travelers so well, I also had a lot of fun at this luxury hotel. The Ujamaa men had never experienced anything like it. They saw for the first time this particular type of opulence as if it were a high-end carnival. I loved watching them being surprised and displaying the exuberance of the young was a joy. We played in two pontoon boats with music blasting and staged a highly competitive dance contest. Old and young danced and boogied around, with all of us showing off our moves, which was very playful and fun. And I, the older white woman, had a lot of moves! Later on, feeling hot and steamy, we cooled off by the pool and enjoyed the cold drinks and hamburgers brought to our chaise lounges. I let go of my initial adverse reactions to the hotel and enjoyed the company of my delighted traveling companions; as we played together, I allowed myself to belong and take in the pleasure of the day.

Colonialism and White Supremacy

Before going to Ghana, I resisted using the term "white suprem- acy" as applied to me. In the workshops on undoing racism that I attended, this term had been brought up and often requested of me. "Isn't that too inflammatory a term?" I objected (to myself). In my Zen community, which is doing racial work, most whites balked at using that phrase. "Certainly, that does not implicate *me*," everyone no doubt thought. "Isn't that reserved for the Ku Klux Klan and extremists?" But having visited Ghana, I now feel the truth of the term "white supremacy" and have no trou- ble using it. Nor do I have any trouble seeing the pervasiveness, centrality, and sense of superiority that goes along with our whiteness. Having learned of the roots of colonialism, impe- rialism, domination, and exploitation within the history of Ghana, I began to understand the deep-seated consciousness of white Europeans. These "conquerors" definitely felt superior to the citizens of Ghana and had a crushing effect on the coun- try's indigenous cultures. In Ghana, it is so obvious, even five centuries later, that the European mindset left much destruc- tion in its wake. The extreme aspect of this position was the slave trade. The slave traders only needed a certain percentage of their human cargo to make it across the Atlantic in order to make their needed profit, so they didn't go out of their way to keep the slaves on their ships alive; when someone died, he or she was simply thrown overboard, like garbage, into the sea.

I can see the consequences of that state of mind in my and other white people's consciousness when we ignore the fact of deeply embodied racism. Some of us may think we are "color blind," yet we are still protecting our white privilege by not acknowledging the repercussions of systemic racism on people of color—and on white people too—or by not taking a stance to fight for change.

The first shock I experienced in Ghana occurred on our very first day there, when I went to the Black Star Square in Accra, which is the site of Ghana's independence from Britain. A huge black star is placed on top of an archway in the center of an island of grass in a traffic roundabout. We were allowed to climb up to the top of the archway to be close to the black star. It was there that I began to learn of Ghana's great revolutionary leader and first president, Kwame Nkrumah. Ghana was the first country in Africa to achieve independence and was liberated in 1957. Oh my god, I thought, that was so late—it actually occurred in my lifetime. It alarmed me that imperialistic domination was so recent—and in Ghana I felt that not only intellectually but viscerally, and I began to understand how fresh the wounding is that produces today's racism. It is the continuing folly and justification of our European and American white cultures to persist in believing that spreading our cultures—and in doing so, trouncing other societies—is good for the world. This lie covers up our protection of our own self-interests and greed; it is a terrible conceit, and it was scorched into my body through my experiences in Ghana.

Ghana is a developing nation with pockets of scarcity and poverty that were evident to us as we traveled through it, but I also found, as a modern Westerner, a kind of restoring groundedness there. The mindset in Ghana was distinctly different from America's materialism, which seems to be obsessed with acquiring more and more money and goods and chalking up more and more achievements. In Ghana, I felt a deeper connection to nature and the earth, and this provided a healing embrace for me. I got to walk in the heat on dirt roads with vast open blue skies above me. I got to eat simply prepared meals of tubers, grains, and plantains. I got to experience the Ghanaian heart, which prides itself in the value of "ackwabaa," which means "welcome." The people's warmth seemed genuine to me through their everpresent smiles and their strong sense of communal kinship, so unlike what I've experienced in America.

In Ghana, I was identified as an *obroni*, which is what white people are called in Twi, the country's traditional language. The root of the word "obroni" is also associated with "trickster" or someone who cannot be trusted. Given Ghanaians' history, I don't blame them for not trusting white people. I also heard "obroni" casually translated as the "white man devil," emphasizing Ghanaians' history of being dominated by white men even more.

In Senchi Ferry, I experienced a poignant incident associated with the word *obroni*. There, while visiting a nursery school, our group saw the level of poverty in which many Ghanaian children are growing up. The school was a low-slung wood building using boards with spaces between them to make up the walls with a corrugated metal roof on top. There were small wooden desks but no school supplies, although most kids had a backpack hung on pegs on the wall. They all wore uniforms provided by the school—orange-checkered dresses for the girls and checkered shirts with solid orange shorts for the boys. Most of the children wore sandals or torn sneakers. We were told that the uniforms were necessary so everyone could be dressed appropriately for preschool. While we were there, the children's main activity was singing, accompanied by small arm gestures and perhaps some dance steps for us visitors; the performance took place in the dirt-floored courtyard under the shade of some large trees.

What caught my eye was a single white plastic baby doll, measuring about two feet long, with no clothes. There was one doll for all the children. The children's main play activity was to pull out the doll's arms and legs and then put them back. I watched as four kids grabbed for the doll, wanting to have their turn, and felt dismayed to see that this was practically their only form of play: the dismemberment of a toy baby. I didn't get the sense that this was a consciously enacted cruelty—it seemed more like an urgent necessity, born out of a near desperation on the part of the children to play and be stimulated. But this activity seemed to me to be a form of violence, not the loving enactment of a mother/baby relationship that I have always thought was the reason to play with dolls—and yet it seemed that this was their play habit. When I was a doll-loving child, our play was to put on and off the clothes that came with the doll but here, there were no clothes. The children themselves did not have a lot of clothes, so they probably took it in stride that the doll was naked. Plus, there were so many children and so very few teachers that I think this disturbing form of play was not high on the teachers' list of behaviors to notice and control. I remembered clicking dolls' arms back into their sockets from my own childhood play, but that was done very infrequently and usually only because some accident had happened. The little girl within me was in shock. But I also remembered that I, as a little girl, had owned an abundance of dolls with a lot of clothes and even doll furniture. What I was witnessing here was the stark reality of these children's lives: There were no toys, but they still felt a driving pressure to play with the one toy they had.

One little girl was quite possessive of the doll. Maybe it was hers. When she saw me, she ran up to me, and shook the doll in my face, "Obroni, obroni!" she cried. She had noticed that the doll and I were white-skinned. Had she realized her doll was obroni before she identified it with me? Had she even been aware of the doll's skin color before my visit? She was very proud of her doll, and perhaps, because of her doll, she felt she had some special connection to me, the white visitor. "Obroni, obroni!" I returned her enthusiasm for her doll and smiled and admired it. I wished each child had a toy. I noticed a few balls scattered in the courtyard, but those were the only playthings around. When we walked into the ramshackle classroom, there was barely any educational paraphernalia there either.

The pain of this grim scarcity has lingered in my heart. I wish there had been more dolls, and that all the dolls were Black, and that they had clothes. What can I do to help? How I would like to fix this situation. The strategy of starting a not-for-profit organization with a title like Black Dolls for Africa seems to fall so short of making a real contribution, although sometimes small things do help. My understanding is that a Western woman is supporting the preschool, the school, and the library in the small village of Senchi Ferry. I still feel overwhelmed by the barrenness and impoverishment I saw. It was the undeniable face of a paucity of resources.

* * *

One day on the tour bus, we all got out to look at a little shopping village, where round tables with large umbrellas stood jostled together on either side of the road, forming a kind of make-shift market. Many of the women there were wearing small, flat turbans as cushions for balancing on their heads huge trays of food and commodities for sale. Many of the women also wore aprons with big pockets, which worked as fabric cash registers, so they could walk around selling their wares. This was such a sight for an American that I dug out my cell phone and began taking a video of the scene. Soon I heard one of the woman saying,

"Obroni, obroni. Aye, are you pay me? Uh?"

"Pay you for the picture?" I asked.

"Pay me for the pictures, pay me," she insisted.

"Okay!" I called out.

She laughed and smiled wildly, running over to hug me. Before I knew it, three or four women were hugging me and wanting money too. The first woman defended me and helped me get out of the cluster of women. She insisted that I take a bag of what she was selling, some kind of grain, and I did take it, even knowing that I had no way of using it. Our group went to look at a newly constructed bridge and on our way back to the bus, one of the other women recognized me from the previous encounter and came up to me again asking for money. I smiled and said, "I'm not going to give you money, but I will give you a blessing." She beamed, looking me straight in the eye, and said, "I'll take your blessing." And then quickly, she disappeared back into the crowd.

During the whole trip I felt very uncomfortable with people asking me for money. The disparity between my wealth and their insufficiency really disturbed me. I have had little experience traveling in developing countries. How were you supposed to handle this? It had started as soon as I got off the plane with maybe fifteen cab drivers aggressively surrounding me, wanting to push themselves into my face and win the prize of giving me a taxi ride. There were always hawkers clogging up the exit from the bus, trying to sell us their wares. I felt uncomfortable, not knowing how I could say no, nicely, as one human to another. Usually I just pushed through the crowd, making no eye contact, ignoring everyone. This happened several times a day and this behavior of mine also distressed me. But my encounter with these women had a different flavor. There was a human connection, an exchange. There had been a real back-and-forth with the first woman, and I appreciated her aid in helping me get out of the pack of women crowding in on me from all sides. The second woman and I had also had a mutual, kind-hearted exchange. "I will give you a blessing"— that at least I could do as a Zen teacher.

I had learned by then that in Ghana, older women gave blessings, and I was the oldest person in our group. Sometimes I was called Miss Judith, and sometimes still I'm called Miss Judith at Ujamaa Place in St. Paul. I've learned to receive this name with affection within a culture that still actually honors their elders. After my acceptance of this honorary name, I thought back to my family home, and began to know that it was an insult that I called the maids by their first names. All the names we give hired help—housekeepers, maids, domestic workers—seem wrong and degrading. Our workers called my parents of their same age Mr. and Mrs. Ragir. Had that been a daily microaggression (or not so micro)—a way of denigrating their position in society? Sadly, yes, it was. These aggressions are seen constantly in daily life. A Black person being followed in a store is seen as a potential thief. Black people are often dismissed in conversations, or passed over at work, or not picked up by a taxi cab, and on and on.

* * *

In Ghana, our group had the great opportunity to talk to one of the most powerful kings in the area and the queen mother. In our interview with the king, I heard him utter the African proverb: *"Until the lions have their own historians, the hunter will always be the hero."* I also saw this saying painted on the walls of one of Ghana's slave castles, and it stuck in my mind even after I returned home.

The local leaders in Senchi Ferry offered us a welcome ceremony that was both formal and informal. The first night, we went around the circle and shook everyone's hand and said hello. There was an exchange of gifts. Each visitor got up individually, entered the center of the circle, and said their names. Then there was a little discussion between the elders, who would come back with what tribe they thought the person might be from, judging by the sound of their name and the look of their features. Next, someone in the audience who was from that tribe would get up and welcome the person and give them a big hug.

Oh my, it was getting closer and closer to my turn. There was only one other white person in the assembly—a man from Denmark who did video work for the village and had been living there for a while. Was he going to get up to hug me? I silently chuckled. When it was my turn, I got up with my heart pounding, went to the center of the circle, pronounced my name, and with a joking tone said, "I'm very curious what tribe you will put me in." Everyone laughed. But still they placed me, perhaps due to the sound of my name, into one of the northern tribes, and someone from the north got up and gave me a hug. He was a young thin man and I knew enough by then to give him a blessing. Everyone was laughing and quite pleased and I sat back down, shaking. At breakfast the next morning, Otis, the CEO of Ujamaa Place, leaned over and told me I had done really well and he would take me anywhere. I was greatly relieved.

But one thing became clear: the Ghanaians don't need advice from white America. Wherever we went, self-sufficiency was the optimal phrase. They told us repeatedly that they need our resources, which they often said we stole from them, but they don't need our advice. One of the saddest statements I heard from a tribal leader was: "You not only stole our gold and minerals, but you stole our strongest, most able men." On another occasion, one chief said, "The Americans are smart and we, Africans, are dumb." Quickly, without hesitation, another chief, quite insulted by this statement and mad at his friend, retorted, "I will never say that Africans are dumb." Ah, the deep consequences of self-worth being eroded by imperialism and domination.

The Politics of Race

Each day of our trip to Ghana was more powerful or poignant than the one before, often overwhelming my ability to take in more. In Accra, we went to the Kwame Nkrumah Memorial Park and Museum in the morning and to the Du Bois Center for Pan-African Culture in the afternoon. And in both of these places I was introduced to a history that was entirely new to me, and disheartening.

The Memorial Park and Museum honors Kwame Nkrumah, the first president of an independent Ghana, who is considered a Ghanaian hero. Most of the exhibition was photographs on the wall. Often old, important objects were simply laid out on a table with a tablecloth. But the museum emphasized the high regard and great respect the Ghanaian people have for Nkrumah. A monument, statue, and water fountains were found outside.

The photographs told the history of Ghanaian independence. An especially poignant photograph showed Nkrumah and his closest associates at the opening of the New Ghanaian parliament in 1957, all of them wearing their black-and-white-striped prison jackets and caps as Nkrumah made his acceptance speech. Nkrumah and his ministers had previously been imprisoned for encouraging sedition from British rule. They were released after mass Gandhi-like nonviolent protests of their incarceration. Martin Luther King, who was in Ghana for all the liberation proceedings, said that he cried at the sight of them in their prison garb coming forth to open the new parliament and lead the nation. The next picture was of Nkrumah dancing with Her Royal Highness the Duchess of Kent, who was the representative for the British government at the inaugural ball. Martin Luther King commented that seeing them dance together after the long fight for freedom was an affecting moment of the beneficial consequences of a nonviolent transference of power.

There was a whole slew of photographs of Nkrumah shaking hands with all the communist leaders of that time. Almost every leader I had feared as a child was also on the wall: Fidel Castro, Nikita Khrushchev, Che Guevera, Mao Zedong, etc. I walked up to Otis and asked him, "Otis, is my historic fear of these communist leaders a white thing?" My next-door neighbor in Chicago's wealthy Highland Park suburb had built a bomb shelter in the days of the Cuban missile crisis, and my classmates and I had practiced "run, duck, and cover" in grade school. Otis chuckled at my question, shaking his head, and said, "Not a white thing." He, too, had been taught to fear these men. The politics of our growing-up years, which included the Cold War and the Viet Nam war, was based on the fear of a communist takeover and the so-called Domino theory that was being played out all over the world by war, secrecy, and spies.

This American terror of communism played out in Ghana as well. As the tour guide told the story, Nkrumah was president of Ghana for seven years until there was a military coup, apparently backed by the CIA, while he was visiting the communist countries of North Viet Nam and China. Even though the United States government denies its participation in the coup, the tour guide presented the CIA's involvement as a fact and Nkrumah as a hero of the Ghanaian people, the leader of freedom and independence. This reinforced my exasperation with American politics, which seems often to support the wrong or more despotic side during power struggles in developing countries.

Later the same day that we visited the Memorial Park and Museum our group also went to the Du Bois Center for Pan-African Culture in Accra. That museum provided a shocking reiteration of American persecution of Black civil rights activists. Though I had heard of W. E. B. Du Bois, I really knew very little about him, as the American educational system dismisses Black history. Du Bois was one of the foremost American civil rights leaders and helped create the National Association for the Advancement of Colored People, the NAACP, becoming prominent as the editor of its journal *The Crisis*. In 1895 he was the first African American to receive a PhD from Harvard. The first time his passport was revoked was because of his stance against the nuclear bomb, and the United States continued to renew or reject his passport for the rest of his life, according to his current political stances. He moved to Ghana in 1960, was granted honorary Ghanaian citizenship, and lived out the rest of his life there. The Civil Rights Act of 1964, enacted almost a year after his death, embodied many of the reforms for which Du Bois had campaigned throughout his life.

W. E. B. Du Bois wrote a document, the Genocide Proposition of 1951, which he submitted to the United Nations in 1951 using the Genocide Convention's human rights treaty signed in 1948, to support his claim charging genocide as a crime of the US government against the Negro people. He used the UN's own definition of genocide: "any intent to destroy, in whole or in part, a national, racial or religious group." Du Bois listed the following actions as demonstrations of genocide: lynching, legal discrimination, disenfranchisement of Blacks in the South, incidents of police brutality, and the systemic inequalities in health care and quality of life between white and Black Americans. But the Genocide Proposition of 1951 was ignored by the United Nations. Du Bois's paper lost out to the Cold War politics of the time: because it was supported by the American Communist Party it was suppressed. The UN did not even acknowledge that it had received Du Bois's petition.

At the Du Bois Center, many of my fellow travelers gathered around a small desk in a corner of the lobby showcasing a copy of the five-inch-thick FBI file on Du Bois, which had recently been released. Du Bois's every move, phone call, and meeting were recorded by the FBI. Looking at this document, I felt a visceral change in my understanding of the power structures of racism in America and understood the insidiousness of protecting white privilege in a way that I had never had to confront so directly before.

The History of Enslavement

Visiting the slave castles in Ghana in July 2018 and then going to the Legacy Museum in Montgomery, Alabama, in January 2019 bookended my experience. I began learning about the transatlantic slave trade in Ghana and continued to discover it at the Legacy Museum in Alabama about the Domestic Slave Trade in the United States—along with the slave trade's aftermath, which has extended into the mass incarceration of African Americans that is still occurring.

At the University in Accra we listened to a lecture on slavery by a leading scholar. Slavery has always existed throughout history because of political and economic reasons in a society's quest for control of land and resources, which includes human beings. Slaves were often the prisoners of war within the warring tribes of Africa. But the idea of a "slave" was quite different than in the Western World. After a certain point of serving a family, the so-called "slave" or POW became part of the family and was incorporated into the life of the community. This is not the same type of denigration and inhumane treatment that occurred in Western slavery and did not produce the dislocation, brutality, and terrorism that marked American slavery.

In the eighteenth and nineteenth centuries, Ghana and its neighboring countries in the bulge of West Africa running across the northern coast of the Gulf of Guinea was then called the Gold Coast. It was nicknamed the Gold Coast because European traders could see gold just strewn across the streets and the land. The commodities being traded came to include humans. Europeans also started involving themselves in politics beyond trading. Europe began its takeover of Africa through diplomacy, but eventually European colonization was driven by force. The invention of the magazine gun, a repeating firearm, really marked the end of the final defeat of the African tribes. Soon the tribal cities were being bombed by cannons and, by 1860, the British controlled all the coastal towns and had bombed the Ashanti strongholds in the north of Ghana. Christian missionaries were also cultural domination agents, and the establishment of British courts saw the end of tribal rule.

Between 1525 and 1866, 12.5 million people were enslaved and transported across the Atlantic. About 10 million actually landed in the New World after surviving the dreaded sea voyage and its inherent illnesses and mistreatment that often brought death. In 1808, the transatlantic slave trade was made illegal in the United States in the Act Prohibiting the Import of Slaves. This was succeeded by the domestic slave trade in the United States, a movement of a million enslaved people taken from the upper South to the lower South from 1810 to 1860 to labor in agriculture. In this trade, more than half of the Black families were broken up and sold to different owners. The Legacy Museum itself is in a warehouse which once housed enslaved people who had gotten off the ships and were waiting to be taken to the slave market at the Court Square. I stumbled upon the Court Square on one of my walks. Newly built civic public markers made me realize that I was standing at an intersection that had once been a major slave market.

W. E. B. Du Bois was famous for saying that "the end of slavery was not going to solve the myriad problems of slavery. If you didn't develop previously enslaved people then slavery would not be over." The American Civil Rights Act of 1866 released enslaved people into freedom, but the soil that needed to be sown for the economic advancement of former slaves was not developed or enforced. Freed slaves were forced into sharecropping and worked on white-owned land in exchange for food and lodging but no wages.

This began the system of "Black Codes" in the South that eventually became the Jim Crow Laws. Developing out of these new laws was an increase in incarcerated Black people based on unfounded and exaggerated charges in which the era of convict leasing began. Prisoners could be leased to work in coal mines, lumber mills, and road construction. In 1898, 73 percent of Alabama's state revenue came from convict leasing, which was sometimes called "the second slavery."

The prejudices that still exist are an extension of this history of trauma. I think about the inmates who come to the Unpolished Diamond Sangha. How many of them were behind bars for exaggerated charges or because they were dark-skinned who had the misfortune of standing in front of a white judge or white jury? I have read that the so-called War on Drugs in the 1970s produced soaring arrest rates that disproportionately targeted African Americans. There are so many ways that the police departments and the prejudicial judicial system is still disrupting Black communities and other marginalized people of color. This is now coming out more and more to the surface of the dominant white culture's awareness.

Truth and Reconciliation

In 2018, the Equal Justice Initiative (EJI) built two centers to bring awareness to slavery and its consequences in Montgomery, Alabama: the Legacy Museum: From Enslavement to Mass Incarceration and the Memorial for Peace and Justice, just a few blocks away. EJI's fundamental philosophy taken from their website is that "you can't get reconciliation until you first tell the truth." EJI's founding director, Bryan Stevenson, author of *Just Mercy*, explains: "Our nation's history of racial injustice casts a shadow across the American landscape. This shadow cannot be lifted until we shine the light of truth on the destructive violence that shaped our nation, traumatized people of color and compromised our commitment to the rule of law and to equal justice."

The whole Legacy Museum is filled with densely layered information about the history of slavery, the Jim Crow era, the civil rights movement, and the mass incarceration of Black people today. The walls are filled with information, photographs, holograms, and videos.

One display that really struck me was a photograph of the lynching of a mother and son, Laura and L.D. Nelson. The photograph showed their two bodies suspended by rope from a bridge on which hundreds of white onlookers stood. As I stopped in front of this horrific photograph, I wondered if Malissa had witnessed anything like this. Then I realized that, yes, of course she had! She was born in the early 1920s in the South. She probably, as a young child, saw the Klu Klux Klan parading down her street. Or she could have seen someone in her neighborhood lynched. Besides the strenuous work of the cotton fields, were devastating images such as these also what she was referring to when she said, "If you only knew the suffering in my life and what I have seen"? The museum placard said that the photograph of the mother and son being lynched had been made into postcards which were sold for monetary gain. Oh my god! Each photo on the wall was as abominable as the last one. There were men and women chained to posts, beaten to death, hung from trees. Was it possible that Malissa's father or mother, grandfather or grandmother, or neighbor was one of these people? Oh, I wish I had been able to hear the deeper story of Malissa's life from her when she was alive.

The Legacy Museum was filled with many layers of sound that created a jarring clamor of noise. One thread of sound was the recordings of deeply sung spirituals and work songs that emanated from two of the six holograms of enslaved people positioned in alcoves that stopped me in my tracks as I turned the corner from the foyer into the museum. The hologram figures looked and sounded so real, so alive—men and women, old people and children, handcuffed or in rags, all of them telling their stories, looking directly into my eyes. I was completely stilled and, holding my hands over my heart, putting my nose to the bars of the alcove, I listened to every word of their stories. The singing of spirituals pervaded the whole of the museum, leaving a deep expression of the humanity that can persevere through outer harm and expressing the voice of both profound grief and the overriding sound of faith.

There was a kind of din in the space—a mix of many speakers and music. On a large screen hanging in the center of the space were displayed videos of white Southern politicians giving speeches supporting segregation and denouncing civil rights, and their diatribes pervaded the din. One horrifying voice, which I write about because I want us all to face directly the truth of this terrible racist mentality, came from Leander Perez, who died in 1969 and was a judge and district attorney in Louisiana. His voice boomed out, "Don't wait for your daughters to be raped by these Congolese. Don't wait until the burrheads are forced into your schools. Do something about it now." What an atrocious statement when the truth is that Black women were being consistently raped by white men and when

Black violence during that era was being provoked by white violence.

Black people were allowed to vote after the Voting Rights Act of 1965. I was fourteen years old then, and did not realize then that most of the maids in my childhood were not able to vote. This is so shocking to me! It also reminds me of the men in the prisons where I have worked. Convicts lose their right to vote, and since a Black man is six times more likely to be incarcerated than a white man, that means that one in three Black men are in prison, and when they get out, they can't vote.

The Legacy Museum brings forward the fact that lynching has left a profound legacy and there are deep consequences resulting from this brutality and violence. The Memorial for Peace and Justice sits on six acres of land within the city limits of Montgomery, Alabama, and is a large and peaceful park dedicated to these four thousand and four hundred documented lynchings. The memorial is a low-slung building that rises up from the crest of a small hill. In this open-air pavilion, there are eight hundred and sixteen six-foot suspended columns that suggest dangling corpses. These pendent slabs are made from a steel that produces rust bleeds that run down the sides of the columns, which makes one think of the blood flowing from lynching victims. Each hanging column represents a United States' county, from both the North and the South, in which one or more lynchings occurred and is engraved with the names of that county's victims or "anonymous."

The memorial itself is a very quiet place with one wall cascading water so that the sound of water runs throughout the space. I sat down in the courtyard at the center of the space, which was created to acknowledge the fact that many lynchings were conducted in town squares with as many as ten thousand people watching. Sitting on a bench in the sunshine, I listened to the soothing sound of the cascading water and breathed deeply, relaxing my shoulders and putting my hands on my heart, feeling their warmth reaching into the deep inner pain of all that I had seen that day. I tried to digest even a little bit of the astounding stories of cruelty I was witnessing. What were the repercussions of lynching to the African American community? These lynchings were not only ritualized killings to protect whites from Black "criminals" but were also used to traumatize the whole Black community. The Equal Justice Initiative named this as terrorism.

I felt such despair in my witnessing, but I also felt inspired. I felt awe for the uprightness and determination of the Black community and for those who consistently fight for racial justice. So much determination was felt and work was done to produce this exhibit filled with the power to affect people's minds. *You can't get reconciliation until you tell the truth.*

As I walked the streets in front of the museum and opened my heart to the pain of this history, I felt all of my maids' presence with me. The civic placards on the sidewalks told the history of the Montgomery bus boycott, a seminal event in the civil rights movement. The Black maids of Montgomery largely led and sustained the boycott for over a year. Black women have been political activists in their community for their entire history on the American continent— central pillars of strength, steadfastness, and love for their communities all through such unimaginable suffering. They have passed down their spirituality and perseverance from generation to generation, and they have instilled their integrity and love in me.

PART THREE: RETURN—THE SLAVE CASTLES

I went to Ghana with our maids in my heart. My connection with their humanity, and in particular Malissa's, was my impetus for wanting to go to Africa and to expose myself to the terror of the slave castles and what they mean to Black Americans. As I made the journey through Ghana, I could hear my childhood caretakers' surprise, delight, and despair as voices in my head.

All of the emotions and revelations I experienced throughout the trip came to a climax at the slave castles. We went to two of these buildings: Elmina Castle and Cape Coast Castle, both of which are on the shores of the Gulf of Guinea. Both fortresses were built by the Portuguese and then later taken over, first by the Dutch and later by the British. These "castles" were warehouses built for storing merchandise but soon they were filled with human beings. The warehouse rooms were not large but often housed hundreds of ill-fed people. The rooms have no windows, so there was no fresh air and the captured human beings often lived in complete darkness. There was often standing room only, and in order to lie down, people had to pile up in layers. The people's urine, feces, and menstrual blood seeped down from the top layer, and the people on the lower layer often died. The tour guide said that when anthropologists analyzed the dungeon floors, that's what they found: compounded urine, feces, and blood. The enslaved people usually spent one to three months in the dungeons before being shipped across the ocean. Many people died right there in the dungeons, and of those who survived to board the ships, many died on the transatlantic voyage.

At one moment during the tour we stood in what was called the women's courtyard. There were several tour groups in the courtyard and it was quite crowded. The sun beat down on us.

Several tour guides were talking all at once, in different languages, but we all got the gist of what they said. This was the place where the women were gathered and reviewed to see who would be raped by the white European Governor. He would look over the balcony and choose a woman to be humiliated by being undressed and cleaned by the soldiers in front of everyone. The woman would then be led into a small alcove, which was used as a waiting room, until she was summoned to be raped. I went with some of our group into the alcove, where our guide explained that the chosen woman would go into the alcove naked and be redressed and surrounded by the guards. There was a trap door with a ladder, and when the time was right, the woman would climb the ladder into the governor's bedroom.

In this alcove, Monique, one of my fellow travelers, came over to me and said, "We should say a prayer, don't you think?" Being one of the two clergy on the trip, I was often asked to pray for the group, before meals, and at strategic moments. All of the power of what I had been seeing and the issue of rape converged into this moment. I definitely lost control. I didn't cry, but I heard my voice ringing out very loudly and I saw that I was gesticulating with my arms. The small group in the alcove was a bit taken aback by my fervor. One woman put up her hands, palms together, in prayer position in front of her mouth. I expressed my ardent wish for healing and for such atrocities, which are still occurring throughout the world, to stop. This prayer expressed my impassioned and vehement reaction to rape, in my own life and others. It seemed for me at that moment that there was a constellation of circumstances coalescing: there were all the Black women who had been raped by white men and their bosses, in that very alcove many African women had waited to be raped, and lastly, there was my own rape by a Black man in the Chicago streets. I was over-come with passion, the heat, and the buildup of my emotions from listening to that building's walls and floors and feeling its history, knowing that there were many, many more buildings just like this one. Not even knowing what I was doing, I tried to express my horror out loud in front of everyone, in the form of a wild prayer. I took from the Jewish Holocaust history this phrase: "Never again, this should never happen again." I wailed this out, beseeching the universe to hear my cry.

Afterwards, Monique took me in her arms, and we all left the alcove. She knew something had happened to me and I told her about my own rape in Chicago. Then I cried. But it seemed that everyone understood this intensity, and that all of us felt devastated and overwhelmed by this place of abomination. I felt that I had expressed that for everyone.

But these scorching feelings were not to be dampened down yet. We had one more room to experience the building's shameful history. Finally, the tour guides led us into a space which my fellow travelers and I had known about and prepared for: the small, dark, windowless room containing what's called the Door of No Return, a little door leading out to the sea. The enslaved people would be led through the dungeons and out this door onto a boat, never to return. The room was filled with floral wreaths that people had left in memorial. One of the rituals that my tour mates were doing, which I hadn't known about before the trip, was to bring pictures of their relatives and ancestors and lay them down on the floor near the Door of No Return so they could pray for them and allow their spirits to return to Africa. When I had learned about this ritual, I had wondered how I could participate. And then I knew: I would bring my Black mothers back to Africa.

The night before, with the sound of the waves of the gulf

coming through my bungalow window, I had prepared a symbolic offering. From lined notebook paper, I made the origami envelopes that Zen priests use to house their lineage papers. I'd had many years of experience making these envelopes, and inside of this one I wrote my African American mothers' names down and what they meant to me: Cora, who had sung spirituals over my sick body when I was a young asthmatic and liked to sing songs to Jesus while she was ironing, her voice floating up the stairwell from the basement. Mary, my parents' last housekeeper, who was an example to me of a dignified, powerful, aware, awake woman. Mary told me a story once about the beginning of her employment with my parents: she walked into my dad's home office, stood in front of his desk, and said, "If you can't treat me with more respect, I'm leaving." Mary was the only one in my parents' world who supported my spirituality and who encouraged me to become a priest.

Then the question arose: *Should I include Carrie?* I sat for a long time in contemplation, looking blankly out the window at the sea. *Should I include Carrie who sexually abused me when I was thirteen years old?* Her actions had had very deep repercussions which have lasted my whole life. I sat and sat. I then realized that of all people, Carrie was a wounded person who needed to reconnect with her roots in Africa too. She needed my forgiveness and my understanding of all the causes and conditions that had produced her actions and resulted in my unfortunate experience with her and its lingering impact. So, I wrote down Carrie's name too.

Writing the name of Malissa, the mother of my heart, I strongly felt her presence. Malissa, with her inner strength and quiet exterior, was with me, putting her invisible hands on my shoulders and saying, "Yes! Do this and remember me." I folded up the envelope in its intricate way and carried it in my purse.

When we finally arrived, near the end of the tour, at the Door of No Return, everyone—men and women—was crying. People were lining up their pictures on the floor and praying. Others were stooping down and going in and out of the little door. I was asked to say a prayer, and I spoke out loud an impromptu prayer for the group, hoping that the spirit would move me since my conscious mind had no idea what to say, and some words did come out of my mouth and my heart. At Cape Coast Castle, a sign had recently been installed on the opposite side of the Door of No Return, saying, "The Door of Return." This was an invitation for all the Africans of Diaspora to return to their roots, and in doing so achieve some sort of healing. Would going back to Africa heal this deep intergenerational wound? Would it provide a partial insight or a soothing medicine? I knew there was no easy solution to the tear in the fabric of Black identity or the devastation brought on by the construction of whiteness, but nevertheless, I stooped down and placed my small envelope amidst the flowered wreaths, opened my heart, and said my private prayer. I brought my Black mothers back to Africa and prayed that this gesture might bring them some kind of rest.

EPILOGUE

The journey of transformation is to confront our
shadow and embrace it. What's done can't be
undone—but it can be healed; it can even become the
instrument of our healing.
—Rabbi Alan Lew

Throughout the writing of this book, as I turned toward the rough, unhealed terrain of my inner life, I was struck by how often I found myself looking at the larger environment of our rough and unhealed world. I found the private sorrow of my young life mirrored in the great world of war and oppression and mired in the swamp of sexual exploitation, and I encountered it in the history of the enslavement and brutalization of vulnerable people everywhere over the centuries. This awareness informs my increasing understanding of interdependence. The personal is the political, and vice versa. You and I mutually affect each other. My inner life and the outer environment undeniably resonate together. Is it possible for us to find and believe in the goodness in our world and that this goodness can heal us?

I have found myself, surprisingly, in a new period of growth. The writing of this book has unexpectedly produced a welcome metamorphosis in my psyche. In a cocoon, the caterpillar completely turns into liquid before it starts restructuring itself as a butterfly. At some points in my review of the stories in this book, I felt as if my previous structure had dissolved and I was swimming in an amorphous stew of historical brutality and suffering. But now I can visualize a new creature peeking out of its cocoon and starting to emerge as a butterfly.

Previously I had thought that you didn't grow after the age of sixty, but these last few years have taught me that spiritual life is a never-ending process. I have leapt over a chasm in my psyche, with my arms outstretched. A woman leaping—that is something I have wanted for a long time. Through my leap, I have landed somewhere else, outside many of my habituated patterns. I am still absolutely Judith, but I feel different inside.

The Authentic Tea Bowl, Broken and Mended

How do we pick up the pieces of a life or a community after it seems to have shattered? Shattering is actually considered in Buddhism to be an essential part of growth. It is an awakening to life's transitory nature and the limitations of human knowledge. Those moments when the rug is pulled out from under us provide the catalyst for transformation. Illustrating this is an exquisite koan about the Japanese art of Kintsukuroi, in which broken pottery is repaired by the cracks being filled with gold, silver, or platinum.

In the koan, a student prepares a tea ceremony for her teacher and one unexpected guest. This interloper deliberately smashes the tea bowl, and everything, every thought stands still. And then the teacher says, "I gave you this tea bowl, but now, I would like you to give it back to me. Before you do, gather up the pieces, glue them back together, and fill the cracks with gold. Name this new bowl 'the Authentic Tea Bowl Before Birth.'"

For me, both the shattering of the bowl and its being glued back together are the integration of wisdom and compassion. Both the visitor's daring wisdom to smash the bowl in a demonstration of impermanence and the teacher's kind advice teach us that we can put our world back together with care. The smashing of old forms is sometimes necessary. This repair does not replicate the original bowl, but is the beginning of something new. Our brokenness is an opportunity for rebirth and can evoke the deep emergence of Avalokiteshvara, the bodhisattva of compassion, herself. Each piece of the broken tea bowl is valuable in and of itself. We put it back together with all the wisdom of its breaking apart. The repaired bowl is often considered more beautiful than the original one. Our scars are golden—the symbols of our transformation, integration, and healing.

I have learned that it is during the dark times that I must trust the flow of my life the most. It is difficult and necessary to trust the total dynamic working of the universe and our karma. When we open wide our eyes and look deeply into what's around us, we see the world of impermanence and loss and we encounter the truth that nothing lasts forever. This teaches us. We can't even hold onto the idea of progress if we enter into the Sun-face Buddha's world of timelessness—there is no before and no after. But it is also true that our intentionality might be strong enough to effect change in our circumstances. Maybe we can influence the world with our actions, without even needing to smash anything. And maybe not. Life and events emerge, they endure, and then they shatter and pass away. For me, trusting in the rhythm of the revolving cycle of birth and death is the deepest level of my spirituality.

Life is and always will be very messy, and we are always right in the middle of it. There are many smashed teacups everywhere. When one issue gets resolved, the next dilemma arises. But recently in my life there have been small and somewhat ordinary incidents in which I have felt a vaulting into a different mind-state. A shift is occurring in me as old karma fueled by hatred has started to release. Writing this book has brought me to a place of integration where no part of myself needs or wants to be cut out or excluded. I am learning to accept and be tender to myself as I hold hands with my shadow. It seems that recently I have been carried along in some kind of healing flow. All the energies have aligned and some deep letting go has occurred. It has felt like a rollercoaster ride in which I've sometimes tried to hold onto my seat but at other moments I've put my hands in the air and let go.

Reexploring Judaism

Sadly, for me, internalized anti-Semitism has exerted a force of self-hatred and fear in me—a deep root of intergenerational trauma. When I returned from the Auschwitz/Birkenau retreat, I was very confused about my relationship to Judaism. I was a Jew, but I had done nothing to honor my ancestors. I was a Jew who was still traumatized by our history and I had become estranged from the spiritual practices of my people. After the quite stunning retreat at Auschwitz/Birkenau, I found myself in deep bereavement for everything lost in my history. My eldest brother said, "Oh, Judith, don't worry about it. It's too late for you. You're too far gone into Buddhism." At the time I believed him and just shoved down, once again, the pain of being Jewish. But during the process of writing this book and taking a break from my role as a Zen teacher, I found I just couldn't bury it anymore.

I have always had Jewish friends who have been important to me. Maybe through them I have maintained a fragile connection with Judaism. My friend Barbra always found opportunities to include me in her Jewish life. She was a shining example for me that there could be deep spirituality in Judaism and that there could be wonderfully warm and sane Jewish households. She has continued to invite me to participate in Jewish retreats with her, year after year, and I have always refused. But last winter, I experienced a glimmering of possibility: Could I go to a Jewish retreat and investigate my lost connection with my lineage? Barbra chose for me a Jewish Renewal retreat at which Rabbi Shefa Gold would be leading chanting, and my long-standing friend Rabbi Diane Elliot would be leading bodywork and movement. Of course, I feel so much more comfortable with women rabbis: their teaching reflects their embodiment of spirituality and remarkably aligns with my understanding.

Before and during the retreat I worked to internally rearrange my prejudices. I was expecting that which I had always experienced in the past: a kind of dismal atmosphere of a punishing Father-god and guilt-producing finger-wagging. My past was filled with thoughts of "you can never do it right," which I had learned in the halls of my Hebrew school and from the *Bimah* (the pulpit in a Jewish synagogue) and my family and relatives. The first get-together at this retreat, however, surprised me with a different Jewish experience. Our gathering was about joy, singing to god, gratitude, and healing. The group singing sounded like a chorus of angels and penetrated my very soul. I belonged to these people. They looked like me. They expressed themselves with the same gestures I use. Some knew Yiddish, and most of us had gone to Hebrew school. That was a remarkable feeling—one of belonging. Oh, such a deep grief arose as I experienced my estrangement from my roots. I realized that experiencing the vitality and joy of the Jewish community was making me aware of how sad it had been for me to have missed the comfort of this deeply loving fellowship.

I have talked quite a bit with Rabbi Diane about what the Jewish community was like in the '50s and '60s—the years of my childhood and young adulthood. Diane often refers to the undigested rage from World War II that seeped out wherever Jewish people gathered. The Jewish communities were unable to process the horror of the Holocaust individually or collectively, especially since it had so recently occurred. No wonder many of my generation, raised in that atmosphere, had turned away from Judaism. Jewish renewal is one effort to return Judaism back to spirituality and deep healing. Interestingly, the Renewal movement often includes people who have studied Buddhism and meditation and can bring these teachings back to the Jewish community. My generation had to look outside its own group to find a mystical tradition, although a mystical path has clearly always been available in traditional Judaism. It is a fact that in the Holocaust, the rabbis were the first to be taken into the gas chambers because the Nazis wanted to eradicate the Jewish leaders. This left the community bereft of spiritual guidance, causing a deep chasm in the belief system and spirituality of the people. The terrible, unanswerable question was, "If God loves the Jews, how could he allow this to happen to them?" The path to spiritual recovery and faith within the context of the horror of the Holocaust seemed almost impossible.

Jewish Renewal began in the '60s and '70s as a countercultural attempt to revitalize the Jewish spiritual experience. If I had been introduced to this type of Judaism instead of the shaming rabbi at my Bat Mitzvah or the mean old man pounding on his desk at my Hebrew school, perhaps I would have ended up as a rabbi instead of a resentful, alienated Jew. It took the rest of the twentieth century for Jewish Renewal to find some footing in the Jewish institutions, and it took me even longer to look at my relationship with my ancestors.

One of the celestial moments at the retreat happened for me when we were singing in trios. I sat in the middle of my trio. The two other people in my trio sat on either side of me and sang the chant sweetly into either ear. The chant we sang is translated as: *Grace me, Yah (God), for I am disconnected. Oh, healer to the broken-hearted, you bind up our wounds.* As I was listening to the beautiful voices of my fellow group members, I heard another voice, God's voice, if you will, saying to me loudly and clearly, "It's not your fault, it's not your fault." As the two people sang into my ears, I sobbed. "It's not my fault." It is not my fault that I have lived with self-hatred. It is not my fault that there was a deep and toxic schism in the psyche of my community and in myself as the results of the Holocaust. My father's rage and its consequences are not my fault.

In a moment I had, for the first time, come to understand that my deep aversion towards Judaism came not simply because I had suffered an embarrassing and shaming Bat Mitzvah. I suddenly realized that Carrie's sexual assault and my Bat Mitzvah occurred a month apart. That poor thirteen-year-old Judith, after being sexually violated, had to stand up in front of the whole community and her whole class of acquaintances and friends in her special dress and Jackie Kennedy pillbox hat and pretend that nothing had happened. That was a searing moment in my young woman's lockdown, as my soul padlocked itself in and built walls around me like a fortress. Those two traumas had become intertwined and those barricades had remained in place for a long, long, time. At the Jewish Renewal retreat I began to "run the rapids," as rape consultants call it—reexperiencing the trauma bodily and allowing it to run itself out and release. This discharge did not happen so much in my head as it did in my quivering, nauseated, vibrating body. I couldn't concentrate and I certainly couldn't follow the schedule of the day. For the rest of the day, I could do nothing else but process that long-ago experience. My mind was either going round and round my narrative and the scene of being violated or my mind was frighteningly blank. Could anyone see the upheaval that was happening inside me? A deep inner blockage was breaking down and I could not rationally control it, nor did I want to talk myself out of it. I was able to tell Diane and my friends who were present what was happening to me. I didn't participate in the retreat for the rest of that day, but I took care of myself. Because it was Saturday or Shabbat, the Torah was out on a table covered with a beautiful scarf. While the other retreatants wandered off on a break, I crawled under the table, under the Torah, and slept. Even though I had very little relationship with this scroll of holy words, I felt protected by the forces of spirituality, and I knew I was safe.

After the retreat, I began my day with the chants I learned from Rabbi Gold. There was an emotionality to the melodies which soothed me and which I don't find in Zen. Having continued to talk to Rabbi Diane, I decided to put up a *mezuzah* on my doorpost—a recognition of faith and a sign that a Jew lives in this house. I was so surprised when I realized how difficult it was for me to identify myself publicly as a Jew. No Jewish star around the neck for me! I continued by encouraging myself to experiment with going to the High Holy Day services at different local temples. Again, the Jewish Renewal service was the place I felt most at home, but I don't really know where I will end up or how my spiritual practices might change with this current exploration. What I do know is that I am willing to unravel my deeply ingrained habit of hating all things Jewish, which implodes into hating myself.

Yom Kippur is a holiday dedicated to forgiveness. Kol Nidre, the Yom Kippur service, is a beautiful entreaty for healing. At one point in the service, people knock with a fist on their chests as they go through the various things the collective "we" need to be forgiven for. In a blink of my eye, I saw my mother across the aisle—all dressed up with a new fashionable hat, a new suit and heels; she pounded on her chest, asking for forgiveness. I forgive you, Mom. I forgive myself.

David Kaye and My Fiftieth High School Reunion

Sometimes we hold onto our bitterness with a strong aversion to reconnection or to any possibility of forgiveness. With a lot of inner violence, I used to go through the remnants of my history and slash and burn what I wanted to forget. But avoiding these situations doesn't heal them. One of those "I will never forgive" barriers was reconnecting to my high school and all the people in it. When I received the invitation to my fiftieth high school reunion, I noticed this hardened hatred in my body. I was embarrassed that my thirteen-year-old's oppositional defiance should remain so strong in me, even as an older woman. If I lumped everyone together, I could just hate the city of Highland Park and Highland Park High School. I could forever be the victim of my childhood rejections, the victim of my own hate. When I received the invitation, in the spirit of making "I will never do that" amends, I thought, "Okay, let's go and see if we can forgive everything and everybody." I prepared by meditating on the forgiveness and kindness contemplations in

Buddhism and by talking a lot about my long-held hatred in therapy. I came to understand that my high school classmates are no longer children but actual grown-ups who have lived long, complicated lives, just like me. Could I actually touch their hearts and see who, after fifty years, we all had become?

I told my therapist that I was still afraid that I would reexperience the ostracism that I had suffered in high school. My therapist leaned her head a little to one side, and, smiling, challenged me. "Is that a real threat?" she asked. "Now, in this present moment, would those people react that way?" Still, I made preparations. I had reconnected recently and become friends with someone from my high school who was also going to the reunion. He knew my history. I asked him if I could come to him, stand by him or sit by him if I started to feel excluded. He agreed to that role wholeheartedly. I also asked my husband to come with me to the reunion as my witness. I dressed up in my party clothes and went with open arms and some quivering trepidation. I wanted to meet each moment and each person with a unique curiosity. Interestingly, I was greeted quite warmly by others. Also intriguing was the fact that all the stories they told about me had happened before seventh grade, the year of the sexual violation and my Bat Mitzvah. Everyone knew me. I realized then that I had been a public figure even in high school. Everyone knew me because I was often the lead dramatic actor in the school plays. I was known and unknown at the same time.

At the reunion, I hoped to find two men, David Kaye and Sam Friedman, so I could ask if they remembered Aspen. An experience we shared in Aspen, Colorado, in 1969, had been the only time I had felt recognized or seen by people from my high school, and I had been so grateful for that healing moment.

In 1969, after graduating from high school, I spent the

Summer of Love and the summer of Woodstock in a small, abandoned mining cabin just north of Snowmass, Colorado. There were about ten of us living as a commune. To make money, our two male leaders, who were Viet Nam Vets, sang and played guitar as strolling minstrels—sometimes on the street, sometimes in a bar. We girls danced around in our swirly skirts and held out the hat for money. My friends nicknamed me Isadora Duncan.

While driving one of my sons to Los Angeles a few years ago, we stopped in Aspen. We walked through what was, to my eyes, unrecognizable streets crowded with gourmet restaurants, designer boutiques, and people dressed to the nines. It left a very chic and swank impression indeed. We heard some music coming from the park where I used to hang out at the gazebo and headed over to it. There were several young people, dressed very similarly to hippies, singing there. We walked by them. The only girl in the group held up a sign to me that said, "Smile." She really didn't have to hold up the sign, because I was already smiling straight from my eighteen-year-old heart. And then she flipped over the sign which read on the other side, "You are beautiful." I bowed the bow of a Zen teacher, and one of the other musicians bowed back. And my son turned to me and said, "There you are mom, that was *you*."

At the end of the summer, the commune broke up, the musicians moved on, and the girls headed back to college. I had a few days, maybe a week, before I would fly home and go off to my first year of college, and I decided to camp by myself on a riverbank outside of town. Ivan, my dear older friend who owned the bookstore in town, drove me out there in his red convertible jeep and dropped me off at his favorite camping spot. I had no tent, just a sleeping bag, and fortunately it never rained. Every day, a young fly-fisherman would stop by my campsite and give me a cleaned rainbow trout. It was quite idyllic. I wrote home to my father that I had found God by sleeping in the moonlight in the Rocky Mountains near a stream. In my naiveté, I wasn't even afraid to be alone. I embodied the cliché of young people thinking they are invincible.

One day, when I had hitchhiked into town to go grocery shopping, I recognized two young men from my high school. They told me they were in the last days of a camping trip. David and Sam had belonged to the cool group at my high school, and I was surprised they would lower themselves to recognize me. I was also astonished when they asked if they could camp with me. But they did. We had a fun time and flew home together. On the plane, I sat next to David and he told me about the pain of his recent breakup with his girlfriend and other rather intimate things. I listened. I was a young woman in full bloom, that girl who had never appeared in the landscape of my high school.

I wanted to find David and Sam at the reunion. Would they remember those few days together with the same fondness and beauty? I found Sam first and very sweetly he said, "I'm so sorry, but I don't remember that." Okay, that was to be expected— that's life and that's reunions. But finally, I found David, who is very tall and was towering over everyone, standing in a corner of the large hotel auditorium. Charley and I approached him. He smiled, and then I said my name. "Do you remember me?" "Oh, I remember you all right!" he said, "To this very day, I remember you. You were the kindest, most compassionate person, and at such a young age. I remember that whole weekend very vividly, and you were one of the people I really wanted to find at this reunion." We talked for a little while about where we had ended up in our life. Then he leaned over and out-of-the-blue said, "You know, I've always wondered, what happened to you in seventh grade?" He actually asked me that! My parents didn't, nor did my brothers or my teachers—in fact, no one had ever asked me, "What happened in seventh grade?" Even when I had told my parents and my brothers decades later about the sexual abuse, they hadn't quite believed me or didn't want to acknowledge the impact that those experiences had had on me. Only David Kaye, when we were both sixty-eight years old, said anything about it. He had been a young man back then, yet he had seen that something had happened to me, and so many years later, cared enough to ask. I felt at that moment, the threads of this knot of hatred in my chest untwine. I looked at Charley, my husband and steadfast friend and confidante, who was standing next to me, and saw empathy in his eyes. Then I looked back at David who was offering me his loving acknowledgment, and I answered him: "I was sexually violated in seventh grade." He blanched. "Oh my god, I'm so sorry. By whom?" "The maid." "Oh my god, I'm so sorry." He was very sweet and attentive. He had become a psychiatrist—I guess he understood suffering. For me, that moment of recognition was an enormous gift. Someone from that time had witnessed the results of that life experience—and someone else, my husband, who was holding my hand, had witnessed my being seen.

That moment brought me a great starburst of opening and release.

GLOSSARY

Anja: A personal attendant to the Zen teacher who does household cleaning, laundry, and making tea, and may also perform some ceremonial functions.

Avalokiteshvara: One of the most important bodhisattvas of the Mahayana tradition. Literally translated as the one who listens to the cries of the world, the embodiment of Great Compassion. Out of a tear of Avalokiteshvara, Tara is born. In Sanskrit, we call this bodhisattva Avalokiteshvara; in Chinese, she is Kuan Yin; in Japanese, she is Kannon or Kanzeon; and in Tibetan, she is Chenrezig.

Bodhidharma: The first Chinese Buddhist ancestor, who lived around the fifth and sixth century. He brought Buddhism to China from India. He is sometimes called "the barbarian from the West."

Buddha: A person who has awakened to the truth. I have always been taught that there are three levels of understanding Buddha: 1) The historic Buddha, who was born in 563 BCE and left us teachings and a story of his life. This is the highest development of a human being that we all can aspire to. 2) The omniscient and energy-body Buddha, which is the life force that flows through everything. 3) The Buddha that is no-Buddha—beyond thought, beyond time, beyond construction and conceptualization.

Gatha: A short verse. In the Zen tradition, it is usually a three- to four-line stanza that is chanted or said as an offering before certain events, times of day, and daily activities.

Jukai: Receiving the precepts. The ceremonial initiation into Zen Buddhism as a lay person. One receives a *rakusu* or prayer shawl, a Buddhist name, and lineage papers. The initiate becomes part of the lineage.

Karma: The universal principle of cause and effect. Everything that is created has an underlying cause or seed. The past conditions the present, and the present plants seeds for the future. And this coincides with the fact that the past is gone and the future is still a construction of our thoughts and does not exist. The historic (or karmic) self is entwined with our Buddha-nature. Cause and effect are not separate but mutually benefit and produce each other. We can also say that our habituated habit patterns can change by our own actions and nonactions.

Koan: A teaching story that points to the nature of reality. These stories are often paradoxical, which helps us break our attachment to conventional thinking, logic, and conceptualizing. The understanding of a koan is an intuitive leap expressing an awakened understanding that is now embodied.

Koromo: A black garment worn under a Zen priest's okesa or Buddha's robe. It was originally designed in China.

Kyosaku: A waking up or encouragement stick is a flattened piece of wood that is used in Zen monasteries to encourage and stimulate the sitters. A sitter is hit on the shoulders or back during long periods of sitting.

Makyo: A Zen word used for dreams, hallucinations, visions, thought constructions, and involuntary movements that arise in meditation. Its use is mostly in Rinzai Zen.

Manjusri: The Bodhisattva of Wisdom, who dispels the darkness of ignorance. The bodhisattva is often depicted holding a sword that cuts through illusions as well as holding in the other hand the book of *Prajñāpāramitā.*

Okesa: A rectangular patchworked robe of priesthood, symbolic of the skin of Buddha, which is worn on top of all other garments. Its pattern is expressed through rectangular shapes arranged like a rice field—that give nourishment to all. Each okesa is handsewn by the individuals being ordained and presented to them at their ordination ceremony. The okesa's various colors often indicate the maturity of the teacher. The okesa is a universal symbol used throughout all of the Buddhist traditions for members of the Buddhist Sangha.

Oryoki: A set of nesting eating bowls used at formal, silent meals in a Zen monastery. The translation of oryoki is roughly *that which holds just enough.* The Japanese Tea Ceremony is patterned after the Zen ceremonial meal.

Prajna: Translated as wisdom or insight, Prajna is referred to in the Mahayana tradition as the immediately experienced intuitive wisdom that cannot be conveyed by concepts or in intellectual terms. The definitive moment of prajna is insight into emptiness.

Precepts: A set of principles that form the basic moral code of Buddhism. They are a teaching that forms a trellis that will support practitioners and give guidance to the Sanskrit word Sila, which is translated as ethics. The precepts offer directions influencing Wise Behavior, Wise Livelihood, and Wise Speech. In Soto Zen, there are ten Grave Precepts:

1. Respect life: Do not kill.
2. Be giving: Do not steal.
3. Honor the body: Do not misuse sexuality.
4. Manifest truth: Do not lie.
5. Proceed clearly: Do not intoxicate the mind.

6. See the perfection: Do not speak of others' errors and faults.
7. Realize self and others as one: Do not elevate the self and blame others.
8. Give generously: Do not be withholding or stingy.
9. Actualize harmony: Do not indulge in anger.
10. Experience the intimacy of things: Do not defile Buddha, Dharma, or Sangha.

Raiban: A raised, rectangular ritual platform placed in front of the altar on which priests perform their bows and ceremonial functions.

Ryaku Fusatsu Ceremony: A repentance ceremony that is practiced twice a month in a monastery at the new moon and the full moon. It is a ceremony abbreviated from the long, traditional Vinaya Precepts ceremony. We gather in community to appreciate, recommit to, and recite the precepts as a group. The core element is repentance and renewal of our ethical practices.

Samsara: The world of suffering or dukkha, the wandering-in-circles world that goes around and around the cycle of existences and our habits without being able to interrupt the flow of karma. We are imprisoned by our own unacknowledged greed, hate, and ignorance.

Sangha: The Buddhist community. On the first level are the ordained members of the Buddhist community; on the second are all people in community; the third comprises the omniscient community, which includes all beings.

Sesshin: Literally, collecting the heart-mind. It is a Zen retreat that involves the especially intensive, strict practice of collecting the mind. Practitioners meditate all day long and often have meals brought to their meditation cushion; sometimes the schedule includes liturgy and work practice.

Sila: One of the three bases in Buddhism, which are prajna, samadhi, and sila. Sila is Buddhist morality or wise conduct and comprises three components: wise speech, wise action, and wise livelihood.

Zafu: A round sitting cushion used for meditation.

Zazen: Literally, the name for sitting meditation performed in Zen. *Za* means sitting. *Zen* means absorption or concentration. Zazen is resting in a state of alert and wakeful attention without being stuck in conceptualization. It is being here and now, open and unrestricted.

Zendo: The meditation hall, a community area put aside for silent sitting.

WORKS CITED

Anderson, Reb. 2001. *Being Upright: Zen Meditation and the Bodhisattva Precepts.* Berkeley, CA: Rodmell Press.

Blondin, Sarah. "When We Must Endure" (guided meditation). Sydney, Australia: InsightTimer.com. Accessed November 17, 2021, insighttimer.com/sarahblondin/guided-meditations/when-we-must-endure.

Brewer, Dr. Judson. 2017. *The Craving Mind: From Cigarettes to Smartphones to Love—Why We Get Hooked and How We Can Break Bad Habits.* New Haven, CT: Yale University Press.

Caplow, Florence and Susan Moon, eds. 2013. *The Hidden Lamp: Stories from Twenty-Five Centuries of Awakened Women.* Boston: Wisdom Publications.

Chodron, Pema. 2007. *Don't Bite the Hook: Finding Freedom from Anger, Resentment, and Other Destructive Emotions* (audiobook). Boulder, CO: Shambhala Audio.

Cleary, Thomas, trans. 1998. *Book of Serenity: One Hundred Zen Dialogues.* Boulder, CO: Shambhala Publications.

Du Bois, W. E. B. 2007. *Black Reconstruction in America.* Oxford, UK: Oxford University Press.

Elliot, Rabbi Diane. 2019. *Unbounded Heart: Poems and Prayers.* Republic of Moldova: Hakodesh Press.

Glassman, Bernard and Rick Fields. 2010. *Instructions to the Cook: A Zen Master's Lessons in Living a Life That Matters.* New York: Harmony Books.

Gold, Rabbi Shefa. 2013. *The Magic of Hebrew Chants: Healing the Spirit, Transforming the Mind, Deepening Love.* Woodstock, VT: Jewish Lights Publishing.

Halifax, Joan. 2009. *Being with Dying: Cultivating Compassion and Fearlessness in the Presence of Death.* Boulder, CO: Shambhala Publications.

Hanh, Thich Nhat. 2002. *Teachings on Love.* Berkeley, CA: Parallax Press.

Levine, Stephen. 1987. *Healing Into Life And Death.* Garden City, NY: Anchor Press/Doubleday.

Lew, Rabbi Alan. 2003. *This Is Real and You Are Completely Unprepared: The Days of Awe as a Journey of Transformation.* Boston: Little, Brown and Company.

Lord, Audre. 2018. *The Master's Tools Will Never Dismantle the Master's House.* New York: Penguin Modern.

Morrison, Toni. 1993. *The Bluest Eye.* New York: Alfred A. Knopf Publishing.

Reps, Paul and Nyogen Senzaki, eds. 1957. *Zen Flesh, Zen Bones: A Collection of Zen and Pre-Zen Writings.* Rutland, VT: Tuttle Publishing.

Ryōkan. 2006. *One Robe, One Bowl: The Zen Poetry of Ryōkan.* Translated by John Stevens. New Haven, CT: Weatherhill Press.

Stevenson, Bryan. 2014. *Just Mercy: A Story of Justice and Redemption.* London, UK: Oneworld Publications.

Sutherland, Roshi, Joan. n.d. *Flashcards for the Radiant World I: Mind of Winter.* Santa Fe, NM: Cloud Dragon—The Joan Sutherland Dharma Works, joansutherlanddharmaworks.org.

Tucker, Susan. 1987. "A Complex Bond: Southern Black Domestic Workers and Their White Employers." *Frontiers: A Journal of Women's Studies.* Salt Lake City: University of Utah.

Walls, Rose. 2017. Foreword to *Elmina: The Castles and the Slave Trade,* by Ato Ashun. Cape Coast, Ghana: Nyakod Printing & Publishing.

ACKNOWLEDGMENTS

I am deeply indebted to and grateful for Sandy Boucher, my writing coach. She not only gave me a private tutorial on how to write a book, but she was also an involved and committed editor. Perfect for me. She was very encouraging and supportive when I was in the midst of tough personal material, and she was also extremely strict. Sandy has high standards of writing and encouraged me to live up to them. I could not have written this book without her.

I'd like to thank my family. My husband, who supports me, perseveres through everything I dish up, and saves my life on a daily basis through his acceptance of me. My sons, who bring me so much joy and challenge me to walk my talk. There is so much opportunity and growth with my most intimate ones. This also includes my girlfriends, all of whom I adore and are behind me every step of the way.

Lastly, I'd like to acknowledge my Zen teachers: Katagiri Roshi and Shohaku Okumura Roshi. A big bow to my transmission teacher, Joen Snyder-O'Neal. And thanks to my communities—Zen sanghas and twelve-step and nonviolent communication groups—and to my students, who draw out the best in me. All of these supportive people and communities are braided into my aliveness and my understanding, and so to them all, I deeply bow.

ABOUT THE AUTHOR

Judith Ragir (known as Byakuren in Buddhist circles) is a Dharma teacher in the Zen lineage of Katagiri Roshi. She was instrumental in founding Clouds in Water Zen Center in St. Paul, Minnesota, where she was the Guiding Teacher for nine years and is currently Senior Dharma Teacher Emeritus. An accomplished artist, Ragir makes Buddhist-inspired quilts that are on display in Buddhist Centers throughout the US. Her writing has appeared in many anthologies, including *The Eightfold Path, Zen Teachings in Challenging Times, The Hidden Lamp, The Path of Compassion, Receiving the Marrow,* and *Seeds of Virtue, Seeds of Change.*

In the 1970s and '80s, Ragir was a dancer in the Trisha Brown Dance Company in New York City and appeared in two one-woman shows of her own choreography. Following her dance career, she worked as a doctor of Chinese medicine, using acupuncture, acupressure, and Chinese herbs, until becoming a Zen priest in 1996.

Ragir lives with her husband in Minnesota, where they raised two sons, and where she runs Mirror Lake Temple, a small Buddhist temple in the woods.

CPSIA information can be obtained
at www.ICGtesting.com
Printed in the USA
JSHW031054110522
25735JS00001B/1